They Did the Best They Could

Discovering Your Path to Compassion

Marnie Vincolisi

We see our stories filtered through the lens of our life experiences. Therefore, my family members may see the situations highlighted in this book differently from mine. Their recollections are valid and have worth.

The guidance herein is from knowledge gained from the author's experiences and should not replace medical or psychological intervention.

Library of Congress Control Number: 2021913774

ISBN: 978-0-9823732-4-8   0-9823732-4-4

DEDICATION

To every person who has felt
abandoned, in some way, in their life.

Table of Contents

PART ONE

Family Tree

PART TWO

Introduction . . . 161

Courses of Action: Chapter One
HIDDEN LOVE . . . 175

Courses of Action: Chapter Two
IF THE TRUTH BE KNOWN . . . 177

Courses of Action: Chapter Three
SUPPRESSED LOVE . . . 185

Part 1

Family

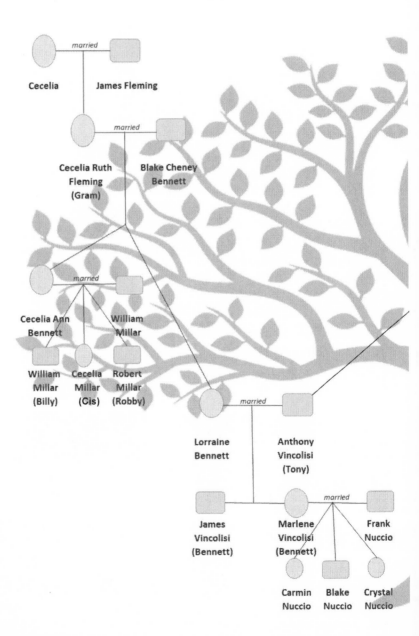

Cecelia — *married* — James Fleming

Cecelia Ruth Fleming (Gram) — *married* — Blake Cheney Bennett

Cecelia Ann Bennett — *married* — William Millar

William Millar (Billy) Cecelia Millar (Cis) Robert Millar (Robby)

Lorraine Bennett — *married* — Anthony Vincolisi (Tony)

James Vincolisi (Bennett) Marlene Vincolisi (Bennett) — *married* — Frank Nuccio

Carmin Nuccio Blake Nuccio Crystal Nuccio

Tree

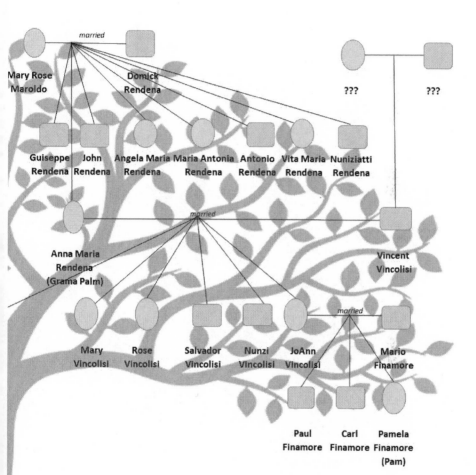

Mary Rose Maroldo — *married* — Domick Rendena

??? — ???

Guiseppe Rendena
John Rendena
Angela Maria Rendena
Maria Antonia Rendena
Antonio Rendena
Vita Maria Rendena
Nuniziatti Rendena

Anna Maria Rendena (Grama Palm) — *married* — Vincent Vincolisi

Mary Vincolisi
Rose Vincolisi
Salvador Vincolisi
Nunzi Vincolisi
JoAnn Vincolisi — *married* — Mario Finamore

Paul Finamore
Carl Finamore
Pamela Finamore (Pam)

Chapter One

HIDDEN LOVE

HAPPY TO HAVE NOTHING ON MY AGENDA, I RELAXED. THE
gurgle of the water trickled over the rocks by the pond. The crisp air filled
my lungs. When the phone rang, I ran inside. It was my mom who delivered her
news in such a calm voice, yet her account shattered my world. I dropped into
the chair and wondered, didn't Mom realize how life-changing this would be for
me? But then again, I had never known her to put my emotions into the mix. The
chain of phone calls is what began my search.

Macy, a kind Italian woman whose kitchen often has the scent of biscottis
and pizzelles wafting in the air, was Mom's high school buddy and attendant at
her wedding. She called to report what she had heard at church. She said, "The
priest asked us to say prayers for a seriously ill man, Tony Vincolisi. Do you think
this is your former husband?" Mom answered without a second thought, "I'm
sure that's him."

My parents had not contacted one another for decades. Mom did not know
his whereabouts but suspected he lived somewhere on the north side of the
city. I wondered why she was so sure this was him. Italian names are common in
Chicago. This man could be anyone, but still, my mom felt this was her former
husband, my father.

My parents had fallen in and out of love within a blink of an eye. They were
introduced by their families when my father came home from World War II. A
few years prior, Mom's high school sweetheart perished in the war, a heartache

that stayed with her. My father also saw death from the war and was anxious to leave the sorrows of combat behind him. They were both primed and ready for love. Unfortunately, they were not prepared to make their relationship last. They had one boy, and before I, their second child, was born, a fight broke out that ended it all. One year after their battle, he disappeared and was never heard from again.

Mom did not talk of her past. It was taboo to speak of him; so I know little of this man. I secretly wanted to meet him but never felt I could share my hidden, heartfelt desire. Those concealed questions stayed in my heart as I pondered, "Who is he? What is he like? Did he ever love me?"

Mom's confident reaction that the man spoken about in church was her only lover showed me she could still connect to my father, even now. Mom never married or dated after her marriage ended. She had never expressed an interest in my father in the last forty years, yet at this moment, hearing about him stirred up old memories, memories she had ignored. By hearing his name, her dormant recollection of the man she once adored activated; but I, on the other hand, was not so sure the man mentioned in the church was my father. Even though Mom understood the man was quite ill, she gave me no assurance that it would be acceptable to contact him. I would be unlatching the rusty lock on the cobweb-covered Pandora's box. Mom had sealed those stories away long ago. Do not open the door to the past.

I felt Mom always wanted to be part of something greater than what her life turned out to be; therefore, I'm not surprised that she did not share Macy's discovery in a kind and compassionate way. Her comment is etched in my memory; I know I did not mistake what I heard; yet months later, I reminded Mom of her words on that day, and she emphatically denied ever saying them.

Her words still echo in my head as if she had spoken them moments ago, "Your father is dying, not that he was ever a father to you." I was stunned by her callous remark, and it felt like a knife cutting into my heart. Her turmoil with him happened forty years ago, but the mention of him now took her back in time, and she spewed out her anger. She wanted validation for the decades of disdain she held for this man, and she wanted me to harbor her resentment as well. I could not. I needed to discover if he had ever loved me

Two weeks after receiving the information about my apparent father's whereabouts, coincidentally, I had a business trip planned to the city where he might be living. I wanted to meet him, but the thought of encountering this stranger made me apprehensive, though not so anxious that I was not going to attempt to find him. And how would I even start this process? Do I call a detective?

As an independent woman in my forties, I had learned how to create a life opposite of Mom's even though we had one similar trait. Mom had large, beautiful blue eyes; mine were also large but as a child were dark brown, and later turned green in my late teens. Probably the most significant difference was my attitude. My bring-it-on, I-can-do-anything temperament made meeting this man seem like an adventure I should take on, and my husband Frank agreed.

At the time I heard Macy's message, my 20-year marriage had lost its spark. For years I was determined not to follow in my mother's footsteps and be a single woman with small children. I was going to break the family pattern and make this relationship a success. Frank and I looked happy from all outer appearances, but I was fooling myself and those around me by becoming passive to its unbalanced parts and deluding myself into thinking everything was fine. We had the 'perfect marriage.'

As I considered how to act on Macy's news, questions plagued my mind for the next two weeks. Forty years of no contact, why pursue this relationship now?

Is this man my father?

Why didn't he come to find me?

Why did he leave?

What if he does not want to see me?

Could Mom have been right? Is he not worth knowing?

Will I be hurt when I confront him?

Does he love me?

After all, he had never contacted me in all these years. He granted us no financial support; evidently, he had no interest in me. Finding my father and possibly being rejected by him was something I had never faced before. I hadn't spent time thinking about it. He abandoned me long ago. Did I want to test those waters and feel the coldness of his heart? Early on, I had let go of the dream of finding him. I accepted it was just the way things were. Nothing would change. This was the life dealt to me. So be it.

Well , that is not entirely true. I recall early in my twenties I considered trying to find him, but the thought of the wrath I would incur from my mom and gram made me reconsider. I can't blame all my reluctance on them. My fear of rejection is also what kept me from looking for him, and then life took its course. The days were filled with motherly duties and work schedules. Soon, the fantasy faded, and the path to my father dissolved, perhaps until now.

I held a romantic tale in my head of a beautiful, loving reunion. Meeting him just might burst that bubble. By keeping this myth in my thoughts, his love for me would stay real. Over the years, this pattern was evident in all my relationships. I would think I had a loving partner, but in reality, they did not accept me or love me the way I felt they should. The truth is my relationships were a reflection of the way I saw myself as not valuable or lovable.

The haunting question remained, if I met my father would I fall into the same trap? Would the bond I had imagined with my father be something that it was not? It was time to step up to the plate, time to find out if this was my father, and if so, what kind of man was he? If this man might be dying, I had not a minute to lose. If I didn't see him now, the opportunity to know who he was would be lost forever. I faced my fears and made the decision. I was determined to meet this man, whoever he was, in two weeks.

But how was I going to orchestrate this meeting? Constructing the plan took some maneuvering. I remember having visited Macy; I assume she would know me, but I did not have her phone number, and certainly, I could not ask Mom for it. She would question why I needed Macy's contact information, and it was difficult enough to persuade myself to see this strange man, let alone convince Mom this was a good idea.

The only way I could get Macy's phone number was to locate Mom's address book, but how would I access it? So, I created a diabolical plan to sneak into Mom's condo and comb through her papers. I wasn't too proud to include my family in my devious plan. I asked my two older children to take their grandma out for lunch. Two of my three children were in their late teens, able to understand my dilemma, so they willingly became part of the plot. Perhaps they even noticed how devious my tactics were, but they said nothing and followed my lead.

With Mom gone, I entered her private space, and even though she wasn't there, I was ill at ease and anxious. I had butterflies in my stomach, and I could feel her presence in every room, watching me. I looked in cabinets and drawers, on shelves, and finally, I found the small metal box filled with index cards with names neatly typed. Frantically I rifled through each card in Mom's address box, visualizing each face as I read their names. Some were vivid, others only a faint memory, while some were just a blank. I needed to be quick yet not too hasty; I did not want to miss the critical card. I peered at the two cards I had in my hand. I wasn't sure which one belonged to the voice on the phone that repeated the priest's words which might lead me to my long-lost father. I wrote down both names. At least two contacts were better than one. I quickly made my exit with the deed completed, highly aware of all this treachery, in broad daylight no less. I sensed how those involved in the Watergate break-in must have felt.

I went home, mustered up my courage, and made the pivotal phone call. Luckily, the first woman called didn't answer. I left no message, for I knew I could not explain my intentions in a short phrase. I hung up the phone, dialed the number of the person on the second card. Could this be the correct number? My relief overwhelmed me when Macy, not her husband, answered the phone. Her bright voice rang over the line, "I am so delighted to hear from you." With my tension released, I listened intently to the words of a woman eager to help me discover who the man in her parish was. My secret was safe with her, and she would not share my plan with Mom. Macy became my partner in crime.

Macy, being of Italian descent, believed the family is of the utmost importance. Therefore, she hoped that this man would connect me to my lost Italian heritage. I breathed a sigh of relief, knowing I did not need to attempt this venture alone; perhaps there was a divine presence directing me.

IN TWO WEEKS, I was on the road, driving to an art fair, trailer packed with my hand-made toys, and the van filled with my anticipation, husband, and three children. We were eager to arrive in Chicago to see if Macy had clues to this mystery man, so the wheels did not stop rolling all night. We were going to spend a few days with my cousin Cis, daughter of my mom's sister Ceal. We arrived at her home at 2:00 in the afternoon. Frank and I took showers to recharge. I knew that if I didn't go to Macy's right away, I would lose my nerve and my chance to discover the truth. We were ready to encounter my father, if this was even him.

Wondering what we would find, Frank and I proceeded without our children. I wanted to spare my young family any awkwardness or rather my humiliation, in case this was my father, but he had no interest in a reunion with his daughter. I contacted Macy and shared my intention to meet the man from her parish that very day. She encouraged me to come to her home, so I said adieu to my cousin, who had little to say about my escapade, and with trepidation, Frank and I drove to the north end of town.

Driving from dry Colorado to the usually humid Midwest, I was pleased to be embraced by a pleasant summer day. There was little humidity or stifling hot air, just a lovely gentle breeze. I knocked on the door, and Macy, whose curly hair was now salt-and-pepper, greeted me with the loving embrace I had come to appreciate from my Italian friends. I was at ease for a moment but not for long. With strong determination, we began to figure out how to find this man. Macy had no clue to his whereabouts; she only assumed he lived in the area. She pulled out the phone book and turned the tissue-thin yellow pages to the name of the man mentioned in church.

I was shocked; how could this be my father? Neither my mom nor my father had ever listed their phone numbers. Mom wanted nothing to do with my father, and he apparently wanted to be incognito as well. On occasion, I would become curious about him and search for his name in the city phone book, but his listing was never there. Yet here, on this odd day, standing in the bright yellow kitchen, peering into the phone book that rested on the 1950 Formica-top kitchen table with the metal legs, next to the woman who began this treasure hunt, I saw the name, Tony Vincolisi, in black and white. Ah, but was he the same man I was seeking?

We looked with disbelief at the address. We looked again. We were speechless. The address could not be correct. This man lived around the corner, only half a block away from Macy. If he was my father, the man whom Macy had once known, how odd that they had never passed each other on the street. Impossible. Being his old friend, surely she would have seen him at some time and recognized him. Indeed this could not be the man I wanted.

"What a cloistered life we lead." Over the years, my mom had visited her old friend on numerous occasions, when, on hot summer nights, they had taken the customary stroll in chase of a refreshing breeze. The coincidence of the proximity of his home to Macy's was just surreal. Perhaps this was all planned in some cosmic order. Were we not supposed to meet until now. I assumed this man had lived there for years, which meant my mom and Macy had walked past his house many times, yet had never seen him or known how close they were. Only a dozen houses away, and they never met, or perhaps they had passed and did not recognize each other because he was not the right man.

Macy suggested we call the number, but that did not sit right with me. I responded, "What would I say?" I knew I had to face him to see if he was the person who abandoned me as a baby. It took no time at all to make my decision; the task was at hand. I had to move forward. To reveal the truth, I had to go to the house around the corner and knock on the door. Some evidence pointed towards the idea that this might be the man I had been wondering about all my life, but there was only one way to be sure. Trusting my gut feeling, we left the safety of Macy's kitchen to confront the person whose name we had found in the telephone book.

There was no need to go alone. My troop consisted of Frank and Macy, who did not want to miss the drama if it occurred. As we walked along the sidewalk that lined this small community stowed away at the edge of a large metropolis, I focused on the golden mosaic pattern on the ground from the sunlight filtering through the trees' full green branches. All my senses were at attention. I could smell each flowering bush as we passed by the well-maintained but meager yards. We three were on a quest, moving into the unknown.

My heart was racing. What would I find? "Oh please, God, let him answer the door." What if a woman came to the door? What would I say? I would have to leave. We continued silently along the sidewalk, turned the corner, crossed the street, and stood before a home with the same numbers on the brick façade as we had found in the telephone book. I walked up the stairs to a screen door that revealed a solid wood door fully open behind it. Because the main entrance seemed accessible, I felt safe; this man did not lock his doors. He was not afraid an intruder would harm him. Perhaps he wouldn't see me as a threat. I knocked on the door and waited with apprehension. I had imagined this scene in my mind for years, but now I searched for words to say. There was no dialogue running.

A white-haired man, small in stature, slowly shuffled to the door. His demeanor showed that he was ailing and weak. He looked at me through the closed screen door. "Hello," I said with a shaky voice, "Are you Tony Vincolisi?" "Yes," was his reply. But that was not enough information to attest that he was the man I wanted. I inquired again, "Were you married to Lorraine?" He paused for a bit, looking puzzled, wondering why I was asking questions about his past. His voice came back again in the affirmative.

My heart was in my throat and simultaneously pounding in my chest. This is him! This is my father. Now what shall I do? I might as well continue. I probed, "You had two children. I am your daughter Marlene." He looked even more puzzled than before. Shaking his head, he said, "A daughter?" I realized my greatest fear. He did not know me, and he never cared. All of this for nothing. My heart sank. I was forlorn. I was just a forgotten child. How could he love me? He didn't even remember me. There was nothing to do now but leave.

I stepped back, ready to set this experience behind me and go on with my life as it was: abandoned, fatherless, and unloved. Then I felt my husband's presence behind me. The pressure of his hands felt comforting on my back, giving me the strength to continue, and his encouragement surprised me.

Though we were married for almost twenty years, his support had diminished to nearly nothing. Frank stood about five feet eight inches tall, with brown wavy hair and a soft voice, not because he was gentle but more because he was afraid to make waves, perhaps the result of being a Vietnam veteran as well as the son of a blind alcoholic. Frank had a good reason to hold back his feelings, but it did not nurture our relationship. However, on this day, standing at the unknown man's door, Frank became my hero.

Even though we had our troubles, there was a nonverbal communication built over the years. At this critical moment, I could hear Frank's thoughts in my confused little girl's head. "Go ahead, you can do it," rang from Frank's heart. I took a deep breath and did not retreat.

Again, my father spoke, "Yes, I have a son named Jimmy." His response put me in turmoil. I was back in time, in my childhood, recalling how I was not the favored sibling. He remembered his son but not me! All my life, it was Jimmy, Jimmy, Jimmy. My brother could do no wrong, he was deemed the man of the house by Mom and Gram, and I was just a girl.

With Frank's gentle encouragement, I decided to pursue my quest for the truth one more time. I had come this far, why not go all the way? So I persisted. With apprehension, I said, "I am his sister, Marlene." My father seemed so confused; it was all happening too fast for him. First, the remembrance of his first wife, Lorraine, then his estranged son Jim. What next?

Again, he just gazed at me, as the wheels in his head raced, trying to make sense of what was happening. Time stood still. The seconds felt like minutes. I could hear a clock ticking away in the disturbing silence. My thoughts were quiet. I could not entertain the idea he might turn and walk away. That was oh so frightening. I had to do something to keep him here, but what?

At last, he responded, "I had a baby girl; I held her only once in my arms." I do not know where my words came from because, without second-guessing, I spoke from my heart, "Open the door; you can hold her again." I felt as if I was in a movie, and I had no control over what might happen next.

He did not immediately react. He was stunned and did not move or say a thing; he just stared at me. Finally, someone broke the spell. Macy spoke in her heavy Italian accent, "Tony, I am Macy. I was in your wedding party, this is your daughter, open the door." Macy's directive seemed to be what Tony needed to move him out of his fog. Still dazed, he opened the screen door, and for the first time I could recall in my life, my father was holding me.

Father and I both began to sob. As we embraced, he kept repeating, "This is a miracle, this is a miracle, I thought I would never see you again, God brought you to me, this is a miracle." I had waited a lifetime for this moment. I did not want it to end or to let go of him, fearing that this dream would vanish before my very eyes. He was so thin; I felt he would break if I hugged him as tight as I wanted.

We composed ourselves, Macy returned home to give us some privacy, and my father invited Frank and me into his living room, where we sat on the sofa. I call him my father because Dad is an endearing name saved for the one you have known. I never knew this man.

It was all a blur; I don't know who spoke first. We sat, we cried, we talked; it was more than I could have expected. He did remember me. I felt truly blessed, for some reunions such as these are not so joyous. There was no time for small talk; we didn't ease the tension by conversing about the weather or baseball; those were of little importance now. I cut to the chase.

This man looked too weak; I felt he could drop at any moment, especially with the shock of meeting me. My words were chosen carefully but not consciously; they came from deep inside, a place I did not know I could access. I am not sure where my courage came from, but I boldly asked the question that I ruminated about for years. Without a preconceived thought, I blurted out to my father, "Why didn't you come to see us? Didn't you care, didn't you love us?" His tears flowed in streams down his sunken cheeks. When he regained his composure, he responded, "I have always loved you."

I was overwhelmed. My entire being was trembling. I was filled with relief and joy. His words of love were the only words I needed to hear; my life was now complete. I knew my father loved me. He continued, "They would not let me take you for visitations; you were too small." I knew his recollection was correct. I weighed a mere five pounds at birth, and I heard that my weight gain during my first year was very slow, probably because my mom struggled as a single mother on her own. As he spoke, the story unfolded. The history I had longed to hear my entire life, answers to questions I dared not ask my mom, and now the gaps about my father's were going to be filled in.

What was odd to me was the emerging feelings of compassion I had for this stranger. It is difficult to miss someone you never spent time with; their energy is so foreign. I did not know what a father's love felt like, so I hadn't missed it. Or so I thought. Over the years, people asked me what it was like to be fatherless. I could not tell them; it was uncharted territory. Perhaps buried deep in my psyche was the love for my father, but it never stood out in my conscious thoughts. I accepted what I was given and understood it was pointless to question my circumstances. There was nothing I could do to make my father appear, so I moved on. But in my subconscious mind, I was stuck in the uncertainty of being abandoned. It colored how I acted and thought in all my relationships.

My father's name rarely came up in conversation, but the few stories I heard were rooted in my mind because I wanted to hold onto them, feeling that somehow then he would be close. The story about my birth did not warm my heart. I recalled my mother telling me about one of her friends who saw my father in a store after my birth. The friend said, "Congratulations Tony, you have a sweet baby girl." My father responded, "I don't have a baby girl." Over my life, embedded in my memory, his denial of my existence was repeatedly told. And if perchance I had pushed it away, my mom stepped up to remind me. I know she did not do this with malice; she was only expressing her pain, unaware of how it continued to injure me. The feeling this story instilled in me was not right, yet it endured. "Your father did not love you, he would not even acknowledge your existence, and you are not worthy of his love." It drilled in the belief that I was not worthy of anyone's love, not a sturdy foundation for building loving personal relationships.

My father's recollection was different from Mom's; he told me my mom did not even tell him when I was born. He shared how he wanted to be at my birth, but Mom never offered him an invitation. They were already separated and not on speaking terms. The way he found out about me was from that friend who approached him in the store. He gave me the key to understand the story from 1948 that I had assumed was correct. Now, as a grown woman, I could begin to clear the regret and pain that the story had caused. All I had ever wanted to hear was a story other than the one that had hurt me for so many years. As he gently disclosed the truth, it made sense, and I did not have to blame him for what he had or had not done. When he first heard about my birth he was shocked, and it appeared once again that my presence had jolted and awakened him.

Father wished Mom would have reached out to him in her time of need; he would have driven her to the hospital and shared in their baby's birth, but that was only his dream. That would not happen; he did not consider that Mom was under duress, caring for one baby and another about to be born. Needing financial support, she had no choice but to move back with her mother and father in their small apartment. Her mother was a woman who was determined to keep my father from reconciling with Mom at all costs. Why I don't know, this was just the way my gram was. She was controlling, and I do not think she even knew why she acted that way. Perhaps Gram thought her actions were protecting my mother's heart, but that was not the case. Nonetheless, living with her mother, Mom had to follow her guidance and not call my father when I was born.

Listening to my father, I found I was not the only one impacted by the non-existent relationship between us; the effect on him was far more significant than I had imagined. Yet he had done nothing in our time apart to change it. Why? That part of the riddle began to unfold.

Sitting on the sofa, our hearts open, my father continued as he recapped the events after the divorce. "I came to see your brother and you, but your mom was at work, so I had to face your grandmother. She barely opened the door wide enough to reach her hand out, take the child support check, and snap back, 'The babies are sleeping!' before shutting the door in my face."

Father continued to contact us by hand-delivering the child support checks until his heart did not let him return. Later, I shared this story with my mom to receive clarification. She did not take responsibility for the refusal of a father to see his children. She said, "Your father did not come to visit at the times designated by the court." As for the door that was closed in his face, again, she took no blame. "It was not my fault," which was right. My gram ruled the roost. No one told Gram what to do.

Gram was a stocky, headstrong woman you did not want to cross. She felt my father had deeply hurt Mom and made sure he would not have a place in her life. I can only speculate how insecure Gram was because her opinion was always the correct one, and she rarely heard another person's perspective. She carried her rightness so far that there was no room for anyone else's idea on how to live their own life. I later found my father was like my mom, weak against their influential family members who ruled them. For Mom, it was her mother; for my father, his authoritarian was his oldest sister, Mary, their family's matriarch. Like Gram, Aunt Mary felt her family member had been mistreated and counseled her brother to walk away from his marriage. If they had only known how their actions inhibited my parents' reconciliation and injured my brother and me, I know they would have advised them differently.

My father continued his story. "They would not let me take you on visitations; you were so tiny. I held you once in my arms," he again reminisced. "I could carry you only as far as the curb to my mother, who was in the car; she wanted to hold you. That was the only time I held you." The explanation of why he stopped coming to see us continued to evolve. My father's voice shook as he recalled the last time he was with my brother, who was one and a half at the time. "When it was time for me to leave, Jimmy did not want me to go and held tightly onto my leg. As I walked away, Jimmy held his arms outstretched to me, but my time was up. I had to depart. His actions tore at my heart, and from that point on, I could not bring myself to go back."

My father once again lost his composure as his breathing deepened; he began to sob, and the tears rippled down his face. I sat by his side where I could feel his grief. I wanted it to be different than it was. I wanted him to be reliable, to be my knight in shining armor, to come and rescue me long ago from the house I had to live in, but being with him revealed the truth. Father was not strong; his will was broken, perhaps before his marriage. He ran away, letting go of his family and his responsibility to us, financially and emotionally. But his actions injured not only us, but him as well. His self-induced pain, over time, took a toll on the organs that encased his heart—his lungs. They were giving out, and he was losing the ability to take in the breath of life.

Father turned to me and sadly said, "Perhaps God is punishing me by giving me lung cancer because I left and did not support you and your brother." I hoped it was a comfort to him when I replied, "God does not act in that way; God does not punish." But this was a belief my father had harbored since my birth. My simple statement was not going to wash it away now. It was clear he questioned his actions, and it had put a strain on his ailing heart, lungs, and body for decades. I felt his psyche, not God, held his pain for abandoning his wife and children.

As I sat by my father's side in his living room, tears drying on our cheeks, he looked deeply into my eyes and took a long breath. It was time for him to ask the question that had haunted him for years. I had quizzed him. Now it was his turn. I could feel the pain in his voice as he spoke; it appeared once again I was to be the fall guy for my mom. I wanted him to ask her. Why me? I wanted this to be just about us—our reunion. I did not want to reply to his question. I was not the one who made up the story; Mom was the one that hid the truth. Why was I put in the position of answering for my mother's indiscretions? He probed, "Is it true? Did your mom tell you that I was dead?"

I was more than a little annoyed. It was not right that my mom and gram conjured this tale, and I became the one who had to answer my father. There was no way to avoid the issue. It may have seemed cleverly concealed in the past, but the facts have a way of emerging. This one took decades.

With a sigh of remorse, I affirmed that the rumor he'd heard was indeed true. My brother and I were told, and for a time believed, that he had died in the war. What a cruel lie to tell a child. My father's demeanor became very still. His facial expression was unchanged, telling me that he knew the story was correct but needed to hear it for himself, not from hearsay. Now that I confirmed the gossip he had heard over the years, knowing the truth did not soften the blow; it took him back to the same pain he felt when he first heard the lie, and there I sat wrapped in his agony. Again we cried together.

OUR STORIES REVEALED, my father suggested our next step: to meet his family. Luckily, I found my father was elated to see me, but what about the rest of the family. Would they know who I was, and would they accept me? And then there was Aunt Mary. Mom spoke more of her than of my father. Mom portrayed Aunt Mary as the wicked witch of the west, and now he wanted us to drive over and meet her; this was too much to process in one day. The thought came to me, be careful what you ask for, you might get it, meaning when receiving your heart's desire, it may not appear as you had imagined. What if the others did not share my father's delight? The dream now manifesting called for nurturing and support; otherwise, it might die and fade away. With my wish fulfilled, I had to continue to act upon it.

Still shaken from our meeting and fearful of taking the next step, I discovered life had a way of lightening even the heaviest moments. After my father and I talked for about thirty minutes, he picked up the phone and called his sisters, Aunt Mary and Aunt Rose. The conversation began, "Guess who's here." I would have laughed out loud if I hadn't already been numb from the afternoon's events. Not in a million years would they have suspected who had stepped back into his life and was sitting by his side.

Sadly, my Aunt JoAnn, my father's third sister, had passed away the previous week. Many of my cousins, who had moved away, came for JoAnn's service to support their grieving family. I found it synchronous that I appeared at the time they were all in town. Our drive to Aunt JoAnn's to meet the family presented even more anxiety for me; it seemed I had opened a can of worms.

The anticipation of meeting the stranger who might be my father was daunting enough, but now I had to encounter Aunt Mary. Although Mom never used derogatory words, her sentiments painted Aunt Mary as the meddling woman who was not on Mom's side; therefore, this ride frightened me, though it was not as alarming as my father's driving. He looked too frail to walk, let alone drive, yet he became our chauffeur and escorted Frank and me to Aunt JoAnn's home. What happened next shook my world.

Aunt Rose—Aunt Ceal—Mom—Macy—flower girl—cousin RoseMary
Macy, Mom's high school buddy and attendant at her wedding, called to report what she heard.

Bobby and Mom, dressed for the prom.
Father came home from World War II. A few years prior, Mom's high school sweetheart, Bobby, perished in the war, a heartache that stayed with her.

Mom had large, beautiful blue eyes; mine were also large but as a child were dark brown, and later turned green in my late teens.

There was no need to go alone. My troop consisted of myself, Frank (pictured below), and Macy, who did not want to miss the drama if it occurred.

I walked up the stairs to a screen door that revealed a solid wood door fully open behind. Because the main entrance was accessible, I felt safe. This man did not lock his doors ... perhaps he wouldn't see me as a threat.

Blake—Crystal—Marnie—Frank—Carmin

We looked happy from all outer appearances, but I was fooling myself and those around me by becoming passive to the unbalanced parts and deluding myself into thinking everything was fine.

The problem is not the problem.
The problem is your attitude about the problem.

Chapter Two

IF THE TRUTH BE KNOWN

THE CAR RIDE WAS ABOUT FIFTEEN MINUTES, AND EVEN THOUGH my father was weak and a wisp of his former self, his driving was not as daunting as I anticipated. He parked the car and we walked along the side street, lined with small rust-colored brick bungalows, similar to the ones I remembered from my childhood. It all seemed uneventful until a completely unexpected magical moment shifted the entire scene.

As naturally as breathing, my father reached down and placed his hand in mine, a simple gesture yet so profound. I felt weightless, walking on air, in a dream. I thought to myself, "I am holding my father's hand for the first time in my life; it doesn't get better than this." Even today, I can touch that memory, and my eyes fill with tears.

I can recall an afternoon many years prior that reflected the same feeling. It was also a brief enchanted moment. I can physically feel the effect today, and it sparks my memory and lifts my heart with joy. It happened one day while walking to the store with my two young children, Carmin and Blake, five and three years of age. I held tightly to their tiny little fingers as we crossed a wide busy street. Their short legs were going as fast as they could. Cars were streaming past as we quickly trekked across the thoroughfare.

On that day, holding my children's hands placed me in a blissful state for an inexplicable reason. There was nothing special happening to create this sensation, and I felt it only momentarily. For a passing instant, I was washed with gratitude for having their sweet lives gifted to me to protect and care for, if only for a short time. This sensation of love moved through me like an electrical current. Even though the joy touched me for just an instant, the memory still makes my heart skip a beat whenever I recall that day. Walking with my father towards my aunt and uncle's home became the second similar captivating moment.

We walked up the stairs, shaded by trees, of Aunt JoAnn and Uncle Mario's home. On that bright afternoon, the light changed as we entered the dimly lit living room that held the sorrow of Aunt JoAnn's passing. People were standing and sitting throughout the space, and no one was familiar to me. I entered with my father by my side; everything was happening so fast, and I was still unsure what would happen next.

As I gazed across the room, sitting just inside the door, in a wheelchair, was Uncle Mario with a welcoming smile that brightened the dark room. Covering his head was lush silvery-white hair, and his blue eyes sparkled even with his heart hurting from losing his loving wife a few weeks before. His spirit was light, and he was quite happy to see me.

Next, I met Aunt Rose, a wisp of woman, thin, with a distinctive rather shaky voice; but there was a feistiness in her that told me she knew her mind and was not afraid to speak it. Her small piercing eyes looked right into mine as she began to cry and hold me tight. Her words rang into the room, "Marlene, Marlene, we thought we would never see you again." Yes, my birth name is Marlene. I shortened it at twenty-one, much to my mother's dismay.

As I stood in the middle of the living room, a stranger before them, they raved over me and noted my resemblance to my aunt. "She is just like JoAnn," exclaimed Aunt Rose, as the others chimed in, "Yes, she is." What were they talking about? I had hardly said five words, but they were confident they saw in me the traits of Aunt JoAnn. What could I do? I just followed along.

JoAnn was described as outgoing, ready for a party, quick with a joke, and always smiling. Hmm, she does sound like me; perhaps there is something to this DNA thing—genes and all of that.

"JoAnn brought you to us," said Aunt Rose, "I know it." Was what they were saying true? Thinking back, I wondered, did Aunt JoAnn orchestrate this whole meeting the week she passed on? On the day the priest asked the parishioners to say prayers for my father did she connect with Macy from the other side and whisper in her ear, "This is the day you need to go to mass." Was she the unseen force that kept me pursuing my quest to meet my father and fulfill our lifelong dreams? Was she by my side those two weeks as I searched how to meet Macy? Indeed, somebody was. I certainly felt a presence stronger than myself moving me towards my goal to meet my father. Did Aunt JoAnn stand by my side as I walked through Mom's home, directing me to the address book where I would locate Macy's phone number? Goodness, I thought, could this family be the connection to my metaphysical consciousness?

My mother's family certainly did not hold this strange psychic mindfulness. Heavens, the thought of the dead reaching out to help us in our everyday life was not a thought entertained in my family of origin. My new-found family believed in spirits who could connect to those who were still in physical form. Cool.

A N HOUR BEFORE, I had stunned my father; now, it was my time to be shocked. As I stood in the living room, they greeted me like the prodigal son. I was overwhelmed. The love expressed to me was not expected. Courtesy, sure, but overwhelming affection?

I had never anticipated such a greeting. In all my fantasies of meeting my father, I had never imagined what it would be like to connect with his family or what their reactions might be. What I had envisioned never went beyond the initial meeting with him. I had no idea what I would find in the discovery of my long-lost father, let alone aunts, uncles, and cousins. I was relieved to know that I was never forgotten; I was loved, missed, and even yearned for by my father and his entire family. I had never expected it. Aunt JoAnn's passing gave my cousins, who had moved to the West Coast, a reason to return home. I found it so curious that many of them were present on that enchanted day when I met my father. The magic continued.

Next to step forward were my cousins. One by one, they approached me with open arms and warm smiles. Standing in JoAnn's living room, I thought, "How bizarre that these people who didn't even know me could shower me with such sweetness." How wrong I was. They not only knew of me, but they were acutely aware of the pain my father carried from the loss of me, and each held a story about me, which prompted their adoration. My cousins told me that when the conversation went in the direction of Uncle Tony's children, an adult said, "That is family business," and not another word was uttered. My brother and I were the elephants in the living room that no one spoke about, yet unknown to us, our presence was always there.

Knowing that my father's family would shush the children when they spoke out highlighted how our families were not so different. We all had a silent code: do not discuss your feelings; stuff away your sadness, shame, or guilt. Perhaps it was a sign of the times in the 1950s. But it was time for a change.

Months later, as the day's events sank in, I found their love for me allowed me to acknowledge and feel my worth, which added greatly to my self-love. Up to that point, I had never thought I fit in anywhere, certainly not in the home where I grew up, nor at school, or even in the jobs I obtained. As a lonely child, I was the odd one without a father; my family unit did not reflect those in the neighborhood. This feeling of not fitting in was the same when I was a hairdresser in my 20s. I worked in a prestigious beauty salon in Marshall Fields, a notable department store in Chicago. I was surrounded by thirty workers twice my age. Their ages began at forty and went up from there. Let's just say we did not hang out. Over the years, I found a way to adapt by becoming an entrepreneur. I did not have any co-workers as friends because I worked alone and only met people briefly when I sold my products. In Uncle Mario's home, I was in a group where I sensed I was home. I could see, and they affirmed, that I was a piece that fit into the picture.

The stories my cousins remembered about my brother and me evolved sweetly. Cousin Patty, daughter of Aunt Rose, was like her mom, petite and gentle, almost fragile, with a soft voice that radiated a caring presence that shone out to me. I felt this young woman accepted me. Patty recalled the only time the family was able to be with me was when I was a few months old. It was at a picnic on a warm day. She was playing with her seven cousins, frolicking in the grass, and out of curiosity, she would peek into the baby basket to see if she could make me smile. Whenever she heard "Tony's children," her memory returned to that summer day in the park, with the cute innocent baby in the basket. When questions about us arose, the inquiries stopped with the halting words "Family business," but those words could not erase her memory of me. Now I stood before her, and she could physically embrace her lost cousin. And she did it with relish, her arms enfolding me, and she melted my heart.

Even hairdresser Paul, Uncle Mario and Aunt JoAnn's oldest son, had burned in his memory the last time he saw his little cousin, my brother Jim. He told me he could still see this tiny toddler waving goodbye from the landing of the wooden steps that lead to the back porch. Then my brother slowly climbed up the steps to the third floor. His short legs could advance only one step at a time. Paul was now a self-assured, successful businessman, confident in himself, yet I could sense how the loss of seeing his little cousin had touched him.

My cousin Carl, the second son of Uncle Mario and Aunt JoAnn, moved to the center of the circle next; like his dad, he had a smile that lit up his face. He looked like your typical, handsome Italian man, with thick dark hair and deep-set eyes that pierced into your heart. He was small in stature like his brother Paul, and his stocky form housed a loud voice showing his strength. When he spoke, his whole body acted out his words. His hands gestured, his arms moved about, and his body swayed. Because of his alluring personality, I connected with this animated character right away; there was no way to avoid his dynamic draw.

What a day! I had a whole new perception of love. I had uncovered a family: a father, cousins, aunts, uncles—it was a lot to take in. Even in my absence, I was part of this extended family. I felt so close to them; it was like I had known them all my life; it was a genuine heart connection; I felt blessed, overwhelmed, yet at peace.

At last, I had found where I belonged. I had never matched my mother's family. My mom and brother had beautiful blue eyes and brown hair; my cousins were blue-eyed, fair-skinned, and quite reserved. Not me, I was loud, upbeat, outgoing, and as for the physical appearance, I did not fit that mold either. I had jet-black hair and dark eyes. Mom, Gram, my mom's sister and three cousins were not demonstrative or comfortable showing any form of affection. When I would get excited and happy, my mom or gram ordered, "Don't be so silly," and I would need to curtail my enthusiasm. With them, I felt like a real misfit.

STANDING IN UNCLE Mario's house, each family member wanted their hug. They came forward to meet me one by one, until there was only one left. My head was spinning from all the love I was receiving from my new relatives, so it didn't register in my mind that I had not met the one I feared the most—Aunt Mary. Her introduction came last, honoring her position as the matriarch of the family. She slowly entered the center of the room, her steps uneven yet moving with intent. She stood less than five feet tall, a slight figure who wore a cotton dress, with black laced shoes that supported her ankles. Mary did not look as ominous as depicted by my mom. Mary, like all of us, had grown older. There was a large hump on her back. Her walking was labored, and her body hunched over, which made her look even smaller than her tiny form. True to the day's pattern, I did not have time to calculate my next move if there was a confrontation. I was not in control of my circumstance.

As she approached, I was surprised to find she looked at me with a gentle gaze that made me realize I had nothing to dread. Like Aunt Rose, she hugged me tightly and cried. She met me with the same love I felt from the surrounding family members. I had no choice but to relax into her embrace.

We assembled in the living room. During our conversations, I found no words of ill feelings directed towards my mom; in fact, Aunt Mary expressed regret for intruding on my father's relationship with Mom. She affirmed, "Families should not interfere with the personal ties of their siblings." Then she apologized again for her actions and the consequence they had on my parent's marriage. Aunt Mary had many years to reflect on how my father was affected by the loss of his family. I was shocked and pleased that she was not the person my mom implied, and I was taken aback by her remorse.

That afternoon, each family member had a story to share. If a story arose, pointing the finger at my mom or gram, my father's family would say, "Water under the bridge," immediately dropping the subject. I had never anticipated such a welcome that afternoon nor seeing Mom respected even though she was not there. I found it refreshing. We left my uncle's meager bungalow, agreeing to get together the next day so my father could meet his grandchildren. I was in a trance.

W E DROVE BACK to the west side of the city to my cousin's house, joyously recounting the day's events, but when we sat down with Cis, the mood switched. My mom's sister Ceal had three children, Cis was the girl sandwiched between her brothers. She was a few years older than me, but she never neglected me when we were small and my family was visiting her house. She always included me in her activities, often playing with her girlfriend. Her lifelong best friend Charlotte lived in what I deemed to be a castle. It was a two-story yellow brick house which to me, looked gigantic. I was always in awe as we climbed the stairs to enter Charlotte's private, always pristine, bedroom, with a pink-flowered comforter and dolls neatly placed about the space. We never played with any of those dolls, so I didn't touch them and sat courteously.

I listened to the older girls talk, happy to be there, but not quite fitting in. I was included in part of my cousin's life, but not fully.

Now, Frank and I sat at Cis's kitchen table, where important conversations happen. I began to share the day's occurrence as Cis looked at me with a blank stare. It was so hard to put into words the emerging feelings, and my cousin was nonresponsive, even cold, to my observations of this moving day.

Cis reflected the repressed sentiments so often displayed by my mother's side of the family. Even though I knew they loved me, their hugs were ones where you hardly touched, that is, if you even got a hug. There was only light pressure from their hands, their body's stiff, placing an inch or so between our chests. Our hearts never touched. The contrast between these two families, especially on this day, was alarmingly apparent. I found it difficult to process, and it became unsettling. I had recovered the love that I thought I never had. How could my cousin not embrace my joy? But then, I did not know the stories she heard in her home about my father. I was sure my Aunt Ceal did not paint a pretty picture, and it no doubt tainted my cousin's understanding of my situation.

Unlike Aunt Mary, who exonerated my family, Cis still held anger towards my father. She had no place in her heart for forgiveness. I cannot recall her exact words, but I felt her disdain and ridicule for my father's actions or lack thereof. I felt judged and almost reprimanded for going to see the man who had abandoned me. My compassion for my father fell upon deaf ears.

Cis's callous attitude hurt me and reminded me of one reason why I had left Chicago and my family ten years prior. I felt there was nothing to hold me there. My cousin's cold heart reassured me that in my absence, I was not missing much. When I left the Midwest and headed to a new frontier, the West, I searched for a new and better life. How interesting that I needed to return to the city I had run from, only to find the love for which I had been searching. It's an irony that rings true so often in life: we run away only to find that what we are seeking is back at the place we left.

In private, my husband shared his observation; his words consoled me as he said, "Now the pieces fit. There was always something missing in you." Once again, like when he stood behind me at my father's door, I was blindsided by his support. We were not getting along; our marriage appeared to be coming to an end, yet he shared an insight with me that was completely unexpected. This lack of continuity that Frank observed in me did not show up until my lost fragments were discovered and claimed this day. Now Frank could look at my father's family, see why I had acted the way I did, and perhaps understand what made me tick. Now I made sense to him.

Back at my cousin's home, Frank and I continued to unravel what had happened this day of meeting my father. I looked into Frank's blue eyes as he spoke. The feelings I had were indescribable, and it was consoling to hear someone, especially him, make sense out of what had just happened. And what was the analogy Frank referenced about the pieces fitting? I had always felt like a pretty together person. What was I not seeing? It took some time to process and understand his observation. That day, meeting my father validated my very existence; yet my cousin Cis, who had known me for forty years, did not understand my actions, support me, or comfort me. Did she truly know me?

I questioned my emotions. Was she correct? Was I a fool to let my father back into my life? Could I trust him? Would he hurt me again?

That night I lay motionless for hours on the sofa in Cis's living room, my family around me on air beds on the floor. I did not want to disturb their rest, but sleep was not my friend that night. My mind was scrambling to integrate the happenings of the day. But I must have dozed off, for when morning came, I noticed a soft light entering the room. I turned my head and found my daughter Carmin's compassionate brown eyes looking at me. We whispered, eager to share our thoughts, not wanting to awaken the rest of the family. She was excited about soon meeting her grandfather. I sensed my Colorado family supporting me from every angle, and that was enough for me.

THE NEXT DAY was the fourth of July, one of my favorite holidays. I loved the anticipation of fireworks and driving through the city to see where we would find them. I was always mesmerized by the brilliant colors and light displays in the sky. It all tied in with the exhilaration of our reunion. Now my father would meet his grandchildren, and they, their grandfather. He told me he would call after he and his wife went to a picnic at his stepdaughter's home.

While we waited for my father to show up, we barbequed at Uncle Mario's house, shared stories, and got to know each other. But as the day went on, the question remained, where was Uncle Tony? My happiness dimmed with each hour as the clock ticked away. I lit sparklers with the kids and laughed with Carl to drown out the thought that my father was not going to show up. At nine o'clock in the evening, my father called and said, "I cannot see you, I am tired, and it is too late." Then my heart, which I had been holding together, began to sink and break.

Father did not come by because his wife kept him at her daughter's home until he was too tired to see me. Months later, when I met her, I saw his wife was a chubby woman who wore flamboyant clothes of aqua, hot pink, and yellow, or other combinations that never quite matched. Her novelty sparkling-ball earrings would light up with the press of her finger. A holiday would not pass without her adorning herself with shamrocks, hearts, bunnies, witches, or wreaths. Those behaviors would seem to make her friendly, but that day, she did not embrace our reunion. I assume she was confused about the purpose of our reconciliation and jealous of my one-day connection to my father. She kept him away all day, making sure he would not meet my children.

I found it telling that my father had married a woman who controlled him just as his sisters had done when he and my mom were having difficulties. Once again, I saw his weakness. He did not stand up to his wife and express his heart's desire to greet his bloodline. I can only guess her reasoning. Perhaps she thought I was after his money, of which there was little. I was disappointed but not defeated. I would be in the city one more day, and I was sure we would meet then. Once again, I would need the aid of my family to keep my hopes alive. I kept a positive attitude, so I went to sleep with visions of happy times with my father.

The next day I called to see when we could meet. My children were excited to see for themselves how this man held them in his heart. I felt this was going to be a momentous occasion for them as well. His voice was soft as he informed me, "We cannot meet. I have family problems, and I cannot have you and your children come to my house." I am good at finding solutions, so his remarks did not throw me off. I suggested we meet at the park. Once again, he declined. With a shaky voice, he continued his reluctance to see us, "I cannot see you in a public place; the neighbors will be watching, and I do not want them to see me cry." His words created a sadness that still resides in my heart.

Was I hearing him correctly? Could this be? We had just met, and again, he denied me access to his life because he was afraid of having his actions judged. How poignant to allow the opinions of others to get in the way of our happiness. The old story of our nonexistent life was reenacted again. My father was not strong. He never was.

I had imagined a different conversation of how my father would stand up to his wife saying, "This is my daughter and her children. I lost her long ago.

I need to do this. It does not diminish my love for you. I must go to see them! Please, give a dying man his last wish. Let me have this now." But alas, that conversation happened only in my head. Those thoughts never formed in his mind, and if they did, those words never left his lips. His whole life, he allowed others to orchestrate his choices. Even during his last days, with depleted courage, he did not dare to ask for what he desired. I suspect my father never told his wife how he felt, and he remained under her control until his dying day. When expectations are unmet, if allowed to fester, they can spoil one's life; I was not going to let that happen to me. I accepted the outcome, releasing regrets of how it should have been, took my family, and left Chicago. Sadly, two of my three children never got to meet their grandfather.

M Y FATHER WORKED in the printing industry most of his life, which probably contributed to the physical factor of his disease, but there is never just one reason for the body and mind to disintegrate. I sensed his saddened heart could have contributed to his illness, and I asked myself, "Now that we had met, was there time to repair his heart, or had too much time passed? Could our meeting heal a lifetime of remorse?" Time would tell.

Once reacquainted with my father, I spoke with him every week, but the conversations were short, uneventful, and in secret. My father's wife, Dolores, still had concerns about our bond, so he was afraid to phone me from his home because of her rule. I could see she did not want him to share his love with me, a stranger to her. She did not understand that when love is shared, it expands, and she too could have profited by our relationship. She had a daughter, and even though her daughter was in her late teens when they married and was an adult now, Dolores still felt he was her daughter's father and was not going to share him with me.

I was left out in the cold, denied his love, and he was not physically or emotionally strong enough to make his voice known. He had been battling lung cancer for the last year and did not have the stamina to fight anyone anymore. Would he ultimately give in to cancer? It appeared to me that my father never stood up for, or perhaps knew, what he wanted. Keeping the peace in his home was paramount, much to his discontent. But then there was Aunt Mary, who tried to keep a bond between us.

These two siblings' custom was to attend mass every Monday morning and then return to Mary's condo, where she would tempt his palette with hot syrup dripping over warm buttered pancakes. But the chemo had destroyed his taste buds, and he said all he could taste was metal. Nonetheless, on those days, she had other ways to brighten his spirit. I would receive a call from Aunt Mary, and her conversation would always begin the same. After a quick hello, she would go into her refrain: "Guess who's here." She would then hand the phone to my father, and we would talk. Once again, Aunt Mary took control of her brother's life, but this time, it proved beneficial.

Because cancer had eaten away much of my father's lungs, his dialogue was labored. The chemo injected into his body depleted his short-term memory, hindering our conversations as well. He would seem to have an important subject to address but would begin to cough, and by the time he could speak again, he could not collect his thoughts. Our conversations often were cut short, making it quite exasperating for both of us. I could see time was taking its toll on him.

When I returned home to Denver from my life-changing trip, I contemplated my next step, and it kept me awake at night. Telling my mom about how I had happily discovered my father was out of the question. My cousin Cis had shown me what the reaction of my mom's family would be. I wondered if I should even tell my brother what I had discovered about our father. If I did, how would he take the information? I was not ready to be judged again for my decisions. I wanted more time to relish the joy of my reunion before I needed to justify my actions.

My hair was always cropped short in a pixie for summer swimming.

My cousin Cis was a few years older than me, but when we were small, upon our visits to her house, she never neglected me, for she always included me in her activities.

Care about what other people think and
you will always be their prisoner.

LAO TSU

SUPPRESSED LOVE

BACK IN DENVER, I REACHED OUT TO MY BROTHER THREE times before I had the courage to tell him about my experience with our father. On the third phone call, I omitted a salutation and blurted out, "On my trip to Chicago last week, I met our father." "I knew you would go see him," he calmly answered. I was shocked. I didn't know that Mom had told him about the call she had received from Macy and that I would soon be going to Chicago on business. Why didn't he reach out to me to discuss the news? What did his aloof demeanor mean? Have I mentioned, we rarely discussed our personal issues?

In his authoritative way, Jim, playing the role of the older and wiser sibling, demanded, "You need to tell mom you saw him." I defiantly said, "No, I am not telling her." Mom's comment, "…not that he was ever a father to you," led me to believe that she didn't have an interest in my feelings about my father. I didn't want her to feel blamed for what had taken place over the years or rather what didn't occur, so I was always afraid to approach the subject. There's no way she would understand how I have felt about these lost years.

Mom had a father, a kind and gentle one at that. Didn't she know that I wanted to see what kind of father I had, besides knowing that he had run from me? Good or bad, I had the right to confront this person and determine if I desired to let him stay in my life. Now that I had discovered he loved me, I did not want Mom to rain on my parade or make me feel guilty about my actions.

I hung up the phone with my brother and walked back and forth across my sunroom floor to the sound of the waterfall by the pond outside the windows. The typical Colorado summer afternoon clouds were forming, reminding me of the gloom that now hung over my confused head. Rats. Jim was correct. I needed to talk to Mom, but I didn't want to face her discontent. I recalled how she had acted during her brief phone call to me on that day she dropped the bomb about her former husband. The picture became clearly defined. She wanted me to have nothing to do with him. Mom, I don't need your approval. I'm a grown woman! But unfortunately, I was still running my old patterns. Keep your mouth shut, Marnie, don't make waves, be a good girl.

When conflicts arise, I feel an urgency to face them, so I let Jim's counsel sit for a few uneasy hours, and later that day, I made the decision to release my fears,. Reluctantly I climbed into my Ford van and drove through the rain, to confront Mom face to face with my news. She had moved to Denver a few years prior and lived just down the street.

Mom's door was open, so I called to her as I entered the kitchen. I found her sitting by her afternoon cup of coffee with knitting needles in hand. A long confetti-colored scarf trailed below the table. "Hi, Mom, how's your day going?" She smiled at me and said, "I'm good. How was your trip to Chicago?" Great, a segue into my next step. I told her, "The weekend was hot and humid, so the turnout at the art show was low and did not give me the income I wanted, but it paid for the trip. The kids had fun with their cousins, and Carmin got to see her new university in Minneapolis, but there was something else that happened while we were there." Mom put the knitting needles down and moved to the edge of the chair. Her eyes were upon me. "I went to visit Macy and looked up my father. I saw him, Mom."

Mom stood up, her eyes flared with anger, and I thought she would strike me, but she walked on past. "Young lady! I can't believe you went behind my back and saw that man, after all he did." She walked into her bedroom, slammed the door, leaving no room for discussion. All I could do was go.

I drove home on the wet streets, to the sound of squeaking windshield wipers, past the empty park, sad and hurt. Over the years, I had never felt compassion from Mom. She never said I love you, so why would this event be any different. Silly girl!

It was difficult to fathom why she never thought I would search for my father. How bound Mom had become to her misguided memories, not even entertaining the ideas that her children might be affected by her story as well. Once again, I recognized a familiar family scenario. Neither she nor my brother was acknowledging or talking about the high level of emotions stirred up by the appearance of our elusive father.

While in Chicago, a few days earlier, while sitting at my cousin's kitchen table, moments after I had met my father, my cousin Cis, questioned me, "You went to see your father? After he abandoned you and gave your mother no support?" The air became chilly when she rose and stepped outside. I was stung by her remarks. She could not understand why I thought finding my father was appropriate to investigate. I was out in the cold. When I talked to my brother, he did not ask any questions about the event or how he could meet his father. It was becoming clear that neither my cousin or brother, nor mom was in favor of how I searched for and found my father. It had made me angry then, and can sometimes still bring my raw emotions to the surface.

On the other hand, I needed to give them time to process and hopefully empathize with this dying man. They needed time to unravel their feelings about my invitation to allow our father to reappear in our lives. After all, I was still processing my emotions. This was all new news to them.

The next day Mom settled down. After all, what could she do? The deed was done. Our bond was solid, but my father's appearance had put a block in our path, and we were both uneasy when we tried to discuss the situation. Our relationship was taking on a new form. She had to see me as the adult I had become, and we both needed time to adjust and hopefully grow. But I wondered how long my father had left and if amends could be made before he passed.

I NEEDED TO know how serious my father's condition was, yet I felt uncomfortable asking him. It's curious how empowered I had become, knowing that my father was ailing and weak. I released my inhibitions and took charge of the matter at hand. I had met Aunt Mary only once, and I felt uneasy calling her, but I did it and asked her if she would share her brother's prognosis with me. There was silence on the other end of the phone as she took a long breath and responded, "He has lung cancer, and it is a terminal condition. The doctor gave him a grim report six months ago. He told him that once diagnosed, most patients live only about a year." My heart sank, but I had hope. Meeting my father and his family changed my life; perhaps reuniting with his children would extend his!

Driven to continue my quest and solidify my family, I saw that my next duty was to encourage father and son to meet. Jim had not yet seen the regret I found in our father's eyes, so when I proposed the idea to him, he coolly responded,

"I will think about it." I understood his resistance; I had asked him to meet a stranger. Jim had often said that he did not remember much of his childhood, so I wondered if he recalled the same scene that our father had described. As a baby, Jim was crying, with his arms outstretched, as our father walked away. I'll never know. Jim never said.

Meanwhile, my father had time to anticipate how his son might react when and if they did meet. During our weekly phone calls, initiated by his sister Mary, I tried to approach the subject of how he felt about meeting his son. My father said, "It makes me nervous." And that thought brought on a coughing spell. When it ended, his next idea was gone. His coughing happened so often that it made our conversations spotty and brief. Trying to read between the lines, I wondered how he saw the pieces fitting together for him and his son.

These were the same things I had thought about before knocking on my father's door the first time. When I showed up at his bungalow, there was no preparation on my father's part to know how to greet his daughter, and I had had only two weeks to design in my mind what might unfold. Neither one was prepared for what happened. As I had stood before the frail man with the thin white hair, observing his confused stare, reluctantly I had to tell him I was his daughter. In that delayed moment, where I thought he would close the door, I heard, "This is a miracle, I thought I'd never see you again," and we then fell into our first loving embrace.

Not seeing the opportunity that lay at his feet, Jim let time tick away for two months as he contemplated whether to reconnect with our father. After all, Jim had not invited him into his life; I had. Challenged to be tolerant, my father and I were emersed in Jim's resistance to connect. Oh please, let Jim have the gift of love that I received. Don't let our father die before he meets my brother. And then the phone rang. It was Jim. "I'm booking a ticket to fly to Chicago. Pat and I will arrive on Friday night, and we will see what happens." Having Pat, his loving wife of twenty years, by his side made sense. She was a kind soul, who would naturally give him the moral support he needed. Still, this weekend would be easier for him than it had been for me when I met our father. All the pieces were in place for Jim. He did not need to wonder if this man was his father or where he lived. I had already laid the groundwork.

The plans were sketchy, but because I was the one who had opened pandora's box, I also wanted to be part of this event. My husband Frank had been my strength as I stood on the doorstep of the unknown man. Frank had encouragingly touched my back to tell me to continue to probe whether this man was my father. Once again, in this last part of my quest, I needed Frank with me.

I hoped that my oldest daughter Carmin, who was now attending the University of Minnesota, could now meet her grandfather and be part of this reunion. A week before, Carmin called with exciting news. "The sorority I hoped for has accepted me. My days and nights are packed full." Then I told her, "I too have news, Uncle Jim has finally decided to meet your grandfather, and it is happening in a week." There was a pause on the phone. She sighed and said, "I recall meeting Uncle Jim only a few times. He has always been kind, but I can't say we have a close bond, and this time may not hold the positive outcome you had. If I come, it will be for you, Mom."

Carmin did decide to join us and took a bus to Chicago, and upon arriving at our hotel, she wasted no time. She dropped her bags and said, "I'm anxious to meet my grandfather. Let's go." Frank, as our chauffeur, escorted Carmin and me to Aunt Mary's condo, and he knocked on the door. Aunt Mary's welcoming smile and warm embrace greeted Frank and me, but as she looked at Carmin, I saw a twinkle in her eye. To Aunt Mary's delight, Carmin, with her long brown curly hair, aptly carried her Italian heritage. Aunt Rose was right behind her sister and exclaimed, "Carmin, you look just like your Mom," and hugged her and held her hand as they walked towards the sofa where her grandfather reclined, shivering under a blanket. He looked at Carmin with love in his eyes as he began to speak, but then coughed and could say nothing. Later he told me, "She is beautiful. Seeing her gave me a glimpse of how you might have looked when you were nineteen."

Carmin appeared somewhat bewildered and then later back at the hotel said, "Mom, this was a lot to process, I didn't know how to act in a room with a family I never knew, and my grandfather, he looks so weak. He was so pale. He looked like a shell of a man. I have never seen anyone so close to death. They sure don't teach you about this in college." "You're correct, Carmin," I replied, "there is very little life left in him—mainly his soul."

Frank and I joined Carmin and sat next to my father, whose eyes filled with tears. Frank joined in the joy of seeing his family so happy. Having us by his side may have warmed my father's heart, but his body remained icy cold, indicating the pain from the disease that riddled through him. I had hoped the sight of me and the touch of my hand would soften his stress while waiting to meet his son. My heart went out to him, but I could do nothing to help, so we chatted nervously, waiting for Jim's arrival.

From the corner of the room, another person stepped forward to introduce herself. It was Dolores, my father's wife, a stocky, round-faced woman; and the thought of meeting her for the first time made me uncomfortable. I did not want to like her. She was the one who had kept me from bringing my children to see my father in July. Did Dolores consent to this evening's arrangement because my brother was not a threat to her? She had no son, no one to compare him to, whereas she might have felt that I, as my father's real daughter, threatened his rapport with her daughter. How could I? He didn't know me. I was not there to dissolve any prior relationships. I wanted only a very small part of his life, the one that I had been denied. However, this night, she gave me no reason to resent her. She quickly took her place, center stage, and I rose to greet her. Her smile was genuine, so I stepped forward. Still, her presence dampened my evening.

The only missing couple was Jim and Pat, so we knew it was them when the doorbell chimed. I quickly followed Aunt Mary to the door so Jim would gaze upon a face he knew. The introduction was cordial, with smiles and hugs, yet I felt a reserved undertone. I sensed that Jim did not understand what he was feeling, and I was familiar with his predicament. At first I also had felt odd around this man called Father. Being a genial man, Jim engaged his father in conversation, and I could slowly see Jim's barriers falling away with baseball being an easy subject for them to discuss. Jim shared, "Even though I moved to California, my baseball team has stayed the Cubs." My father agreed, "I have seen my friends move from the city, but we can always keep a conversation going talking about our Cubbies."

Jim and I grew up on the north side of the city, so there was no argument about the best team in our city. It was the Cubs, not the White Socks who played on the Southside. I could hear them mention names and batting averages that meant nothing to me. When Cub fans moved away from the city, their loyalty and support never waned. Father and Jim were remorseful about how the Cubs had not won a World Series since 1908. Those facts never dampened their spirits or their love for the game and the team.

Sadly, years later, when the Cubs finally captured the pennant in 2016, after 108 years of trying to nail the coveted award, my father had passed, so he was never part of the celebration. That day in 2016, the city went wild; church bells rang, the schools closed, the fans rejoiced, and all was right with the world. This evening, like when the Cubs won the pennant, there was a chance to right things in Jim's world.

Mini conversations were going on throughout the room, but over the voices, I could hear Jim's voice get excited as he described the time he and Pat lived on a small sailboat in a harbor of Los Angeles. Jim's stories flowed like California wine, sharing how they met independent thinkers and entrepreneurs while on their floating home. Jim described their adventures, "I would come home from working in my woodshop, and my neighbor would invite Pat and me to come on board to sail, drink wine, and watch the sunset. We would breeze back under the moonlight and return to our boat. I just liked being rocked to sleep while I listened to the water lapping against the hull. We didn't need to sail our boat because our friends had much grander ones, and we were happy to take off to Catalina with them." The night was going well. My father was happy, as were his sisters, but for me, it paled in comparison to the afternoon my father had introduced me to this family.

True, our first meeting held the element of surprise, which always electrifies a room, but I also had had an immediate sense of belonging to my newly discovered clan. We had had tears and stories, but this night, no one brought up any personal tales in front of Dolores. The usual code of silence stood unbroken, and my father did not change his pattern of concealing his emotions around his wife.

The evening had taken on some of the traits of Mom's family, adopted by Jim, ones of being reserved, proper, and guarded with one's feelings. On the other hand, I approached life differently from them, and on this night, the contrast between my mother's and father's families was blatantly in my face. No one talked about anything meaningful that night.

Father's family wanted Jim and Pat to meld into the group, so they continued to open their hearts, understanding the best way to offer love and acceptance is with food. We all adjourned to the dining room for one of Aunt Mary's simple dinners. "Aunt Mary, this is wonderful tomato sauce," I remarked. "Ah, in our house, we call it gravy," was her reply, as she ladled it over her homemade pasta. Yet, the gravy held so much flavor. Was it the excitement of the night that sweetened our palates? I inquired, "Aunt Mary, how do you make this scrumptious pasta?" "It is easy, you take some flour, a bit of salt, add water until it looks right, and maybe an egg." Oh, I wasn't going to try this one at home. I needed more steps. But it was kind of her to share her secret concoction. One ingredient she neglected to tell me that she had placed in the bowl was amore. That was the element that came from the recipe of the goat farmer's daughter, her mother, Grandma Palm.

WE FINISHED DINNER, and while the others were having coffee, Aunt Mary beckoned my brother and me into the privacy of one of her bedrooms. On the wall were pictures of the countryside of Italy, Jesus, Saint Anthony, Mother Mary, and a wooden cross with a rosary draped over the side. Our father followed. In an awkward gesture, he looked at us and said, "I want to give you something. I didn't know what to buy, I don't know what you like," and he handed us his offering—a one-hundred-dollar bill. I still have it. I knew he was doing the best he could, but I can't think of anything I would purchase that would be a remembrance of his love. He didn't see it, but he had already given me a priceless token. Knowing he loved me, missed me, and that his family had never forgotten me became his legacy to me.

But there was more my father wanted to bestow upon us. It was curious what my father had held onto over the years. He reached into his pocket and, without words, placed in each of our hands a total of three pink checks. Ones that he had never delivered! Now in our possession were a few child support checks that he had withheld because Gram would tell him we were sleeping and not let him visit.

This night, he again hand-delivered the checks, but this time my brother and I were not sleeping. Gram had since passed on, so the stipends went to the ones for whom they intended to serve. Here we stood, in front of him as adults. But these checks were late! Hardly worth the paper we held. I looked at my brother. We were speechless and puzzled by my father's actions.

Baffled, again we peered more closely at the checks, one dated July 9, 1949, ironically my mom's twenty-eighth birthday and over a year since my birth. Embedded in the pink paper, I felt the grief held by my father each time he had to leave my brother and me behind and how often those meetings did not even occur. These were the checks that had kept us apart—never cashed. My father had never thrown them away. He had kept them hidden in a drawer for decades, never forgotten, just like my brother and me.

Back home, I found Jim and I were not the only ones thrown off by these checks. Mom was aware of the trip Jim and I had taken, and when I returned, I shared our visit with her and showed her the checks. Her reaction was startling. Merely seeing these checks ignited a dark memory that took her back to 1949, waiting for the money she so badly needed.

The moment she looked at these checks, any anger she had stuffed away resurfaced. She grabbed the checks so fast the paper almost ripped in my hands. For her, it was still about money, but she was not aware of her patterned behavior. She said, "I will sign them, and then you can go cash them." Oh sure, I'm going to cash a check that is forty years old from a bank that no longer exists. Funny how her mind played tricks on her. Mom thought cashing the meager twenty-dollar checks would be a fine idea. She quickly signed the back, but in her haste, she wrote Mrs. Lorraine Vincolisi. Her mind placed her back in the timeframe when she was married—a Mrs.

I had no way of knowing my mom's thoughts over the years, but I wondered how many times she revisited those tumultuous days when she was still married? Did the memories bring her desire, remorse, or rage?

The other time I had seen her anger rear its ugly head was when she first told me my father was deathly ill. She shared Macy's words and added a little twist of her own. I reminded Mom that she had said, "Your father is dying, not that he was ever a father to you." Later, when I reminded her of those words, she emphatically denied ever saying that and responded, "That is a terrible thing to say." Then, as I saw with the checks, her actions were so automatic, so instilled, she had no conscious awareness of how her pain from the past made her react so negatively.

These checks were not a lot of money, but that was the price put on our heads. Pay it, and my father might get to see us. If not, he wouldn't. My father's ability to leave us made me wonder how traumatized this man might have been by the separation from his wife and children. However, it still hurt to think he didn't value his visitations with us enough to push through his pain and see his innocent children, no matter what the cost.

I had a few hours with my father. How could an entire lifetime be revealed and understood in a time frame that brief? But it was.

After we received the little pink checks, the evening concluded, and my brother agreed to meet with my father again the next day. On that cool fall day, my father filled in a gap to my parent's love story while he and Jim carved out a brief time to be alone. They sat in the park on a hard bench. The wood rails must have dug into my father's thin ailing body. His disease was advancing. His appetite almost nonexistent, his muscles half-starved, unable to receive the little nourishment he gave them, and with no fat to protect his skeleton, his bones protruded as he grimaced with pain. His diminished lung capacity also proved to be an inhibiting factor in their conversation. His words with Jim were labored as they were with me on our telephone calls. He could only recall ideas he wanted to express for brief moments, but there was one last thought he longed to share.

Jim told me that out of the corner of their eyes, they noticed movement. A woman was approaching, her face stern and focused. It was Dolores, quickly walking towards them. My father did all he could do to muster his thoughts together and command enough breath to deliver what he so wanted to express in the precise manner that he intended. Looking my brother in the eye, he professed, "I have always loved your mother." Pointing to his wife, he continued, "... and that is my hell." He had declared his love for our mom in a quick but fleeting moment. And he never touched the subject again.

Is fear stronger than love? Did my mother also love my father all her life? Did their timid natures keep them from reconnecting? Were they afraid of making the same mistake, concerned about what family members might say, scared to open their hearts and be vulnerable once again? They carried that trepidation in their bodies until it incapacitated both of them. My father could not breathe; my mom could not move forward.

I had to wonder if my father had had an undying love for Mom, why did he not act upon his feelings? My mom was available. She never remarried or even dated, but I don't know what her reaction would have been if he had shown up at her door. Aunt Rose told me, "Grandma Palm never accepted Dolores as your father's wife, and I suspect, like your father, was waiting for your mom to come back to him." But after fifteen years, the silent dream of my parents' reunion, held in this romantic Italian family, vanished.

Dolores later confided in me, "Your Father did not eagerly enter our marriage. Tony and I had been dating for quite a few years. I had gotten tired of waiting, so I asked him, 'When are we going to tie the knot?' " Dolores knew he was reluctant to make a permanent commitment, but she continued to press for more. So, to keep their relationship intact, he agreed to be married.

The weekend with Jim gave us some time to bond with our father. On Sunday, Carmin left to go back to college, and my father invited my brother and me to his home. I found it different from the first time I entered his small yellow brick dwelling. On this day, there were no surprises. My father's energy was up from Friday night, for he was on familiar territory now, aided by knowing that his son accepted him. In my eyes, Jim had made peace with whatever demons he had harbored about our father. I listened as my father and brother talked about how they liked to watch bowling on television. How strange, bowling is not a popular sport to watch, yet my brother and father enjoyed this pastime. It appears you can't run away from your genes. Later I would discover that I too held preferences that my father had.

With the reunion a success, we all flew back to our homes, holding onto the love we had found in my father. I was grateful that Carmin had gotten to meet him, connect to her roots, and perhaps see what makes me tick. Frank seemed content to have found more pieces to the puzzle that made up his wife, and the weekend gave me hope that Jim had found peace in knowing that his father had always loved him.

O NE MONTH LATER, back home, on a sunny warm October day, I re-ceived a call from Aunt Rose. The disease had taken its toll on my father's body, and he had passed away. Perhaps once he had met us, there was no reason to hold onto a body that had become so compromised. It appeared his journey on earth was complete. Standing in my bedroom, I sobbed with my husband by my side, but my sadness did not last long. I had worn the badge of grief from not knowing my father all my life, and now I felt my grief letting go. Meeting my father had filled that void. The years of uncertainty about his love had eaten away part of my heart, and now it was time for my healing. The softening of my heart came in patches, a little at a time. I was grateful that the next year continued to build loving connections with me, my brother, and my mom.

I did not have a lot of experience attending wakes. When I was twenty-three, my gram had passed away, making my father only the second close relative to die. I did not know how to be when sitting with the body of one who had gone, especially one that I had hardly known. It felt odd. My brother, his wife, and I were the only ones from my side of the family that attended my father's memorial service, but I felt supported in the company of my newfound cousins, aunts, and uncles. A couple from Chicago, who had been my friends for decades, came to the service, and though I did not think I needed anyone, their appearance filled my heart with gratitude. Jim, Pat, and I rode to the gravesite, and the sorrow we shared rebuilt a bond that I thought we had lost. My father's death brought many gifts, but one stood out from someone whom I did not expect.

After the burial, my father's wife Dolores invited us back to her home, where she was quite kind. To keep his memory alive, she shared things I did not know about my father. We sat in the living room where I had noticed on the wooden end table, sparkling in the sunlight, a cut glass candy dish. It had cellophane-wrapped caramels with a white sugary filling, Bulls' Eyes, my favorite candy. "Who likes these?" I asked Dolores. "Your father," she replied as I smiled and confirmed, "They are my favorite too." She asked us to join her in the kitchen, where she offered us a cup of tea.

Interesting, because in most homes, the beverage of choice would often be coffee. Even when I worked as a hairdresser, I always had drunk tea, whereas coffee was the fuel that kept my fellow cosmetologists running. I had never developed a taste for that tart-black liquid. Apparently, neither had my father. Dolores placed a cup of hot water on the table before me. I dipped the tea bag into the water and quickly back out. "I like my tea light," I said. "Then it is not bitter, and I don't need sugar." With her resistance to me dropped, she commented, "You're your father's daughter. He drank his tea the same way," she reminisced, "Tony and I would always share our tea bags." It consoled me to know that even though we had spent our lives apart, we were still alike in some ways.

How do these things happen? My brother and I knew nothing of my father's preferences; they were never a subject in our home, yet here we were mirroring his likings. What other habits did we have that were anchored so deep in our subconscious that we were utterly unaware of them?

Father's rooted traits were not limited to me. My cousins searched through their memorabilia to find pictures of my father so that I could have a photo journal of his life. In the images I received, I noticed that my father was always up to the latest fashion. In the 1960s, he wore bellbottom pants topped with a paisley shirt with a long-pointed collar. In the 1980s, curly hair was in, so my father got a perm, and as his hair greyed, he dyed it so he would look younger. Looking remarkably similar to him, at the same age, was my son Blake. His mannerisms reflected how my father walked, how he moved his hands, and how he had a keen eye for style. All these characteristics were a natural occurrence within Blake. So sad, he never had a chance to meet his grandfather and see this for himself.

The year after my father's death, Jim received a package from Aunt Mary that had a few items he thought I'd like to see. Therefore Jim invited me to his California home to see what Aunt Mary had sent. Frank and I loaded the kids into the van, and we drove to the land of palm trees, movie stars, and beaches. We settled into my brother's home, and seventeen-year-old Blake disappeared with his Uncle Jim for a short time. They reappeared with Jim entering the room first, smirking. With a Cheshire cat smile on his face, Blake walked in wearing my father's Navy uniform. It came from Aunt Mary. It fit his body to a T.

Father had his Navy uniform fitted with zippers on each side of the shirt, pants taken in to adhere to his sleek body, and adjustments for the sleeves and pant length. After noting how my father had watched fashion, the tailoring did not surprise me. The changes made were perfect for Blake. The entire uniform clung to his body as if it were adjusted for him. The smile on his face told me, in his grandfather's clothes, he could now feel his grandfather's presence embracing him. Blake's only comment was, "It fits." There was nothing more to say. My father fit: he fit into each of our lives in his unique way. This man was never physically present, yet he was, in some way, always with us. Unseen and still some of his traits were embedded into my family.

As a child, I had overheard conversations about my father late at night when I should have been sleeping. They were rare, so my memory is vague, but one story sticks in my mind. It highlighted my father's fear of dogs. The tale was never embellished, only that my father's father had been bitten by a dog, instilling in his son, my father, his deathly fear of dogs. After I was acquainted with my Italian relatives, they filled in the missing pieces about my Italian family. The story about my grandfather gave the dog scenario a whole new light.

Father reached into his pocket and, without words, placed in each of our hands a total of three pink checks. Ones that he never delivered!

With a Cheshire cat smile on his face, Blake walked in wearing my father's Navy uniform that had been sent by Aunt Mary... It clung to his body as if it was made just for him.

Father had his Navy uniform tailored to show his slim form with zippers on each side of the shirt, pants taken in to adhere to his sleek body, and adjustments for sleeves and pant length.

The first and great commandment is:
don't let them scare you.

ELMER DAVIS

IN THE STILL OF THE NIGHT

IN ITALY, GRANDFATHER VINCENT LIVED IN MURO LUCANO, THE
same small town as Grandma Palm, but he was not from that region. He
was an orphan, a foundling discovered wrapped in a blanket, discarded in the
street: abandoned, relinquished, and forgotten. In the late 1800s, disgrace and
humiliation accompanied an unwed mother, so to protect the reputation of my
great-grandmother, Grandfather Vincent's mother, her family removed her from
the comforts of her home and kept her hidden until his birth.

I cannot envision my great-grandmother willingly releasing her baby to the
cold streets of this village of goat farmers. But how did her family strip their
young charge from the life she had nurtured and carried in her body for nine
months? Did someone sneak into her room and remove her infant while she
was deep asleep, exhausted after arduous labor, only to wake up distressed and
find her once-warm bundle of joy gone forever, leaving her to lie alone in a cold
empty bed? Or did they tear him from her arms to the sound of baby and mother
wailing? How many nights did she cry out begging for his return to no avail and
finally fall asleep at dawn, regretting how she had allowed her passion for a man
to ruin her life and strip her of her newborn infant.

Did she return to her home, where no one knew of her plight? Was she
dismayed and angry because she had no choice but to abide by the previous
arrangements her parents had made? Perhaps she sadly married an unloving but
wealthy man and kept her secret buried in her broken heart until her dying day. Or

was the father of Grandfather Vincent his mother's true love, but tradition kept them from marrying? There was no way for her to mend her broken heart and find her son, nor could Grandfather locate her. Or did it happen another way? All these questions remain unanswered mysteries, and her family's plan to hide him remained a success. Their secret was buried forever. Over a hundred years later, there was no way to find out who they were.

When Vincent was three years of age, a judge gave him the name Vincolisi. It was not a name the judge picked without thought; he perceived this tiny boy's personality and gave him the name that suited him. His name translated to little strong one, and indeed he was. The village did not have an orphanage, so Grandfather was sent to live with a farmer's family in the town. They did not see him as a child to love and care for, but rather as someone who needed to carry his weight. They physically abused him, did not allow him to sleep in the house, and put him in the shed with the animals. They gave him enough food to survive, and then at five years old, turned him out into the fields to shepherd the sheep in the cold of the night.

What was Grandfather's plan if a wolf appeared? How could he protect the sheep, being no bigger than the lambs himself? I suspect his eyes remained open during the long nights for fear a fox might devour him along with the animals in his charge. Still, this never dampened his spirit; he found the unconditional love he sought for in animals and carried that admiration throughout his life, pouring the fondness of animals into his DNA that would filter into cousin Pam and Uncle Sal.

Even though Grandfather Vincent had been treated like an animal, he did not act unkindly to the creatures in his care. He nurtured and loved his four-legged family. The farmer moved his family, Vincent, and the animals to another village, but the uncaring farmer gave no heed to their confused cat, which kept running back to the old house. Vincent knew the cat would die without food, so he hitched up the wagon, trotted miles over the rocky roads to fetch the feline and bring it back to the new farm. The cat continued to run back to the old house, and each time Vincent would make the arduous journey and retrieve the cat until the cat remembered its new home. He made sure that both he and this pet would not be abandoned.

It was hard to deny Grandfather Vincent's Italian genetics; he had a dark mustache, a head adorned with thick black hair, and an unusual red beard. He never knew his heritage, but my relatives believed he came from a wealthy household in a distant town, for he possessed wisdom not found in the farmers of his surrounding communities. My aunts assumed that some family member dropped this little one off in a remote town, where no one could find him. He easily could have died, but his strong will allowed him to survive, and thus emerged our family lineage. It was clear to me now that my brother and I were not the only ones discarded by a parent. Locked within our genes is the poignant tie to abandonment.

As Grandfather Vincent grew, his intelligence was evident, as was his confidence. Sitting with goats did not fill his passion. He did not fit the mold of his meager community, so he gathered what books he could and taught himself to read and write. In the village, the talk he had heard said America was the land of opportunity, which started him thinking that there he could build a better life. With no connection to the people in the town where he was discarded, he set his sights high and started plans to venture across the sea.

Grandfather Vincent manifested his dream, but one trip to America was not enough for young Vincent. He sat rocking in the holds of ships numerous times to and from America until he could attain his dream on the shores of that distant land. He kept returning to his motherland, searching for a wife and a new life. In New York City, he had self-educated himself in the same fashion as in Italy. This time he used the publications of the city rather than books. Walking the muddy roads, dodging the horses and buggies, with a newspaper in hand, he would ask an unsuspecting passerby's the meaning of words. From these kind strangers, he soon mastered English.

Vincent married a woman in his town but wanted to offer her security before he asked her to join him and venture across the rough seas to America. It was important to him that he had work and could support her. In America, a letter arrived that told him that his wife had discovered she was pregnant. Tears of joy streamed down his face, for a family was also part of his dream. Mail was slow, so it took months before he learned that his wife had developed a heart condition and had passed away in childbirth, but thankfully his baby son survived. His mother-in-law had cared for the infant long enough and she requested that Vincent return to Italy to fulfill his duty as a father.

After losing a spouse, the custom was for women to wear black and for the men to mourn by not shaving. Vincent abided by this tradition of the 1800s. When Vincent returned to Italy after his wife's death, his wavy red beard with orange touches reached his stomach.

Vincent's mother-in-law told him that his mourning time had ended and that it was time for him to remarry. He was not interested in marriage, but he shaved his beard, consented to his mothers-in-law's wish, and hired a matchmaker. Matchmaker, what an intriguing concept, a person with the ability to find your true love. Could that work today? Maybe that is what we are missing. I, for one, would give it a try.

M Y FATHER'S MOTHER, Anna Marie, was one of six girls. She was nicknamed Palm because she entered this world on Palm Sunday. She had had many suitors, though she refused them all. At that time, girls married in their teens, so at twenty-eight, Anna Marie was considered the family's old maid. Her sisters called her the nun. One brisk fall day, walking with her five sisters, Anna Marie gazed at Vincent as he sauntered near. He looked her way, and their eyes met momentarily, which elicited the sound of giggles and teasing emanating from the group. Just that gaze was all the fire needed to ignite their romance. Her sisters worked in the fields with the goats, but Anna Marie's hands stayed clean, for it was her job to cook, and her meals were the best in town.

The matchmaker brought Vincent to Anna Marie's house, suggesting he marry one of her younger sisters. Vincent arrived at the house and found all the family girls in a line, waiting or him. The suggested farm girl did not call to his heart. Vincent looked across the house's dirt floor, where his eyes stopped at the sister who did not work in the fields, he picked Anna Marie, the cook for the family. He was smart. He knew what he wanted. His hand raised, pointing directly at Anna Marie as he professed, "I want that one."

Still, she did not jump at the opportunity of his conjugal request. By looking away, her coy demeanor reflected her avoidance of answering him. She never said yes, and she never said no. This nun was playing hard to get.

Vincent looked at her and spoke the words that his family still recalls today. "I will be at the courthouse steps in a week, "If you desire to be my bride, join me there." Then turning, he walked out the door. There was no courting, no flowers, no words of adoration. Asking for her appearance on the steps was his awkward way of telling her, "I want you to be mine."

I can imagine Grandpa Vincent arriving early at the courthouse, not wanting to miss the opportunity of marriage. Perhaps he was concerned that she might have arrived early, become nervous, and left. He wondered, "Will the woman I desire appear? Will my proposal be ignored?" He anxiously waited. Then he saw in the distance a single image walking along the dusty road, her skirt blowing in the breeze as she glided towards him, but it could have been any villager. As the figure moved closer, he could see this was Anna Marie. His wish granted, she stepped up to him and placed her hand in his. It was not a romantic beginning, but over the years, their love grew strong. Aunt Rose said that her father would always say, "I had two wives, and the second one was the best."

Vincent and Anna Marie had a simple but happy life. Their first child, a girl they called Mary, was the apple of his eye. But Vincent would not let go of his quest for life beyond goats, so he left the dusty town, Anna Marie and their baby behind, and boarded a ship heading to America. For three years, he sent his new wife letters, asking her to join him, along with money for a boat transit. Conflicted, Anna Marie would reluctantly discard his requests holding onto her fear of what might await her on the unknown shores of America. She felt safe in her village, close to her family, and could not envision herself crossing the sea. Eventually, she received a letter from Vincent that made her realize that she now needed to fulfill her marital duties.

Grandfather's words made an impact, "I will not force you to join me, but if you do not come now, I will consider our marriage over, and this is the last letter you will receive from me." That correspondence lit the fire needed to get this woman into motion. She turned away from her fears and made the necessary arrangements for the tumultuous trip across the sea. Anna Marie gathered up what little she owned, took the hand of three-year-old Mary, along with Vincent's first son, and boarded the next boat.

THEY HAPPILY UNITED in New York, but the city was overflowing with immigrants, so they piled onto the train heading for Chicago. In ten years, they were blessed with six rambunctious children who scampered through their small apartment. Leading the pack were Mary and Rose, who reluctantly helped their mom by guiding, or perhaps controlling, the younger ones. As the family grew, the younger children took on their parents' gentle nature, unlike Mary and Roses' tough exteriors. Sal came next and was different from the others; his abilities did not center in his brain but in his heart. Because of his special needs, he showered transcendent love to his family and animals. Next was Nunzi, an independent, know-my-mind kind of guy, and the middle child who kept the peace. Then came JoAnn, who was as loving and kind as my father, the last child.

Grandma Palm had longevity in her bones; she lived in her healthy body until one hundred and four. With no coiffure to speak of, this round white-haired lady, usually in a simple cotton dress, never learned to speak a word of English. Even though she had teeth missing, it did not inhibit her smile. Pam described her as genuinely selfless, kind, and compassionate, a saint walking on the earth. Pam recalled, "There always seemed to be a glow around her as she greeted you with her radiant smile. Upon entering the apartment, she would call out in Italian, 'Come Stai, Vieni da me.' How are you? Come to me. With a tilt of her head, she would spread her arms wide open, gesturing for you to approach and receive her loving embrace. She did not need language to express her feelings."

Grandfather Vincent held to the custom of being the sole breadwinner of his home, with eight mouths to feed. To uphold his position, he needed to work two jobs. His long hours away did not stop him from spending what little free time he had with his family. Grandfather Vincent would come home from working in the sewers and say to Grandma Palm, "Let me be with the children. You have had them all day. Now it is my turn. You go do what you like." Aunt Rose had shared, "We always knew he loved us, but he was still a strong disciplinarian. You did not step out of line. I heard in the inflection of his voice, 'You better mind your father.' So I did."

M Y FATHER'S OLDER brother Nunzi, at the young age of eleven, thought that he would like some cash of his own, and the best way to accomplish this would be to start a small business and acquire a paper route. The city's news was to be on the citizens' doorsteps, while the stars still twinkled in the sky, just before the sun came up. Grandfather Vincent was not in favor of little Nunzi's plan. It was the 1920s, and the streets of Chicago were rough. There was trouble often brewing from the dark dealings of the syndicate, run by the mob. These men thought nothing of leaving bloody bodies lying in the alleys, and Grandfather knew this was no place for a young boy alone.

Uncle Nunzi was fourth in the line of six children. Any reasoning Grandfather presented to Nunzi did not sink into this boy's strong head. He was determined to have and income, though meager, and he did not relinquish his plea. Grandfather knew how much it meant to Nunzi to have money jingling in his pocket; so as not to begrudge his son his dream, he consented to Nunzi's request. Grandfather demanded one non-negotiable condition. Grandfather was to join Nunzi on the paper route to keep him out of harm's way. Not to be left out of this adventure, the other brothers joined in. When their troop took off in the wee hours of the morning, the lineup began with Grandfather tall and strong, Nunzi, a confident eleven-year-old, Sal at twelve-years-old, a bit slower and often trailing behind, and Tony, a scrawny eight-year-old.

Grandfather would arrive home from his second job at midnight, drop exhausted next to his love in their small bed, and sleep for a few hours. Grama Palm would wake him at three in the morning to escort the excited boys on their paper route. They traversed the streets, and with their job complete, they would walk back home as the sun began to rise. He fulfilled his son's request and did not complain when he had only a brief time to rest before taking off to work in the dark pipes, below the city of his dreams.

Early one morning, while en route with the boys, newspapers in hand, Grandfather was alarmed by a dog's behavior on the opposite side of the street. The dog did not act normal: it was barking, agitated, and heading towards the boys! Grandfather, a lover of animals, thought he could put the dog at ease, so he spoke in a gentle voice, only to see that it wasn't working. Aware of the problem, he did not hesitate. He knew the only thing he could do to protect his sons was to take on the angry creature by himself. The sound and sight of the vicious growling dog froze the children in their tracks. Grandfather leaped in front of the youngsters, putting his hand out to stop the dog from attacking them. The dog lunged at Grandfather, its yellow teeth penetrated his skin, blood oozed from the bite. He slammed the dog to the ground, and then it ran away into the night. With the boys unharmed, his bravery commendable, they returned home, traumatized, frightened, and unclear of what would happen next.

Grandma Palm did what she could and wrapped Grandfather's festering wound in rags so he could continue to work in the filth of the sewers, for he was the only one who could bring home an income. There was no time to sit idle and allow his hand to heal, so he continued his activities as usual with fortitude, but he was not well. The injury was slowly taking its toll. Periodically, his consciousness wavered; the throbbing pain in his hand made working difficult, but he carried on until he no longer could. At that point, he realized the laceration should have healed by now. Something was very wrong.

Grandmother Palm's nurturing was not enough, she needed to enlist a doctor's care, but she could not take him to the hospital. Her duties were tending the six children, and besides, she did not speak English. Mary and Aunt Rose took on the responsibility of finding the help he required. They took him to the doctor and were shocked to learn that this was not an ordinary animal bite. The dog had rabies.

Their father had all the symptoms of rabies: fever, restlessness, blood pressure spikes, abnormal behavior, hallucinations, hydrophobia (fear of water), and insomnia, but thankfully the disease had not yet progressed into delirium. It did not take long for this diagnosis to sink into Mary and Rose's teenage heads; his severe symptoms mirrored the fatal disease. The family nursed him at home, for that was all they could afford, and when he required a bath, no ears were safe from the sounds of agonized bellowing that echoed throughout the apartment.

Grandfather Vincent required advanced medical care, but the family did not have the money for such extravagance. When it became apparent that the care they gave him was not enough, they pleaded to their parish priest for help. The forlorn vicar of their church pulled some strings to get Grandfather Vincent admitted into the Catholic hospital. To combat the virus that was assaulting his body, the nurses gave him tormenting shots in his stomach. The injections were more insidious than the attack from the dog. The medicine did not work as planned, and to the family's dismay, the disease continued to progress.

Aunt Rose recalled how her father would cry out in excruciating pain, but the nurses would only turn their heads and walk past his room. Aunt Rose suspected that, with no insurance, the medication needed was withheld. From her point of view, no one in the hospital helped. Or could it have been that the nurses did administer the proper medicine, but it was too late; his work in the sewer had infected the bite, and the disease ran rampant in his body? The staff, and the family, regretfully knew there was nothing more they could do. The disease invaded his brain, delirium set in, and he suffered horrendously. Before his family's eyes, he went mad.

Grandfather's gruesome death etched a horrific memory into each family member. My father walked away from this tragedy, registering in his mind that dogs are not safe creatures to be around. Nunzi carried the burden of causing the death of his father by insisting on a paper route. Rose and Mary harbored the image of her father screaming in the night. Grandma Palm never got over the grief of losing her loving husband. She cried for months until the priest told her, you must pull yourself together; you have a family to raise. At that point, Aunt Mary took the reins and stepped in to keep the family intact, but I suspect that she never wanted to take on the job. She resented her unrequested position and reacted by controlling her siblings. No family member was unscathed by Grandfather Vincent's death. It affected them for the entirety of their lives.

THROUGHOUT THE METROPOLIS of Chicago, there are neighborhoods of various ethnic backgrounds, like small villages. My father's family lived in the Italian section. Throughout the city were expansive brick apartment buildings containing three and four flats, making it ideal for families to live with their adult siblings. Families would pool their funds and invest in apartments depending on the size of their pack. My father's family was no different; they lived together in a three-flat: Grandma Palm, Aunt Mary, and Sal, none of whom were married, lived in one flat, Aunt JoAnn and Uncle Mario in another, and for a short time, my parents in the third flat on the top floor.

Sal always stuck close to home and the security of his mother. He rode a bike into his adult life because his nerves could not handle driving a car. After working at the bicycle factory in the evenings, he would retreat to the basement of their three-flat home to be with the dog he loved. Like his father, Grandfather Vincent, Sal loved animals, so he always had a pet. Aunt Mary did not share his affection for his four-legged friends and refused their admittance in the main part of the apartment. The only thing that would ruffle the feathers of the pleasant nature of his mom, Grandma Palm, was Mary's constant berating of poor Sal. "Zitto, zitto,"—shut up, shut up, was her cry to Mary. So close was Sal to his mom and her protecting love that when she died, he told the family he could hear her calling him, "Come to me, come to me." He left Mary's angry words and joined his mother on the other side, just a month after Grandma Palm had passed. Even my mom and gram would reminisce that Sal died of a broken heart.

Over the years, my cousin Pam, Aunt Mary and Aunt Rose have shared stories about the family that allowed me to feel more connected to them. I find them colorful characters whose stories need to be told.

Nunzi—Grandpa Vincent
JoAnn—Sal

It was hard to deny Grandfather Vincent's Italian genetics; he had a thick dark mustache, head adorned with curly black hair, and an unusual red beard.

Mary—JoAnn—Rose

Grandfather Vincent would come home from working in the sewers and say to Grandma Palm, "Let me be with the children. You have had them all day. Now it is my turn. You go do what you like."

Grandma Palm had longevity in her bones; she lived to the ripe old age of one hundred and four. Pam described her as genuinely selfless, kind, and compassionate, a saint walking on the earth.

~ *Chapter Five* ~

WHO THEY WERE

U NCLE MARIO WAS THE FIRST OF MY FATHER'S FAMILY WHOM
I met, and I wondered why he had the use of only one arm and not his legs.
What happened to him?

Later his daughter Pam told me that they did not know for sure what caused
the problem in his legs. She shared that Uncle Mario was from the old school;
he did not believe in doctors, so he would not listen to his family's pleas and get
medical attention when the problem began. His response to their requests was,
"I'm strong. I don't need a doctor." The combination of three incidents could
have contributed to his inability to walk.

When Uncle Mario was a boy while running down the stairs, he lost his balance and slipped on the hard concrete steps where the corner pierced his head.
The fall also twisted his neck and spine. His family felt that by placing a little ice
on his head, he would be just fine.

The second accident was when Uncle Mario was a teenager playing baseball.
On the north side of Chicago, baseball is not merely a game played by the Cubs at
Wrigley Field. It was the lifestyle of the city. Walking through the neighborhoods,
in empty lots, schoolyards, and parks, you will see boys and men engaging in this
summertime pursuit. When these lots were vacant, there would still be a bat and
ball lying on the ground, waiting for a game to start and fill the neighborhood
with cheering voices. Uncle Mario was part of this clan, and during a game, the
hard white ball came streaming through the air, colliding with the back of his

head just above his neck, and laid him out flat. His neck and spine were once again injured. This tough teenager stood up and walked away, acting as if he had never been hit. Tragic as these incidents were, I do not think that was why he could no longer walk. There was one more disastrous event that slowly reduced his ability to move.

The last blow to his body came when he worked as an adult for the Silvercup Bread Company, driving a delivery truck. One day, he pulled the long tray of fresh fragrant bread out of the back of his vehicle to the sound of screaming brakes. The car behind him came to a halt, but not before it crushed his legs between the bread truck and the vehicle. Did he go to the doctor? The hospital? No.

Being a tough Italian, Uncle Mario said to the driver, "I'm fine," and drove home. But he was anything but all right. Pam told me as the months progressed, after the accident, there were many nights after dinner where she would observe his intense pain. Unable to walk, he would crawl from the kitchen table, across the cold linoleum floor into the living room, pull himself up on the sofa, and pass out on the couch. For years, he would obtain temporary relief by visiting the hot springs, but his pain never entirely ceased. It appeared that being pinned between the truck and the car began the deterioration of his spine and nervous system.

Over time his mobility diminished to the point where he could not use his legs and one arm. At that point, he finally enlisted medical help. The doctor informed him that he would lose the use of his only functioning arm if he did not have an operation immediately. He agreed to the procedure, but woefully, it did not restore what movement he had lost; therefore, he used a wheelchair.

Paul, the oldest son of Uncle Mario and Aunt JoAnn, learned how to be strong like his dad and survived his teenage years in Chicago's ruthless neighborhoods as part of a gang. When he was a teenager, because Uncle Mario could not walk and Aunt JoAnn was afraid to drive, Paul was the one who drove their car. While driving his parents through the city, he would think nothing of slamming on the brakes in the middle of the street, jump out of the car, and accost a boy from another gang, ignoring his nervous horrified mother in the back seat. Then acting as if nothing had happened, he would leap back into the car and drive off. I find it curious that this callous guy later became a hairdresser.

Paul watched the popularity of wigs grow in the 1960s so he built his company around that business platform. Paul thought he would prosper if he employed his family, so he convinced some of his family to work for him. Uncle Mario kept track of the books, Aunt JoAnn, with her bright smile, was the receptionist, and Aunt Rose's son Billy worked in the back. What started the money pouring in was the glue that Paul's cousin Billy developed. The adhesive allowed men to wear their toupees with confidence. There was no concern that their fake hair would tilt during a fiery conversation, fly off in the wind, or float away while swimming. I can't help wondering how many of those gang members employed Paul's help later in their life, to cover their balding heads with one of his custom toupees. The day my father took me to meet his family, I had admired Uncle Mario's lush hair only to discover later, it was not his real hair.

Pam, Paul's younger sister, told me that his multimillion-dollar business began in their family's home with his employees taking over much of the house and yard. The wigs were cleaned in the sinks, hung on the clothesline outside to dry, while Styrofoam heads with wigs sat on the dining room table, ready to be curled, teased, and sprayed. It was quite a circus.

THE ONE COUSIN I did not meet on the day I met my father was Pam, the third child and only daughter of Uncle Mario and Aunt JoAnn. Ironically, a few days after meeting my father, I was heading up to St. Paul, Minnesota, where Pam lived. This leg of our Midwest trip was so Carmin could visit the University of Minnesota, where she would be attending in the fall. It seemed to be the perfect chance to meet yet another relative, and I wondered what her reaction would be to me.

When Frank, the kids, and I arrived at our hotel in Minneapolis, I called Pam. I was surprised that she immediately jumped in her car and arrived at our hotel in only fifteen minutes. I just assumed she rushed over because she was curious about me. She was dark-haired with a quiet, commanding voice and embraced my family and me just like the rest of my father's family. She sat close to us on the loveseat's edge in the hotel lobby and was full of questions. We were all eager to hear each other's stories. Pam was unmistakably intelligent and open to receiving me into her family. Like Carl, her brother, we bonded at that moment and became life-long friends.

Pam and I saw eye-to-eye, not only in stature but in thoughts as well. We respected animals and omitted them from our menus, which was not trendy at the time. I know we could easily have been girlfriends when we were kids, and maybe we even were.

Uncle Mario, her dad, raised his children in the house where I met him the day my father brought me by to meet the family. I was familiar with the area because I grew up in a neighborhood just south of there. As we shared our childhood experiences, I found my cousins' recollection of her summer vacation aligned with mine. Pam, as I, would spend summers swimming at Portage Park Pool, which was a brief walk from where I had lived.

The hot, humid summers would bring us baby boomers out to splash about in the cool waters, but there was a limit to the number of bobbing heads allowed to enter. To assure that I would get to soak my bones in the crisp blue water, I would walk to the pool one hour before it opened and sit on the warm concrete sidewalk, in line with the rest of the eager girls. I was never bored because I knew what awaited me. I ventured forth with my peanut butter sandwich in hand, along with a deck of cards in hopes of engaging a girl nearby in a game. The fresh scent of Bain de Soleil tanning lotion wafted in the air, making for good times in the sun.

I lived in a neighborhood where Italian girls were abundant. Pam and I embodied all the Italian traits: dark hair, exuberant talking, outgoing personality, and a small body that quickly turned pudgy when eating pasta. We swam in the same park pool, waited in the same line to get in, and played cards with unknown girls. Pam seemed so familiar to me. I questioned if she could have been a girl I met in line at the pool; it is highly likely. With little to entertain me at home, I frequented the pool in the summer for five years. I did the math; I swam at the pool daily during my three-month summer vacations, multiplying that by five years equals four hundred and fifty days. I'd say the odds are pretty good that we had met. Yet, the pool was not the only place we patronized where we could have met.

Malls were not abundant in the city in the 1950s, so my family would frequent locally-owned shops that popped up along the busy streets. We befriended one such storekeeper, Mr. Maximov, a watchmaker we met while I was taking music lessons with his children. On occasion, Mom and I would stop by his repair shop on our way to the local stores.

Mr. Maximov was from Russia and appeared to me to be too old to have children under the age of 10. His hair was thin, and he had a few teeth missing. His wife looked about the same, along with a babushka she tied under her chin. I assumed that all people from Russia looked like that. I was a kid. What did I know? He was the original DYI guy in a time before anyone spoke of doing-it-yourself. His son had fallen and cut his head, so his dad sewed the laceration with a needle and thread. What made it peculiar was that Mr. Maximov used black thread.

We lived about two miles from a significant shopping area called Six Corners. There three major streets intersected, making plenty of retail space for Mr. Maximov's shop, Sears, Woolworths, Walgreens, and various other establishments. Our custom was to stroll and look into the full glass storefronts and admire their wares. Some doors had signs posted illustrating a black and white penguin and words that read, "It's Kool Inside." The advertisement encouraged people to purchase cigarettes and told the public the store had air conditioning, which was becoming popular. Naturally, we would step inside to feel the cool breeze. Pam and her family shopped along those streets as well. Strange that we never saw them, but they were not the only ones we never met on the streets of our adjoining neighborhoods.

My father later told me that he would go shopping at Six Corners on Saturdays. That was the same practice for my mom and me after we cleaned the house in the morning. I had the exalted job of dusting the intricacy of the carved walnut end tables, a task I did not always perform to the perfection required by mom. Even though she still enlisted my help.

I find it odd that my mom, father, and father's family never crossed paths in all those years. Perhaps there is a life plan, and all things happen according to a cosmic clock. I have heard timing is everything. I just don't know why meeting my father was not in the mix until his time on earth was near its end.

I soon found that Pam loved animals, like her Uncle Sal and Grandfather Vincent. Her focus was to embrace animals not only with her heart but by sheltering them. Carl, her brother, proved he cared for humanity with his socialist activism, but for Pam, her philanthropy was with the animal kingdom.

Pam told me that as a young child, one day, she saw a cat run over by a car on Lawrence Avenue. Consoling from her mom, Aunt JoAnn, could not stop Pam's tears. At age ten, Pam said she ran away from home with a stray cat in her arms. It was one that her parents told her she could not keep. She refused to return until permission was granted for the cat to be part of their family. The cat reigned in the house for the next twenty years. Then at nineteen, Pam extended her care for the felines people discarded. She answered an ad in the newspaper to volunteer at a cat rescue located in a small, three-room apartment. She was shocked to find there were one hundred and twenty-five starving, sick, and dying cats. Pam said, "I was baptized by fire. The conditions were horrific." Because she could not change that environment, at twenty years old, she and another woman opened a rescue of their own called Feline, Inc., which is still in existence today.

Over the years, Pam lobbied for legislation against fur farms in Wisconsin, and like her brother Carl, she was not afraid to protest openly. She made sure the people heard her voice crying out as she held posters at rallies against experimentation on animals and laws that did not protect these creatures. Carl, Pam, and Paul made a difference in this world. My three cousins from Uncle Mario's family knew what they wanted. Nothing kept them from manifesting their desires. Their dedication so moved me.

O N A VISIT months later, to see Carmin at the University of Minneapolis, I found Carl, Pam's brother, was giving a lecture on Marxism of all things. Because I did not know a lot about Carl, I was excited to fill in yet one more gap in my family's portrait, so I had to go to the event. Carmin and Pam were interested as well so we drove to the place where Carl was speaking. Leaving the chilly fall night behind, we entered the room's warmth and felt anticipation from the audience in the air. The auditorium was packed, so we took the only seats left in the back. We, along with the others in the room, were eager to hear the talk. What we were going to see surprised us.

Carl joined the stage with two other men. They spoke first. My eyes drooped as these boring orators droned on about the subject at hand. Luckily, I was able to wake up and become alert as Carl approached the platform. The other men exited, their heads towering over Carl; they smiled, nodded, and passed by him. Approaching the podium, Carl had to step to its side because being short, all you could see was his eyes just peering over the top. He began his talk, slowly forming his words, giving historical background comparing Marxism, Communism, and Socialism. He stated their dogmas in their ideal forms that, unfortunately, do not exist. I would do him an injustice if I attempted to paraphrase his speech. Still, the listeners sat captivated by the extensive knowledge delivered by a man who spoke from his heart, being a socialist in the purest sense.

Carl was the only radical in the family and would have heated discussions with his right-wing Uncle Nunzi and unresolved yelling bouts with his brother Paul. Carl was a man who stood against big business, objected to government laws that did not serve the people, and he told me he was as far to the left as you can go. So, in the 1960s, when he saw the injustice in the southern states, he moved there, determined to make a difference. If employees got injured on the job from unsafe machinery, there was no compensation for their time lost or sick leave. They had no recourse. Carl took jobs in factories where the system was exploiting these people. Like the employees of the factories, Carl found it hard to make ends meet when paid well under the minimum wage of $1.60 an hour. Carl knew that the only way to help them was to work by their side in order to fully understand their problems and protect them by starting a union.

His white form stood out in the black communities where on the way to secret union meetings, being the only Caucasian, he had to ride in the back of the car, lying unseen on the floor so they would not be arrested, beaten, or both. He was a passivist, so at sit-ins, he went unarmed, going head-to-head with police who had guns and clubs. They would beat him and then easily lift this short man into the paddy wagon, but his moral strength towered over his size as he stood strong. It could take months or even years to construct a union, but once established and safely in place, Carl knew his efforts had been rewarded, so he moved to the next town and began again.

That night we watched as Carl continued to become more and more engaged with his audience. His voice began to modulate up and down. Soon his arms flew into the air as he pranced across the stage. Every eye was upon him; his words compelled the audience to listen as they moved to the edge of their seats. He was more than just noteworthy. He was convincing. All I could say is that I would have joined him on any crusade. Whatever he was selling, I was buying. This man knew how to grab his audience and engage them. His talk gave me one more reason to adore him. His presence on stage amazed Pam and me, for like me, Pam had never seen this side of her brother.

E VEN THOUGH AS a child I did not spend time with Italian families, I married an Italian, Frank. I had a few years with his father, Frank senior, to give me a sense of Italians. For a brief time, through Frank's dad, I also experienced what it was like to have a father in my life. After we were married, Frank's dad took me under his wing. He'd never had a daughter; I was without a father, so this became our bond. I called him Dad. He was one of ten children, three of whom developed a genetic disorder called retinitis pigmentosa. Dad had poor sight since he was a child, and sadly in his twenties, he and two other siblings lost their eyesight altogether.

Dad's parents were poor immigrants from Italy. When they came to America, Chicago was their destination, and they found what was familiar to them in a location in the city called Little Italy. It was an area near Taylor Street just west of downtown. Dad told me, "Al Capone would give me and some of the other kids money for ice cream." Gee, I thought, what a nice guy.

Dad would say to Frank and me, "Don't get messed up with the syndicate." Frank and I would look at each other in disbelief and respond, "No problem, Dad, we won't." Yet one day, some of the guys from the mob knocked on the door looking for my husband, Frank!

Frank needed a job, and he had heard that sanitation workers received a good income, so he put his name on the list and waited for his turn. Every week he would go to the precinct office and see if his name was getting closer to the top. Weeks went by, and at last, Frank was the next one to be called; but instead of getting the job, someone else got it. Frank was angry. He marched into the office, grabbed the clerk by the shirt, and yelled, "I'm next! I'd better get that job. It's not fair that Mario got the job before me." And he stomped out.

Frank was quite pleased with how he took command, unaware of how Mayor Daily's political machine disbursed jobs in the city. The next day two thugs knocked on the door, but instead of coming to our basement apartment, they climbed the stairs to Frank senior's flat on the floor above us. Dad recognized their voices and invited them in for a beer. They told Dad, "You gotta tell your son to stop pushing around the guy at the precinct. Tell him he is lucky we know you. You get my drift?" They drank their beers, talked about who knows what, and left. The next day, my Frank got a call. The voice on the other end of the line said, "A job has opened up, come in tomorrow to start your training."

Being a new bride, I did not know Frank's family background. From the encounter regarding Frank's new job, I saw that Dad knew people in the syndicate, but I didn't think Dad was involved in any shady dealings. Dad did have a newspaper stand, and perhaps he took a few bets on the horses or maybe ran the numbers. I have no proof that he was more deeply involved. He did appear to have wind-falls from time to time, and once Dad bought me a necklace with a diamond. He said it was from winnings he received on bets placed on the horses, yet he never went to the track. I told him, "Dad, I have never had a diamond before. I love it!" It pleased him so that he continued to gift me with many pieces of jewelry adorned with these sparkling gems.

When my Frank was a child, his dad drank to excess, but Frank's mom was no angel either. Unknown to Frank senior, she cheated on him for years, and he discovered her infidelity shockingly one day. One night Dad made dinner for her birthday, packed it up, got on the bus, and headed to the cafeteria where she was the manager. When Dad arrived, the cook said to Dad, "She has not worked nights for the last seven years," which set Dad in an uproar. At the time of this unfortunate discovery, Frank was overseas, in the front-line of the infantry in

Vietnam. Upon Frank's return to the states, he soon found that the Vietnam war was not the last bloodbath that he would encounter.

Frank arrived home from his tour of duty, but his brother Ricky, not his mom and dad, met him at O'Hare airport. Frank asked, "Where are Mom and Dad?" Ricky looked sheepishly at him and responded, "Let's get a drink." Ricky informed him that their parents were getting a divorce, and their Mom had moved into the apartment downstairs with her boyfriend of the last seven years.

Frank returned home to his dad's house, into his old bedroom that was only a few steps down the hall from his dad's, where each night, Dad drank himself into oblivion. Not long after Frank's return from the war, Dad attempted suicide by slashing his neck and wrists. That day, Dad locked the bathroom and tried to end his life. Ricky was scared and ran out of the house, and Frank had to be the one to break down the door to rescue his dad. Frank was in excellent physical shape from the war, so by slamming his shoulder against the solid wood door, it easily opened. He entered to the horrific sight of crimson walls and his dad, lying in the bathtub, barely alive. My Frank had a soft side, but the horror of war and his dad's suicide attempt shut down his emotions so that, over the years, our communication became non-existent.

Although I was comfortable with what I knew about the family I'd married into and I was delighted with all the warmth and shared stories I was receiving from my newfound Italian family, I still had questions I'd never found answers to about my mom's life. What were the events and actions that had kept my parents apart? Why, over the years, had Mom never revealed her true feelings, and did she even know what they were? Finding out why I was denied the love from my father and his family took some sorting out, and I was ready to give this process time. I found my efforts were about to be rewarded.

Being the only radical in the family, Carl would have heated discussions with right-wing Uncle Nunzi .... So, in the 1970s, when he saw the injustice in the southern states, he moved down there.

Determined to make a difference, he attained jobs in factories where the system was exploiting the people.... Carl knew the only way to help them was to work by their side, understand their problems and help start a union.

Pam—Crystal—Carl—Aunt Rose

The one cousin I did not meet on the day I met my father was Pam... My cousin Carl...like his dad, had a smile that lit up his face.... Next, I met Aunt Rose, a wisp of woman, thin, with a distinctive rather shaky voice.

After we were married, Frank's dad took me under his wing. He'd never had a daughter; I was without a father, so this became our bond.

BURIED MEMORIES

YEARS AFTER I MET MY FATHER, MOM ASKED ME TO HELP HER organize her papers. I drove to the bank to retrieve items from her safety deposit box while she stayed at home. I followed the banker through the massive vault door to the slot that matched the keys we held in our hands. He pulled out the long metal box, and I followed him into the windowless room to a table where I had privacy to view what Mom deemed essential enough to secure from the threat of fire and theft. Resting on the table were the memorabilia she held close to her heart. On the top was her birth certificate, with imprints of her tiny feet. Underneath were two smaller documents with light blue ink, a Christian cross, and the priest's signature recording the baptism of my brother and me with the surname of Vincolisi.

Seeing the name, Vincolisi, printed on this form reminded me of when I was seventeen when I first became aware that my brother's and my surname was Vincolisi rather than Bennett, the name we had used at school. The Vietnam war called our young men to fight against who knows what, and my brother needed his birth certificate to enlist. We had always believed that Bennett was our legal name but found out at that time it was not. Yet, Mom always kept Vincolisi as her name. Another oddity I have never understood.

In my twenties, I made a little adjustment on my own for my name. Marlene, my legal name, seemed too formal and proper for my personality, so I changed it to Marnie, much to my mom's dismay. Mom took it as a personal insult. Frank and I felt it was a good choice. Besides, not a great deal of thought went into my name. My mother first had chosen a name that combined her name, Lorraine, and her sister's middle name Ann. "You have to be kidding. LorAnn—what a silly name," was her sister's flip comment, so Mom tossed that name aside. She sat in the hospital, with no name for her new baby girl, and without my father's input, she didn't have a clue what to call me. How did Mom find my name? Forlorn and alone, confined by the green walls of her hospital room, she looked out the window on a bright spring day where a retail shop caught her eye. The script of the sign read Marlene's Bridal Shoppe. Thus, I was given the name after an unknown proprietor of a local store.

I cannot be upset with Mom. After all, there is an old wife's tale saying that before we were born, as spirits on the other side, we whisper our names to our parents. If this is true, I chose Marlene, and because I created it, I could change it. Frank suggested Marnie: I liked it, I embraced it, and I have always cherished his gift.

I noticed another baptism certificate that did not seem to fit with the other papers. It was my father's. How strange, Mom still had it in her possession. Underneath were more of his personal effects. One paper was dated July 6, 1947. It marked his discharge from the Navy. Why did she keep that, now unnecessary, document for all this time? Were there more than memories of him that she kept hidden in her heart, as he did for her? If so, she never spoke of it. More papers slipped out that showed the things she did not want to forget, ones about me that made me happy.

I recall, at three year old, dancing by the smiling faces at the VFW hall. Mom always had an affection for dolls, so I became the living embodiment of her desires. I recall how she would dress me up with patent leather tap shoes tied with a bow, a bright red cowboy hat, with a skirt and shirt to match. To top it off, she spent hours knitting a white angora vest and matching cuffs to circle my ankles. I loved the dancing part, but I can still feel how annoying the fuzzy rabbit fur was because the yarn tickled my nose and made me sneeze. In the bank vault, I picked up one of the blue-lined index cards that held the steps and poems to my routine, stacked in numerical order, yellow with age, and neatly typed. I could still hear the rhymes I memorized play in my head.

From the cards' dates, I discovered this phase of my short dancing career began when I was three and ended at five. To be assigned a solo performance, I had to practice each week in line with the other tots. From old photos, I could see I was so skinny that my wee form scarcely filled out my leotard, and it sagged at my butt. I did not need pictures to remind me how my black ballet slippers stood out from the rest of the girls. Because I could not remember my right foot from my left, my teacher told Mom to sew a blue star on my left slipper and a red star on my right. I can only imagine how frustrating it was for the teacher to keep me in line with the group.

They thought I had a poor memory, but I had dyslexia, an undiagnosed anomaly in the 1950s. It continued to haunt me through high school, where I found reading and recalling facts quite challenging, so much so that by tenth grade, I gave up the idea of going to college.

Yet, Mom was determined to have a dancer in the family. I found a picture of me at age seven dancing on the stage at the Portage Park field house, that told it all. As part of the performance of "The King and I," I danced along with the rest of the girls, adorned in gold satin fabric, cardboard glittered epaulets, and sparkles in my hair. The performance did not go so well. Mom had to hide her face as she watched me dancing off to the side, in the opposite direction from the rest of the dance company. I was oblivious to my mistake.

A S I SAT in the vault, I discovered, tucked underneath the cards, concealed in an old, cracked envelope, were papers tissue-thin, folded in quarters. To preserve them, I had to peel them open slowly. They revealed the pain Mom and Father had locked away. They were their divorce papers. Time took its toll on these delicate papers, wrinkled from age, like my elderly parents. My emotions were raw as I read the decree. In less than two years after they wed, they found they could not reconcile their differences.

My father's weekly income recorded in the divorce decree allowed me to see that both my mother and father had financial hardships. Mom had to go to work to support her children alone, while the court ordered my father to pay forty percent of his salary towards child support. There was no alimony for Mom as she did not ask for it. Soon after, all the responsibility of raising two children fell upon my mom. But there was someone in my father's family who later tried to make amends for my father's neglect.

Also carefully folded were other court papers. With sadness, I gazed at the warrant for my father's arrest. He had compensated Mom for a short time, and then he had neglected to follow the court order. I can only make assumptions about why. Mom, hoping to obtain help, took the only action she could to encourage my father to fulfill his parental duties. She took him back to court, where the judge issued a warrant for his arrest for nonpayment of child support. My father had hit a breaking point. He stopped delivering the checks, angry and dejected, he took off. He left his obligations and us behind.

Mom did not receive another penny after my father vanished. Knowing that money was what had kept my father away made me angry. Come on, why didn't you just pay the money? This was so stupid.

Once those checks stopped coming, Gram was livid and made sure life progressed according to her design. She decided no one should forget my father's errors, holding his supposedly negative influence in the forefront, implying he was someone whom Mom, Jim, or I should never desire to have around. My father was no saint, but neither did he deserve the harsh treatment he received.

With the threat of incarceration, my father dared not show his face in Chicago's vicinity; therefore, he told no one where he was going and left his close family connections. He missed the traditional Sunday dinners at Grandma Palm's, where the entire family joined together with their spouses and children. For Grandma Palm, this was no casual gathering. She was delighted to spend the week preparing food for her loved ones. Pam told me when she was just tall enough to peer over the top of the wooden kitchen table, she would watch Grandma Palm as she made her scrumptious ravioli. White dust filled the air as Grandma Palm sprinkled the ingredients on the table and went to work. Curiously, when the dough was just right, Grandma Palm would disappear into the pantry and step out with a broom in her hand. She then turned the broom into her makeshift rolling pin, no doubt a custom she brought with her from Italy. Pam stood by Grandma Palm's side with a fork in her little hand until it was her turn to seal the deal by closing the ravioli along the edges with the tines of her fork. Pam said, "Grandma Palm's pasta was heavenly."

Pam had told me that Uncle Tony, my father, was her favorite uncle, for when he returned from self-exile in Wisconsin, he would sit on the living room floor to play with her and the other cousins while the adults chatted in the kitchen. How I wish I could have been one of those children who sat at his feet. After meeting this family, I could see his time away broke their hearts. I was not the only one who lost out on seeing my father, though my term was almost six times longer than the seven years his family missed him.

After the split, Mom did not live the life she desired either. My parents were both in limbo. Mom had no time for or interest in dating. All she knew was to find a way to support her family and attempt to keep peace in the house. Whatever that took. But peace did not always prevail. Gram's control created underlying stress so heavy that it stifled all our fun. Gram kept us all under her rule.

Another revelation I uncovered in these buried papers was the fact that my parents divorced five months after I was born, not before I was born, as I had thought. Knowing they were married at the time of my birth disturbed me. He had a right to know that I was born, yet Mom had never told him.

My mom did not share stories about my birth, but I gathered snippets of conversation over the years, and I envisioned my birth like this. Mom was in labor on a Thursday afternoon just before Memorial Day Weekend. Mom, resting her hands on her round belly, nine months pregnant, keeping cool at the kitchen window when her labor began. My mom's father, Grandpa Blake, was out of town, so Mom and Gram took a yellow cab to the hospital. Even though Mom was married, a fact documented on her admission papers, the nurses paid no mind. She entered the hospital without her husband, and in the nurse's eyes, she was an unwed mother. They treated her as such and looked at her with scorn.

Mom could hear the nurses' conversation, "Let her sit here in the hall for a while." She sat, waiting in the wheelchair while in hard labor. The sling of the seat gripped her hips and pulled on her already aching back. The nurses walked by, ignoring her pain. From Mom's vantage point, she could see a few empty beds through the open doors of some rooms, but the attendants did not allow her the comfort of lying down. "May I please be in a room?" was her request. The nurse said, "There are no rooms ready yet."

This conduct continued until a doctor walked by and reprimanded the nurse. "Why is this woman sitting in the hall? Get her onto a bed. Now!" Reluctantly the nurse rolled her into a room, but she was not happy about being scolded by the doctor, and she made sure this was not going to be the end of Mom's mistreatment.

Mom was not in labor an unusually long time, yet she told me, "Each time I had a contraction, the nurses would pull on my cervix to speed things along." I can't imagine this to be a common practice. I can only assume the nurses wanted to start their holiday weekend, and Mom and baby were delaying it. Bearing a child should be a joyous event, but for Mom, it was an omen of the rough times to come. Upon my birth, there would be no flower bouquets, no outlook for a bright future, only the burden of another child.

All these stories flooded through my mind as I sat alone, in the windowless room of the bank vault, with Mom's locked-away memories. The pieces were beginning to fall together, filling in the holes of my curious life. The family I grew up with had never made sense to me. I did not understand the way they thought and dealt with life. I am sure my father's family had their issues, but I wanted to discover that side of the family myself. And so I did.

Mom had to hide her face as she watched me dancing off to the side, in the opposite direction from the rest of the dance company. I was oblivious to my mistake.

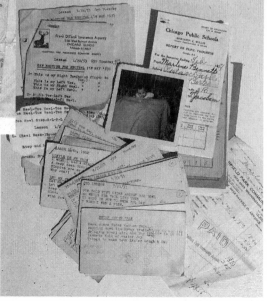

I picked up one of the blue-lined index cards that held the steps to my routine, stacked in numerical order, wrinkled with age, and neatly typed. I could hear the rhymes sing in my head.

Chapter Seven

HIDDEN AGENDAS

MY OLD CONFUSED FEELINGS FIRED UP WHEN I RECALL THE anguish I saw on my father's face as he posed the question that had haunted him for years. "Was it true? Did your mom tell your brother and you that I was dead?" I could not lie. I was the one that had to confess the truth, not Mom. Our years apart hurt to the core, but this was more than a white lie. It created the ultimate separation. Tales of his death created a chasm between us, one that would stop us from ever attempting to search for him. How could Mom and Gram make up such an ugly fabrication? Did they think they were protecting us from pain?

Strange, but I don't recall when I found out that my father was not deceased. To me, it was a story that evolved, and I just accepted it. It was different for my brother, for of all the things he did not recall from his childhood, this fable was not one of them. Precisely instilled in his memory was the time he uncovered the truth.

Jim, being one year older and wiser, did not buy into Mom and Gram's jargon. He was smart enough at eight years old to detect that their story had some holes. In school, he was learning America's history and saw that the date World War II ended was before our father's demise. My father could not have died in the war and sired Jim a year later. Abandonment has many faces, and the injustices from our youth affect us in different ways. This was the wrong that ate away at Jim, not me. But I had others.

How long did Jim sit with his realization before he confronted Mom? Did he ruminate for days and sleepless nights? Did he act on it instantly? Did he declare his findings with anger? Did Mom cry and express remorse? Only my brother knows these truths. That is his story.

When my brother went into military service, he was required to use the exact name on his birth certificate. At that point, I realized the discrepancy. The surname we were using was not our legal name. I had never needed or desired to look at my documentation, so the different name on our birth certificates was news to me. I was shocked, but that subsided because, by seventeen, I had become accustomed to the oddities I observed with Mom and Gram.

My mom had always kept her married name, but we went by my mother's maiden name, Bennett, that of my Grandpa Blake, who passed away five years before we enrolled in kindergarten. Mom could have easily reclaimed her maiden name at the time of the divorce. It is an option given, merely a box to check on the paperwork. Keeping her former husband's name was not an oversight; it was a conscious decision Mom made. Why?

As a divorced woman, I saw Mom acting as if she had been scorned and shamed, especially by the Catholic church, which taught that marriage is a holy sacrament, requiring couples to stay in their relationship no matter the consequences. After the divorce, Mom was not allowed to be part of her parish. The church excommunicated her from every Catholic church, and my Irish gram left the church as well. When I asked my father, "You go to mass with Aunt Mary. Why do you get to attend, and Mom does not?" He answered, "Your mother wanted a divorce. I did not. Therefore, the blame is on her, and she is restricted."

Another stone in Mom's path was the collective consciousness in the 1950s. Then, most women stayed at home to care for the children and obey their husbands. Some observed divorced women as damaged goods, people to avoid because they could not hold their marriage together. So, the judgment that I suspect Mom felt was rampant in society at that time. Perhaps Mom thought it was more honorable to be a widow than a divorcee. Having her name be Vincolisi and our name be Bennett did not indicate that reality.

When we went to school, our names were incorrectly filled in as Bennett on the required forms, reflecting one more way to distance us from our father. I still cannot figure out the convoluted thinking Mom had in this matter. What was the purpose? As an adult, I asked Mom, "Why were our names different?" She took no responsibility. Her reply was, "Your Gram went to school to register you, she filled out the papers, I was at work." But Mom had to sign those papers as our parent. Just another incident to show she was still under the control of her mother. Mom never stood up for herself. She was trapped and could see no way out.

Jim enlisted in the army and, at that point, he had a decision to make. Did he want to legally adjust the suspicious error on his records and take my mother's maiden name, the one assigned to us in grammar school, or did he desire to keep his father's name, Vincolisi? At nineteen, my brother knew he wanted to change his name legally to Bennett. Jim still held the disdain that was prevalent in the family about our father. I was neutral. I did not feel the need to hate a man I had never met.

Our names were just another way Mom unknowingly transferred her unbalanced emotions onto my brother and me. I hoped that it wasn't her conscious intent. She did not know how to keep balanced as she struggled with her oppressive life. Yet, at the beginning of each school year, our false name stayed the same. Questions would arise from secretaries who reviewed the numerous forms, and their query was uncomfortable for a small child to answer. They would inquire, "Why are your names different from your mother? Did you fill this out correctly? You must have made a mistake." I did not know what their questions were implying, only that something felt wrong. I can conjure up ill feelings toward Mom for putting us in those compromising circumstances, but it does me no good to place fault.

AFTER MY FATHER passed on, my relationship with his family did not dissolve. Aunt Mary continued to reach out to my brother and me and, one day, she sent Jim a package with a roll of film. It was one that she found tucked away in the back of a drawer. She told Jim, "I don't know if this film is still good. I have had it for years."

Jim developed the film and asked me,

"What do you think is on this film Marnie?"

"I don't have a clue."

"Father holding you."

That roll of film hid in Aunt Mary's dresser drawer for over forty years, waiting for us to come back. It proved that my father's words were confirmed when I first knocked on his door as he said, "I had a baby girl. I held her only once in my arms." His refrain was, "This is a miracle, this is a miracle." I'd say this film is another miracle.

From the first day I met my father's sisters and all the occasions afterward, I could see they knew mistakes had happened, and they were sorry for how it affected my parents. I found them to be empathic and compassionate. Aunt Mary held grace by seeing the mistakes of her ways and had remorse. She remarked, "I now see it is best when young people get married, that they take some time by themselves, move away from the influence of the family, and form their special bond. Sometimes our wisdom comes too late to make a change." Wise words indeed from a spinster.

How long did it take for Aunt Mary to receive her insight? Was it a few years or decades? And once obtained, why did no one reach out to find us? I guess that action was up to my father. When I met Aunt Mary, she made amends, but my mom was a different story. I never heard Mom speak a kind word about Aunt Mary. Perhaps, I was reading Mom wrong, but her grudge seemed to fester in her mind over the years, fabricating images of her sisters-in-law's opinion of her.

Guided by the realization that my father's sisters did not harbor ill feelings from the past, I thought if Mom met her old nemeses, perhaps she would benefit. I found Mom's stories that had once rung true were now no longer valid, but Mom needed to discover that for herself.

After my father's death, Mom slowly softened to the idea that I had brought him and his family back into my life. I frequently traveled to Chicago for business and pleasure. On one such occasion, I said to Mom, "Join me. You can visit your sister in Chicago, along with some of your friends like Macy." I never requested that she visit her old sisters-in-law, though the thought of reconciliation was in the back of my mind. I had told Mom how kindly Mary and Rose spoke of her, hoping it could begin to crack open a door in Mom's heart.

Mom joined me on my next trip. I kept things light as Mom and I casually went about our day. My children would not have forgiven me if I hadn't brought home their favorite foods. We stopped at the Georgian Nut Company, where high on the shelves, stored in burlap bags, were fresh nuts from far-away lands. We filled our paisley bags with nuts, trail mix, and confections to share back home. I have not found a bakery in Denver to compare to those in Chicago. So we drove to the Andersonville neighborhood for a marzipan cake filled with whipped cream and custard. I chatted with the clerk behind the counter. "I love your bakery. I lived here years ago and would come by often." "Yes," was her response. "I remember you and your two small children." How sweet to know that after ten years, she recognized me. I carefully chose my pastries and watched as she placed them into the white box and set the box on the machine's metal tray that spun white string around the box. I picked it up and walked out the familiar double doors onto Clark Street and back into our car.

We continued our drive and headed from the lake to the west side of town. The Maurice Lenell cookie factory became our next stop. We entered the store enveloped in the sweet smell of baking cookies and watched droplets of colorful dough parade by, cooling on the conveyor belt, behind a glass wall. There was no reason to guess which ones to take home because you could taste every one. There were racks of boxes lining the store and white buckets filled with samples that hung on the ends. I liked the pinwheels with chocolate swirls and red sprinkles on their sides, but I could not come home without a box of stars with red jelly centers. Mom has always looked for something sweet to eat after her dinner, so she too made her selections. We grabbed a few bags of broken cookies and headed to our next destination. I felt the day would not be complete without an Italian roast beef sandwich.

The Chicago Italian Beef comes on a baguette that is soft inside, crusty on the outside, creating a chewy sensation that adds to the flavor. The meat is drenched with beef gravy and covered with roasted green peppers. It is soggy and drippy and makes my mouth water just to think about it. There are places in Denver to find this delicacy, but the dry air changes the way the bread bakes, and it is sadly not the same as back home.

Being content, with our tummies filled and the day packed with tasteful memories, we continued our drive across the city. I felt this might make the perfect segue to mention that we were near Aunt Mary's condo. It seemed like there was no time like the present to encourage Mom to take this step. On a fluke, I asked. "Mom, would you like to go see Aunt Mary?" To my surprise, Mom said, "Yes, let's stop by." All right, now we're getting somewhere.

All the children in a family have their inherent roles. Usually, the firstborn is a leader who blazes the trail for the children who venture after. The middle child is the one who attempts to keep things on an even keel, becoming the peacekeeper. And if there is a third child, he or she usually gets away with much mischief because, by that time, the parents are too busy to notice. I am the second in line, so I took on the role of the family diplomat. I had aptly performed my duties by finding my father and introducing my brother to him. Now I hoped to smooth out the rift between my mom and my father's sister. Such was my intention.

The drive was about ten minutes, so Mom did not have time to change her mind, but I could feel her anxiety as we walked up to Mary's door. Just before reaching the entryway, Mom wavered., "Perhaps we should drive back to our

hotel. It is late, and we do not need to disturb Mary. We should have called first."
I did not react to her reluctance to see Mary. Her agreement was obviously not
thoroughly thought-out. "Well," I responded, "We are at her door now." We were
only on her sidewalk, but I kept walking, "Let's just knock." I rapped on the door
and waited for it to open. I tapped again, with no response. I could hear Mom's
sigh of relief as we turned and walked away. In Mom's mind, we had accomplished the task we set forth to do. For Mom, the mere act of showing up at the
door had the same effect as if Mary had answered. We drove back to our hotel
room, where we retired for the night, and both slept soundly.

The next day, once again, I drove Mom to Mary's condo in hopes of introducing these estranged former in-laws. Mom was relaxed and ready to confront
whatever was going to happen because our actions the night before gave her
peace. This time, when we knocked on the door, Mary was home. She greeted
Mom, "I'm so glad you came by." She embraced Mom, as she would an old
friend with whom she had lost touch over the years. My endeavor had proved
to be effective. I relaxed as I watched them sit over a cup of coffee and reminisce. Months and even years later, Mom and Mary continued their friendship
and phoned each other regularly. I prevailed as the peacemaker once again.

ONE YEAR AFTER my father's passing, Aunt Mary summoned my brother, mother, and me back to Chicago. Now that Mom and Aunt Mary were
friendly, it was not difficult to convince Mom to join us to fulfill Aunt Mary's
mysterious request. With our interest piqued, we departed from separate parts of
the country to see what Aunt Mary had in mind. My brother arrived from California a few hours before us and went directly to Aunt Mary's condo. Mom and I
were curious about what we would find, so we also drove straight to Aunt Mary's
place from the airport. Mom and I arrived just in time for one of Aunt Mary's
mouth-watering yet modest dinners.

Aunt Mary placed her light, airy homemade pasta on the table, floating in
gravy, filled with her love. She had made a special trip to the Italian market that
day to purchase fresh ricotta cheese that she thinly sliced, placed upon Italian
bread, and sprinkled with salt. We sat around the table with no need for deep
conversations. We were too busy enjoying our dinner. Afterward, Mary requested
that I join her in the guest room while Mom and Jim cleaned up the kitchen. I
had stayed in this room a few months prior while on a business trip. It contained

a single bed with a white chenille bedspread covering my father's old army blanket that Mary later gifted me. On the wall there were pictures of Blessed Mary, Jesus with a bleeding heart, the current pope, Archangel Michael with his sword in hand, his foot on the devil's head, and a rosary on the nightstand.

Aunt Mary made small talk, pointing out figurines on the dresser. She seemed uneasy about what she wanted to say next. Then, as if it were no big deal, Mary handed me a check, claiming my father had an insurance policy from the war that she had kept. She did not share it with his second wife, Dolores, feeling that this money was ours. Mary was good with finances, and I assumed she had invested this money and allowed it to grow. My father had passed one year prior, which completed the traditional mourning period, making this the proper time to bestow this windfall upon us. I looked at the check and was shocked to see it was a sizeable amount. We returned to the living room, enjoyed our evening with Aunt Mary, and then the three of us retired to our hotel rooms.

While Aunt Mary and I were in the other room, my brother had handed Mom a check. Mom expressed how generous it was for Mary to give this money to the three of us. "No," my brother said, "this money is for you, Mom. Marnie and I have our checks." My mom was speechless. The woman whom she harbored resentment towards for decades was now giving her money. Mom did not share her feelings with us, no doubt unsure of her emotions as they churned. I can only assume one of those emotions was guilt for how she had blamed Mary with her thoughts and words over the years.

We were not the only ones surprised by Aunt Mary's generosity. Later I shared Mary's actions with cousin Carl, who told me, "You have no idea how special you are. Aunt Mary loves you very much. She is not one to part easily with money." That was an interesting comment because Mary had said this was my father's money—or was it?

Back in Denver, I did a little math and found the funds gifted to my brother and me totaled the sum of the child support checks for eighteen years, the exact amount my father was required to pay. How strange, his insurance policy also contained this same figure. I can only surmise this was not money from my father's insurance policy, but from a loving, caring sister who made sure her brother's soul would rest in peace, taking into account his mistakes of the past. Mary had paid his debt in full.

That roll of film hid in Aunt Mary's dresser drawer for over forty years....
It proved that my father's words were true when I first knocked on his
door as he said, "I had a baby girl. I held her only once in my arms." His
refrain was, "This is a miracle, this is a miracle." I'd say this film is another
miracle.

WORKING ON THE RAILROAD

T HERE WAS ONE PERSON I HEARD ABOUT IN MY MOTHER'S family who bore no ill feelings towards another. He was the leveling force of the family, but I never met him. I learned my grandfather was gentle, kind, and loved by all. He was a balancing force in the family dynamics. From the photos I discovered in a dusty box, it appears that he had been a jokester as well. One such photo shows Grandpa Blake, lanky and tall, wearing overalls, standing over the hole he had dug, holding a shovel. Standing in the apparent grave is Gram, in an old-fashioned cotton dress, like the kind I always saw her wear. The expressions on their faces reflected their whimsical stunt, implying he would do away with her. I'm glad to say I took on his qualities of a playful demeanor and positive outlook rather than the fear, stress, and control of Gram.

Gram's mother was an unhappy, unkind woman, though I cannot attest to that as she passed on before I was born. The stories I heard drew a picture of her as downright mean. I can only surmise that Gram's mother's demanding attitude built the character I saw in Gram. She mimicked what she saw at home, which set her up for failure to nurture her children with loving care. She knew no other way to behave. Control was the way to get things done, which became Gram's reflection of love. But for part of her life, the stars smiled down upon her. She was blessed with unconditional love from the one person in her life that knew how to give it. Grandpa Blake.

I never heard anyone speak ill of Grandpa Blake. Everyone admired him, even my father. Grandpa Blake worked for the railroad, which took him away from the city, where he left early in the morning to board the train that ran from Chicago to Savanna, Illinois. He was the fireman who stood by the engine shoveling coal into the dark hot hole. With black soot on his face, Grandpa would wipe his brow with his red handkerchief and hang his head out the window to catch a cool breeze while enjoying the view of the countryside. He dressed in clean blue jeans, but they were covered with the soot's fine black powder by the end of the day. Gram would wash his pants and hang them on the clothesline to dry, but being an efficient wife, she found a way to dry their heavy fabric more quickly in the Midwest's humidity. The new invention was called pants stretchers. They not only allowed the pants to dry faster, but they gave the dungarees a crisp crease in the legs. The men in the railroad yard would tease him, calling out, "There goes the man with the ironed overalls!"

Traveling over the open land reminded Grandpa Blake of his days growing up on a farm in Minnesota. There he learned the value of a hard day's work. He and his brother would harness the horses, place the leather strap over their shoulders, and till the ground for their father, while his mother would tend to the vegetable gardens along with their domestic help. He appreciated living in his family's full house with farmhands, fresh food, and cards spread across the table for games at night. But once he reached adulthood, farm life could no longer hold him, and he ventured to the big city of Chicago. He kept close to what he knew by living on the outskirts of town, near a few small farms, but never acquired one of his own.

Grandpa Blake met Gram in 1915 when she was nineteen years old, and he was twenty-six. I recall an old photo of Gram that attests to her beauty, trim body, and glistening eyes that hinted at her dream of a better life. Matching the fashion of the day, she piled her dark hair in a knot on the top of her head. I have inherited a few traits from the women in my family. My large eyes come from my mom, and gram's latent genes came to the surface when I was in my teens. When I was small, my eyes were dark brown like my father's but later changed to look like Gram's green eyes. When Mom lost patience with me, I often wondered, was it because I reminded her of her former husband?

Before she married, Gram had a job as one of many young women who worked as runners at Western Union. In the early 1900s, only the elite had telephones, making the quickest form of communication a telegraph. When the messages arrived, they needed to be moved fast to various departments in the building. Then they were retyped and sent to the intended addressees. The job required speed, so to hurry the delivery of these vital memos, the carriers laced up their roller skates, and with agility, they flew from one room to the other.

When Grandpa Blake met Gram, he was smitten and knew he wanted this handsome lady for his own. He wasted no time letting her know his intentions when he found her sitting on the stoop of her apartment in tears one day. That day, Gram's uncaring mother had upset Gram so much that she did not know what to do. Blake took control. He made his decision and taking her hand said, "That is it. You will not go back into that house. We are getting married." And so they did that very day. It appears that both my grandfathers knew their true loves early on and lost no time in making them their wives.

Gram's exciting career was short-lived because after she married, her sole job became housewife and mother. Gram had five pregnancies, but only two children survived—the strong females. Two of the boys died at birth, and Gram never got over the heartbreak of her third baby boy who was in her loving embrace for only a few short months. When their first daughter was born, four years after their marriage, joy-filled their hearts and home, and they aptly named her Cecelia but called her Ceal, making her the third female to keep that name alive. She was a tomboy who loved to go fishing with her dad, climb trees, and get dirty, thus showing the qualities of the son Grandpa Blake never had. Ceal once told me, "I loved to read books, but there were chores to be done, so when it was my turn to wash the wooden stairs, I would place the book on the step above the one I was washing, and just keep reading until I reached the top landing." My mom, born two years later, became the polar opposite of her sister Ceal. Mom carried a doll with her most of the time, wore clean clothes, and made sure that they remained so the entire day. Their personalities stayed with them their whole lives: Aunt Ceal, with a hammer in hand, helped her husband remodel their home, and my mom continued to possess dolls through her adult life, in her immaculately clean house.

Gram and Grandpa lived through the hard times of two World Wars and the Depression of 1929, yet they survived. As families needed to join together to survive, Grandpa Blake opened his home, lovingly bringing his blind mother and his challenging mother-in-law into the fold. I'd say their apartment was crammed full.

Food was scarce, as were jobs, but the railroad gave Grandpa Blake security. Always looming in the background was the possibility there would be no food on the table or money to pay the rent. Their worries were real. The depression left a lasting imprint that carried through Mom and Gram's life, and they transferred the feelings of uncertainty and scarcity to our family. The undertone of their actions was that there was never enough, so they rationed not only food but also loving acts.

I think Mom and Gram felt that if they gave me compliments, I would take their adoration, allow it to inflate my ego, and not form into a proper adult. Therefore, they never mentioned the positive attributes they observed in me. There were no kisses or words of praise, thus making sure I would not be conceited; but as a consequence, I never knew my worth. Once again, their family upbringing overshadowed common sense. To rear my children, I took another approach. I did the opposite of what I had experienced in my youth. I hugged my kids, read stories, played with them, and had fun. I'd say it worked well.

Grandpa Blake was Gram's guiding light. Mom said Grandpa Blake would not argue with Gram. He made the right choice. He did the best he could to maintain harmony in the home, but it was an uphill battle. When Gram became upset, Grandpa would go outside for a smoke. My mom adopted the same tactic years later when she needed space from Gram. When perturbed, Mom would walk down from our attic apartment into the cold, unfinished basement, stand by the washtubs, and puff on her cigarette with a sigh of relief. Gram did not approve of her smoking, so Mom never smoked in front of Gram. Silly, the smell of smoke permeates your clothes and breath, yet Mom thought her secret was well hidden. Funny, but Mom never inhaled. I don't think she wanted to smoke; it was just her way to escape.

With a home packed with females, Grandpa Blake would occasionally stroll down to the neighborhood bar to talk politics and have a beer with the guys. I rarely heard tales about him, but there was one story I heard repeatedly. It was about Grandpa, Gram, and their car.

Gram was coming home from the store, driving the old black Ford filled with groceries. She pulled into the driveway but didn't see Grandpa Blake petting their scruffy, little black and white dog. By the time she saw him, there was no time to apply the brakes. She froze at the wheel and later told me, "God Almighty stopped the car, and I did not hit him." A daunting episode where she let fear take hold of her, and from then on, it diminished her ability to live her life to the fullest. She never sat behind the wheel again!

They celebrated both their daughter's marriages and were blessed with five grandchildren, making their days happy ones; but it all came to an end one October day. The cold touch of winter was in the air. Gram put on her coat and walked outside as she often did to say goodbye to Grandpa as he left for work. He never returned. At the young age of fifty-five, he gently slipped out of his body while resting in a chair at the railroad office in Savanna, Illinois, never to be in Gram's arms again. After he passed that day, she rarely talked about him without a tear in her eye.

Gram had always yearned for Grandpa Blake throughout her life and never looked for, nor was interested in, finding another mate. Her beautiful eyes adorned her stocky form, and one day coming home from shopping, she told me an older man stopped her and complimented her, "Your eyes are so beautiful." Her response to me was, "The old fool." From her comment, I could see this old bird was not going to be won over by flirting.

When Grandpa Blake passed on, I was an infant, and my father told me that he had tried to attend Grandpa's wake, but they blocked him from attending. How cruel. Grandpa was the voice of reason in the family, but even he had little control over what Gram did. Now with Grandpa Blake gone, my father realized there was no longer anyone to support him in seeing his children, and the chance to build a relationship with us was dissolving at his feet. My father knew Gram was drawing a line in the sand. He said, "Sadness overtook me, and I stood alone on the front porch and cried. I know with Blake gone, it was going to be almost impossible to see you."

Forty years after Grandpa Blake's death and after my father's death, my brother acquired a renewed interest in our family heritage. Jim took it upon himself to fly to Illinois to locate the train yard where Grandpa Blake had perished. Remarkably there was an older man at the yard who had worked with Grandpa. The man respected and fondly remembered Grandpa Blake and gave Jim a tour of the yard as he recalled, "Your grandfather would come off the train, walk into the office, sit in a chair, and entertain the crew by telling humorous stories." The man continued, "One day, Blake came in from a train run, sat down in a chair, and passed away." He then motioned to the very chair where Grandpa Blake had made his exit; the old worn-out red leather chair was still in the office.

G RAM DID NOT follow her husband to the other side for another twenty-five years, but her heart always yearned for her gentle man, the one who had left too soon. Gram rarely was ill, only in the hospital once to remove her gall bladder, so it was a surprise when she had a stroke that left her paralyzed on her right side. She spent her last days in a nursing home not far from my apartment building in Chicago, so I visited her often. The stroke impaired her speech, but I could understand her because my children were small and just learning to talk, so I was accustomed to understanding garbled speech. One day Aunt Ceal's husband, Uncle Bill, came to visit her. She looked at him yearningly and said, "I hope you never get like this." He turned to me and said, "What did she say?" I did not respond. I did not have the heart to tell him. Gram did not stay in her compromised body long; she left the earth six months later.

On the way to Gram's burial, we traveled across the northwest part of Chicago in a procession of thirty cars, showing Gram's large circle of friends. The police held back the traffic at every light so that the motorcade would stay together, but no one holds back a train. During our sojourn, not one but two trains stopped the entire line of autos for about ten minutes each. I was sitting in my car, with the sun streaming onto my face, waiting for the trains to pass, when I noticed that this was a synchronistic occurrence. It triggered my emotions and made me smile. Both the trains were the railroad lines Grandpa Blake worked for: the Soo, and the Milwaukee Road.

Grandpa had made his presence known. He gave me a message to tell me that he was there with Gram, but he did not do it with words or psychic visions. He used real physical objects. Spirits can turn lights on and off and send a fragrance through the air, but those who have developed their skills can make sounds and move objects. Grandpa moved trains. That was the power he wielded from beyond.

Grandpa Blake and Gram had a sweet love. No one in the family noticed or gave credence to the coincidence of these trains but me. I took it as a sign that Grandpa was there to escort Gram to her new home. She was in good hands. Once again, romance prevailed.

UNFORTUNATELY, MY PARENT'S did not have a romance that endured. Their vision of a happy union lasted a little over a year. Even with the help of the Catholic priest, their marriage was still on rocky ground, and then it vanished before their eyes. However, even in my father's absence, the lines of communication were not entirely severed. My father did not need telephone wires to connect to us. He listened on an invisible line and stayed connected to us, but to my loss, I never knew.

We lived in a city of millions of people, a place where you would think people could hide their pursuits; not so. My father told me that he would hear things about us from their mutual friends and even his family. My father's sister Mary and Mom's sister Ceal were telephone operators at Illinois Bell. Unbeknownst to my aunts, through their gossip in the workplace, stories spread between our families, something they would not have done willingly. The story continues to unfold.

The stars smiled upon Gram, blessing her with unconditional love from the person in her life that knew how to give it. Grandpa Blake.

Skating was Gram's first and only job. I often would hear Gram nonchalantly tell her story about her former vocation with a reserved demeanor, but I could see the twinkle in her eyes as she recalled the fun.

Grandpa Blake met Gram in 1915 when she was nineteen years old, and he was twenty-six. I recall an old photo of Gram that attests to her beauty, trim body, and glistening eyes that hinted at her dream of a better life.

That day Gram's uncaring mother had upset Gram so much that she did not know what to do. Blake took control. He made his decision and taking her hand said, "That is it. You will not go back into that house. We are getting married."

Grandpa's mother—Gram's mother—Lorraine (my mom)
Grandpa Blake—Gram

Grandpa Blake opened his home and his heart, lovingly bringing into the fold his blind mother and his challenging mother-in-law. I'd say their apartment was crammed full.

On the far right: **Gram—Mom—Grandpa Blake**

My mom, born two years later, became the opposite of her sister Ceal. Mom carried a doll with her most of the time, wore clean clothes, and made sure that they remained so the entire day…My mom continued to possess dolls through her adult life, in her immaculately clean house.

If you want the rainbow, you've
got to put up with the rain.
DOLLY PARTON

Chapter Nine

STRUGGLES

M Y PARENTS MARRIED IN JUNE OF 1946 AND HAD THEIR FIRST child, my brother Jim, in March of 1947, but their home had little joy by Christmas of that year. Troubles were brewing. Mom's heart was depleted of the happiness she had had a brief time before, and thus she made her decision. Mom, four months pregnant with me, exhausted from caring for my brother Jim, who was a nine-month-old, filed her separation papers on December 26. Now what?

Mom could not support herself and her baby; therefore, the only solution she could see was to move back into the loving embrace of her mother and father in their small two-bedroom apartment. No doubt, it was a humiliating act for this proud woman.

Time moved forward, but there was no compromise or reunion for my mom and father. I assume Mom's heart was broken and her emotions were running a-muck. Without a doting husband, she gave birth to her baby girl, my entrance into the world. Mom's strain was reflected in my body: my weight was not quite five pounds at birth.

Being with her parents, Mom had time to be nurtured while caring for her babies, but it did not last long. Though not an ideal situation to begin with, things got even worse. Five months after my birth, while Mom was chasing a two-year-old around the apartment with her new baby on her hip, an event occurred that changed the dynamics of Mom's life forever.

The day Grandpa Blake happily left to go on his usual train run to Savanna;

he kissed his wife on the lips, hugged his daughter, patted his grandson on the head, and snuggled the baby. He never returned. Grandpa, the only provider in the house, a healthy man with no known physical issues, died without warning. He had a hernia that ruptured while he was sitting in a chair at the train yard in Savanna, and he passed away instantly. Gram was devastated that day, and her heart never mended. She had lost the man who had loved her with all her foibles when she was only fifty-two. It did not seem right. From that point until her death, I never saw her recall a story about Grandpa Blake without getting a longing look in her eyes. It was a time of tremendous change for Mom and Gram, and they clung tightly to each other. They were scared, alone, and unsure of their future.

My parents were still married, though not living together when Grandpa Blake passed. The divorce had not finalized until the next month. Without her father or love from her husband, I imagine my poor mom being quite distraught, all within one month. Mom was thrown once again into turmoil, which her fragile physical and mental state could hardly tolerate, and yet she endured. Gram was not going to go out and find a job. She was unskilled and had been employed only once in her life.

Technology had progressed, and in 1950, Gram's work experience from 1914 did not meet current work skills —not that she could recover her roller-skating flair at the age of fifty. Gram did the only job she knew, being a mother and housewife; so Mom had no choice; their roles were clearly defined. It was not in mom's design, but she had to go out and find work. Raising another set of children was not in Gram's plan either.

A few months prior, Gram and her loving husband had been looking forward to their empty nest. With their daughters cared for by their husbands, Gram and Grandpa Blake had time to nurture each other. Now sadly, Gram lay in an empty bed.

Stemming from the pain Gram held from her own mentally abusive childhood, child-rearing was not a vocation she was skilled in, and yet she was back in that role. Gram never spoke of her father, so I can assume he, like my father, had abandoned his family, which could have unconsciously added to her anger about my father. The resentment Gram carried from her childhood overshadowed her kind heart, and now she was thrown into a circumstance that she could not control. Even though she never said it, I know she deeply loved us, but I think she felt life had mistreated her, making it even harder for her to express love to us.

Now, all the responsibility of providing for two babies, plus her mother, rested upon Mom's shoulders. Not an easy task for a single mother in the 1940s. She did have some child support, but would it be enough for four people?

There was even more unrest in my father's camp. My father later recalled, "When your grandfather was around, visitation was easier. After he died, that support was gone. Your grandmother did not like me, and she made it very hard to see you." I read between the lines and could see my father's sense of loss and isolation, a pattern that would follow him to his death.

Mom felt somewhat safe in the shelter of her mother's apartment, but her circumstances were soon going to change again. She was living with the stress of completing her divorce when she was hit with one more devastating challenge: six months after my grandfather's death, my father stopped paying child support, left town, and went into seclusion. Now she was without his financial support.

Jobs were scarce, and the ones available were going to the men who had served in the war. Women's roles were to care for their families, not in the city looking for employment. Companies did not consider women in the workforce valuable and paid them less than men.

Mom never had time to rest. She held down two and sometimes three jobs to make ends meet: a secretary at a small insurance company during the day and selling shoes in two different department stores at night. I do not recall her gentle touch, nor a hug, a kiss on the forehead, words of praise, or her reading me a story. Nurturing was not on her list of things to do. Everything was about how she could feed and clothe her family in a warm, safe place.

WHEN MOM WAS in her eighties, and in assisted care, I found a letter as wrinkled with age as was she. It was to the veteran's administration, hand-typed, in desperation, hoping as the former wife of a veteran, they might see her as a woman in need and lift a hand to help her. The letter, dated June 15, 1951, states:

"I am being evicted from the apartment that I live in with my mother, two children ages three and four, and am endeavoring to obtain a veterans temporary housing unit in our city . . . I divorced my husband, and he was to support his children; when he found this out, he left town, and the court or I cannot locate him. This was two years ago . . . he is now in contempt of court."

Mom told me it all began in the fall of 1951. There was a knock on the basement door of Gram's apartment. Before her was the sad face of her landlord as he spoke, "I am so sorry to do this. You have been good tenants, but my son and his family need a place to live, and you know rentals are scarce. I have no choice. I must ask you to leave." Mom told Gram, "Don't worry, I will find us a place.

I don't work on Sundays, I will look then, and I will contact the VA. Surely they will help."

Alas, the Veteran's Administration did not take pity on her situation or try to help. Their department assisted only the veterans who served our great country. The VA, along with society, did not feel it was their job to help a divorcee. Mom was at the bottom of VA's list, if even on the list at all. Temporary housing was for the families of veterans who were still married. She searched in vain and found no place to live. We would soon be out on the streets.

Mom had nowhere to go. With the eviction in place, she entered a level of fear that put her into a state from which, I don't think, she ever recovered. I've always known her to be anxious, stressed, and waiting for the next shoe to drop, often seeing the glass as half empty, and perhaps for her, it was.

Back then, my vision of Mom was this: Mom was coming home from a long day at work, dropping her exhausted body onto the sofa, her head pounding, the babies crying for attention, and she has no energy to deal with any of this. Her migraines began then and stayed with her throughout her working career.

How telling it was for me to find, in the safety deposit box, these letters of times gone by, the ones that made her life so harsh. Why did she save these papers for fifty years? How could they have helped her process the invalidation and devastating effect on her life? Her future seemed grim, but then someone showed a light on her darkened path.

With no place for us to go, Mom's sister Ceal and her husband Bill opened their heart and home and asked us to stay in their house. They had three children of their own, making nine bodies in their tight quarters. The bedroom, kitchen, small dining room, and living room were all on the first floor. The place in which we slept couldn't be called a bedroom, for we five kids slept in the attic. I do not recall where Mom and Gram slept. Perhaps the sofa was a pullout bed. This arrangement was surprisingly fun, at least for children. We all had someone to play with each day, and I recall giggling at night until we heard the echo of adults urging us to "Go to sleep!" But then again, as a four-year-old, I laughed at anything.

One of my favorite memories is the Christmas we spent living in my aunt and uncle's home. My cousin Cis, the one my family and I stayed with the weekend I met my father, recalls our extended visit to be a fun time for her as well. Surprisingly, as an adult, she claimed that the year we lived with them was the best Christmas ever.

The weeks before Santa's arrival, we would make our wishes known by placing our mark in the Sears catalog. Five tiny bodies, crowded together onto the sofa, so small that Gram could see the soles of our shoes because no one's feet could touch the floor. Billy, the oldest, held the catalog open to the pages of toys, each of us grasping onto our little pens. As the pages turned, we would place our marks next to the toys we most desired, hoping Santa would bring at least one of them to us. I never did get the Easy Bake Oven or the penguin toothbrush holder. I asked for them many years in a row. It is still a mystery how a cake can cook under a light bulb in the Easy-Bake Oven.

As an adult, I shared with a friend the sad story of my childhood void of an Easy-Bake Oven; and one year, on my birthday, she showed up with a package in hand, tied with a big bow and a smile on her face. "Open it," she said. I obeyed and hastily tore into the box, with the paper flying into the air. There it was, at last, my wish came true. There before me, in all its glory, was my shiny new Easy-Bake Oven. We hurried into my kitchen and made a tasty sort-of-flat cake. Fifty years later, that oven was still on the market for the joy of other little girls.

Living with my cousins, I deemed Billy the smart one. Being older, he must be wiser. He would think of numerous adventures for us, the marauding children. One night, while avoiding sleep, he moved the small rug covering a vent on the floor to reveal what we considered secrets the adults were sharing that night. Five little heads, looking down on the four adults who were casually talking in the kitchen about things that were probably not so important, but we felt we were in on a secret. To this day, I have no idea what their conversation entailed.

Mom meant the arrangement at Aunt Ceal and Uncle Bill's to be temporary. Mom was afraid to live in a large apartment building with strangers, so she would diligently search for a place to rent that she considered safe in her eyes. She felt a private home would serve that purpose. Thus, she would tuck us away in a make-shift apartment in an attic or basement of someone else's house. There would only be a few spare rooms, usually three. We had a kitchen, living room, and one bedroom. Somehow, she made it all work. Three months later, Mom found a place a few blocks away from Aunt Ceal's in a small basement flat.

MY CHILDHOOD DID not look like the scenes portrayed on television as in the sitcoms like "Leave It to Beaver." My mom did not wear an apron, bake cookies, or lovingly greet my father at the door as he returned home from work. The scenes on the small twelve-inch screen were foreign to me. Mom worked all day, so she never had the opportunity to attend a PTA meeting, teacher conferences, or the programs our class performed. Mom did not drive, so there were no vacations or trips to the beach on Chicago's north shore. Her life focused on holding herself together, and I admire how she made ends meet.

My girlfriends had fathers, but I rarely saw them with these men. Perhaps it was because I mainly was around on the weekdays when their fathers were at work. It never occurred to me why I rarely saw their fathers. It just looked like what I knew from my home; women and children alone in the house. When their fathers were present, it seemed strange. I did not know how to act around these males. Their energy was so unfamiliar.

On weekends, when I would search for a playmate, I trekked to a nearby house, stood outside the window and rhythmically called out their name, "Yo O Joey." When no one responded, I assumed they were out having fun with their families. I was lonely, and it seemed everyone had a place to go for the weekend but me.

A common question people asked my brother and me was, "What is it like not to have a father?" As children, we would respond in like manner, "I don't know, I never had one." The time we finally met our father was when the real sorrow registered. As an adult, for three short months, I felt what it was like to have both my parents in my life. But, alas, it did not last, and after he passed, I was once again fatherless.

L IVING IN THE city of Chicago, I thought traveling by bus with my family was the norm. My Uncle Bill was a bus driver, my mom did not drive nor own a car; therefore, it never occurred to me that some people did not need to use public transportation. I did not realize we rode on buses because we did not have money to do otherwise. These bus adventures happened only on the weekends and some of them were fun.

The weekends were often the same. Saturday night, we would all wash our hair, put out our best clothes, and be ready for church the next day. Saturday night was also pizza night, but ours was not delivered. Ours came in a Chief Boy-ar-dee box with everything we needed: a can of red sauce, flour in a bag, and parmesan cheese. As I think back, it was not a culinary taste sensation. The crust was like cardboard and the tomato sauce watery, but at the time, it pleased my young palette. Our dining would take place on the green metal flowered TV trays set by the TV in the living room. Mom turned on CBS so we could watch "Have Gun Will Travel." Gram loved to watch Richard Boone play Paladin. I think she had a crush on him, which makes me smile.

Sunday morning, there was no time for pancakes because, at 8:30, we had to leave the house and walk four blocks to church. There I sat completely bored, wondering if it would ever end. I would rest my head on my mom's lap and drift off to sleep. I recall the morning in church when Mom instructed me, "Sit up and don't lean on me. You're a big girl." That was a sad day. One, because Mom directed me to pay attention to the minister's words, ones I did not understand, and two, and most importantly, I sensed her undertone. Grow up, you are no longer a child. I was only seven.

Sunday supper consisted of boiled chicken and dumplings, green beans from a can with cream sauce, and because Gram had loved to bake, fresh rolls. By one o'clock, once again, we were pounding the sidewalk for another four blocks to arrive at the bus line that would take us to visit Mom's adult friends who did not have children. They lived in apartments in the city, so there was no yard to play in; therefore, I did not look forward to these outings.

I recall one of the street corners where we stood in the wind and rain. The Olsen Rug Factory was at Diversey and Pulaski, and the coolest place to wait for a bus. Their corner lot had what appeared to be a huge waterfall right in the middle of the city. As an adult, it surprised me to see its actual size. I had found it had only been gigantic from a three-foot-tall child's perspective. In October, the rug factory would celebrate the harvest with a festival where Native Americans would dress in colorful attire and dance around cornstalks as fires blazed. The waterfall was aglow with orange and red-colored lights. Uncle Bill would invite us to join his family to see this wonderland at night. The nine of us climbed into his station wagon, and when we arrived, the scene was magical.

During our city treks, we would often wait for a bus by one of my favorite places: the candy factory, where ladies would hand-dip chocolates right before our eyes. I always wondered if they ever licked their fingers. Gazing through the window of this small establishment on the bus line reminded me of the "I Love Lucy" sitcom. It was a television show enjoyed by many Americans, and my family was no different. There was an episode when Lucy had one of her many hair-brained ideas. Though married, Lucy portrayed one of the first independent women on television who did not wholly rely on her husband for financial support. She took action to acquire her own money.

In the show, Lucy and Ethel landed jobs at a candy factory. Their simple task was to stand alongside a conveyer belt, and as the chocolates traveled by, all they had to do was place them in wrappers. It at first appeared to be an easy job. The supervisor instructed them, "Now remember, if one candy gets past you and into the packing room without a wrapper, you're fired!" and then she walked away. To make the scene comical, the supervisor saw how well they were doing so she yelled to the back room, "Speed it up!" Lucy and Ethel were not able to keep up and began to panic. Their solution was to pop the candies into their mouths, but the sweets were flying by too fast. With their cheeks bulging, they saw the next option was to stuff candy into their hats, then into their uniforms, until eventually, they completely lost control. Of course, they were fired. Even though the ladies in the factory window did not appear to have Lucy and Ethel's problems, it was fun to imagine they did from time to time.

On below-zero days, which were a common occurrence in the Midwest, Mom would swallow her pride and allow Gram, my brother, and me to step into the entrance of the corner bar. This allowed us to get out of the icy wind while Mom stood outside and watched for the bus. The odor of beer filled my nostrils, and the loud voices of men echoed in the air as we hovered in the corner of this unfamiliar place. No one spoke about this strange-smelling room full of men. I only remember feeling that we should not be in there, but it was better than freezing our little toes. Our sense of smell holds strong memories, and even now, those bars haunt me as I cringe at the smell of beer.

Shopping downtown was reserved for special occasions, like a haircut, new shoes, or maybe a coat; there we followed an unwritten law. The attire for ladies and children called for the appropriate apparel for going into the big city: dresses, hats, and white gloves. I loved to wear my black and white checkered organza dress, with a crinoline slip that made my skirt fluff out. I think my mom liked the chance to wear a lovely dress, her one stylish coat, of course, a hat and gloves.

To stream us quickly through the city, avoiding stoplights and automobiles, we would take the elevated train line. On the outskirts of downtown, the train would whisk back up and loop around the downtown buildings, hence the name, the "L." It was an entertaining way for a small child to travel. My brother and I would run to the train's first car so that we could watch the transformation from light to dark. The train at first flew high above the street, clattered along the tracks, giving a birds-eye view of the houses, stores, graveyards, and parks. Then the train dove down underground, taking us in our Sunday finest, into the grim, dirty tunnel under the city.

Once we arrived downtown, we would exit the "L" at the stop where we could walk right into Marshall Fields & Company. We rode the elevators in the department stores, but our pristine white gloves never touched the brass buttons that marked the floors—or the brass gate. Only the elevator operator could open the gate. Each department store—The Fair, Carson Pirie Scott, Mandel Brothers, and Marshall Fields—had elevator operators trained in charm school. They wore hats and gloves, sat on a small stool, and inquired what our shopping destination would be. The heavy gate clicked as it was pulled closed and clanged as it locked. We could see the dark interior walls on the passing floors. The operator's voice rang out, "Second floor: ladies' gloves, lingerie, hats, hosiery—third-floor: children's apparel, coats, shoes"—as they listed the treasures on each floor. The top floor of the Fair was open only at Christmas. In December, that floor magically turned into a winter wonderland with rides for a child's pleasure. One year, Mom bought me a snowman balloon. He had cardboard feet, so when I tossed him in the air, he always landed upright. At home, I was so sad when he finally lost his air and lay deflated on the floor. I found shopping downtown always a treat.

Most often, our weekly shopping was done in our neighborhood. We walked a mile to our destination, Six Corners, but we cleaned the apartment before starting. One morning, Mom must have had one of her frequent migraines because she became enraged with my inefficiency at dusting the end table with the intricate wood-carved roses filled with dust. I dusted again, but because I didn't know what I missed the first time, I did not get it right the second time. The table looked clean to me. I was confused, but I knew never to talk back to her or voice my opinion. Therefore, I had learned to speak with my eyes. Her usual reaction was, "Don't look at me with those eyes, young lady!" And one of those looks is what prompted the abuse that day.

Embedded in my mind is what happened. I can see the floral sofa in our living room, the green painted walls, and the white lace curtains at the window that faced a passageway between our neighbors and us. The buildings were so close that only eight feet separated them in our community, allowing neighbors to hear what was happening in the apartments next door.

I do not remember the words, just the anger and tension. I was being slapped, which made me afraid and angry. More from fear than pain, I began to cry. As she often did, my mom gripped my upper arm when she was upset with me and shook me; my upper arms are still sensitive to touch. Mom put her hand over my mouth, not knowing her hand was also covering my nose. She whispered, "Stop crying. The neighbors are going to hear." Ah yes, the neighbors, we had to put up a good front for the neighbors. Mom pressed her hand against my mouth so tightly. I can still hear my breath, gasping for air, yet very little could come in. I could not stop crying. I was being hit, shaken, and suffocated. I could not breathe. I don't know what made her stop; I just know that she did because I am here today.

The threat of death is a powerful motivator. From that point on, I did not argue with her and surrendered my power.

On calmer days, after lunch, Mom and I would go shopping and do errands. Our weekend outings were not to the beach or the forest for a hike. Ours were to window shop along the busy streets, and though it was a long walk, my little legs were strong, and it never occurred to me that we were walking so far.

Once we completed our errands, Mom would take me to Walgreens or the dime store, and we would sit at the counter on the red stools that spun around with the slightest motion and order what I saw as delicacies. We always had the same thing. For me, the lady with the white apron and hat would place before me a mini chocolate sundae with whipped cream and a cherry on top. Mom had only coffee, served in the round cream-colored cup and saucer, but she seemed to enjoy her choice as much as I relished mine.

THERE WAS AN order to our week, just like the order that my mom and gram imposed upon our lives. Monday was washday, and even when automatic washers were a common household item, Gram held onto her wringer washer. It was her tried and true appliance, making it her Monday morning companion. When it broke down, as it inevitably would, it was nearly impossible to find a similar one because, by 1957, new technology flooded the US market with ten million automatic washers, selling to eager women who desired to lighten their household load. Not so for Gram. Mom searched and finally purchased a new pink wringer washer and had it delivered, down the basement stairs, to sit next to the washtubs, fulfilling Gram's demand.

During summer vacation, my job was to rinse the clothes by switching them from one washtub to another. If the clothes were white, I would dip them in bleach water, then rinse again in the washtubs. To ensure they were as white as possible, I put them into the adjacent tub, which had bluing. It took only a few drops of this intense coloring to brighten the whites. I liked seeing the indigo swirl, changing the water from clear to sky blue. I also felt my importance when Gram asked me to hand her clothespins while hanging the laundry outside to dry. An electric dryer was not in our budget or necessary in Gram's mind.

Tuesdays, Gram would sprinkle the clothes that needed to be pressed and place them in a plastic bag in the refrigerator. Don't ask me why they went into the fridge. On Wednesdays, Gram would iron. Sometimes I would be awarded this chore, but just the pillowcases and handkerchiefs. Shirts were too complex a skill for my tiny hands and mind; one needed maturity for that job.

I don't recall what Thursday's chores were. Perhaps that was a day of rest. Fridays were the days we headed to the grocery store. I begged to join Gram, giving me time as we walked to plead for lemon cookies, Alphabet's cereal, red licorice candy, and sweet luscious ice cream, which my mom also loved. Gram had a wire cart that she pulled behind us, filled with the food. On hot days we needed to walk fast so the ice cream would not melt. When we arrived home, the ice cream was taken out of the cardboard container and neatly placed into Tupperware, the storage container of the future. My brother and I would locate spoons, scrape the cardboard free of the excess cream, reveling in the process. Not only would cream cling to the edge of the ice cream container, but milk caps as well. Mid-morning at school, one child would carry a heavy wire box, filled with glass milk bottles to each desk, where we would pull out one bottle. Under the pleated paper top was a cardboard disk with a tab, and when we pulled off the tab, there too was a thin layer of cream we licked off. Too bad with today's homogenized milk, the tasty cream no longer floats to the top.

Chores were an essential part of the day. All these jobs, small as they were, gave me purpose, and that is how I felt needed and loved. I'm not sure what my brother was doing during all these weekly activities, except he was always there when Gram was baking, and it was time to lick the beaters from the Mixmaster.

The concept I had been taught and assumed was correct is that busyness is tied to love, and I have followed that pattern my entire life. If I cannot accomplish a task for the day, I feel I have wasted my time. I must have a purpose. I need to have a project. Sitting during the day and reading a novel is foreign to me. It seems wrong. Reading a nonfiction book is permissible in my skewed mind because it gives me the information I can then apply or disseminate to others. Instilled in me from my youth was, "Do, do, do."

In the first thirteen years of my life, we lived in basement apartments. When I moved into my own space as an adult, I made sure my living quarters were above ground for what I deemed a vast view. I was tired of seeing only the feet of people as they passed by.

With Mom at work, it became Gram's job to get us ready for school. Chicago can get below zero on most of the winter days. In our meager basement apartment, the only source of heat was a small oil stove in the kitchen, so from the kindness of her heart, Gram would light the oven with a match, wake us up, and we would huddle by the open oven door to keep warm. Neatly arranged on the iron racks of the oven lay our undergarments, so when we put them on, and for that moment, we felt toasty warm.

Fear held by Gram and adopted by Mom kept us under wraps. We had an unlisted phone number, so my father or his family would not know where we were. Later I discovered that some of my Italian relatives lived in the adjoining neighborhood; we never crossed paths. Our identity always stayed secret. How strange.

My brother and I went to sleep in the same bedroom, where childhood excitement kept us from immediately closing our eyes. Once we heard the click of the door as it shut, that sound was the signal to start lively conversations. Our quiet talking turned into mirth as we kept our legs on the bed and extended our bodies halfway out onto the floor, keeping our heads close enough to hear our whispers. We were not as quiet as we thought. The door would open, flooding the room with light, and the disturbing voice of an adult bellowing, "Be quiet and go to sleep." It all seemed so innocent. Who knew back then that our lives would be permanently impacted by being as poor as we were.

Neither my brother nor I wanted to repeat living in housing that, although clean, was inadequate. Living in cramped environments with little money motivated us to move in a different direction, turning our childhood into a blessing. My brother became a successful businessman, and I became an entrepreneur. I feel our youth was a divine gift, and I am grateful for what I learned from my family experience. I saw my mom move through adversity, injustice, ridicule, and blame, and it taught me to aspire to be a woman who could jump the hurdles in life and not be afraid.

There were no words of praise at home, but there were people who made me feel special. I remember the coffee man who delivered fragrant beans to our small apartment every week or so. Sometimes he would give us candy. I recall one morning when Gram ran to the grocery store after saying, "Don't open the door to anyone!" She had forgotten this was the day of the coffee delivery. The coffee man repeatedly knocked on the door, but my brother and I obeyed Gram's directive and did not open the door. Instead, we sat with our backs hard pressed against the basement door, with the glass window, to ward off our pending intruder, even though we knew he was harmless. Laughter rang out from our little voices as we felt hidden and inconspicuous, but of course, we were not.

Mom worked for Mr. Detardi, who had a private office for Hartford Insurance. Occasionally on Saturday mornings, I would join Mom, scribble on the notepad she gave me that had the Hartford elk in the left-hand corner, and sit under her desk while she worked. I recall on my fourth birthday, Mom came home with a turtle. A gift from Mr. Detardi. To my dismay, it died the next day. Gram said it was because I had held it too much. My heart sank when she implied that I killed it. It's no wonder I don't usually have pets in my home.

Mom had had only a high school education, but she was an intelligent woman. She knew working in a one-person office would not give her security in the future. She feared that when Mr. Detardi retired, she would be without a job after years of service. Allstate Insurance Company's headquarters became the corporation she wisely chose and stayed a loyal employee for forty-four years. She pulled herself up through the ranks and became a supervisor in various departments but unfortunately did not receive equal pay to the men who held the same jobs. But she stayed on. As the company grew, the office moved farther out of the city, into the western suburbs, where eventually it took her two hours by bus to travel to work. She rarely missed a day, venturing out even on the snowy, windy, frigid days, waiting on the cold streets for the bus.

Besides Mr. Detardi, there was another kind soul I recall. Aunt Anna, the sister-in-law of Gram. She would visit in the summer once or twice a year. Her bus ride took over two hours, traveling diagonally across Chicago from the south side to the far northwest corner where we lived. She was quite a character, a woman who was locked in time. She looked as if she had just stepped out of the 1920s. She always wore a black dress and black shoes that laced up to almost her ankles, her hair was clean and neat, and her tresses housed a rat, not the kind that scurries through the alleys but a nesting material that would give her hair body. Its purpose was to enhance her diminishing locks, but with hair so thin, you could see past the few strands right into the rat. It gave the appearance of a bird's nest snuggled on her head. Her hair was pinned back in a bun and always looked the same. I suspected she never combed it out, which was probably not true. I do wonder what traumatic incident stopped her from advancing through time.

Aunt Anna was the gentlest woman I had ever known. Her voice was soft, her manner tender. The conversations between Gram and Aunt Anna led me to believe that Aunt Anna was even more financially challenged than we were, though at the time, I did not see myself as lacking. It was just the way things were. Even though Aunt Anna's funds were few, her heart did not appear deprived, for she was rich with love. She always brought us bear claws, a tasty sweet roll from a bakery in her neighborhood. I suspected this was an expense she probably could not easily afford, yet she gifted us with them. As I look back, I can feel the calmness she brought to me in my youth, and now it consoles me because otherwise, my childhood was a little bit crazy.

June 15th, 1951

Bureau of Navy Personell
Washington. D.C.

Re: COPY OF DISCHARGE PAPERS on
    Anthony James Vincelisi Y/2/c

Dear Sir:

I would greatly appreciate your sending me a
copy or some verification that Anthony James
Vincelisi has been in the service and discharged
from same honorably.

I am being evicted from the apartment that I
live in with my two children ages 3 and 4, and
am endeavoring to obtain a veterans temporary
housing unit in our city. I have been informed
that if I can obtain a copy of the discharge papers
I will be eligable to obtain one of the housing
units.   I divorced my husband, and he was
to support his children, when he found out this
he left town and the court or I cannot locate
him.   This was two years ago.

I do not have his service number as he distroyed
the record I had on this, but the Naval Recruiting
Office in chicago has a card stating that on
April 29th, 1942 he entered the Navy as an
apprentice seaman V3, but they do not have the.
serial number listed.   He was honorably discharged
from the service in 1945, I dont know the month
or day, or from what discharge station, it may
have been somewhere in California.

He was stationed in New Orleans-Africa-and the
South Pacific on a ship which name I dont knew.

I am sorry that I do not have any additional
information that might assist you, but would
appreciate your giving this your earliest attention
as my eviction notice is to go into effect on
July 9th, 1951.

I found a letter wrinkled with age, as was she. It was to the veteran's administration, hand-typed, in desperation, hoping as the former wife of a veteran, they might see her as a woman in need and lift a hand to help her.

With no place for Mom to go, from the kindness of their hearts, her sister Ceal and her husband Bill opened their home to the four of us.

Billy—Me—Jimmy
Robby—Cis
Uncle Bill and Aunt Ceal had three children of their own, plus the two of us makes five.

Mom (center) would relish the chance to wear a lovely dress, her one stylish coat, and of course, a hat and gloves.

Randolph & Michigan

When we went shopping downtown, ...we followed an unwritten law. The attire for ladies and children called for the appropriate apparel, for going into the big city: dresses, hats, and white gloves.

Don't let someone dim your light simply
because it is shining in their eyes.

Chapter Ten

A STRANGE WAY TO LIVE

WE NEVER HAD DOGS OR CATS BECAUSE WE ALWAYS LIVED
IN someone else's house, creating a somewhat restricted lifestyle. I could
not walk on the grass in the yard, there was no running about, especially up and
down the stairs, and I had to keep my voice quiet—all impossible tasks for a small
child whose only focus was to romp and play. Along with these restrictions was the
no-pets-allowed rule. I was never at ease around dogs and later wondered if it was
because I never had a dog or because I had often heard the story about my father's
fear of dogs. Perhaps this is a side of him I took on subconsciously. Animals, therefore, have never played a significant role in my life, except for chickens.

I was only five years old when we moved into a lowly basement apartment
near Belmont and Harlem on the edge of the city, where some parts of the land
still had a rustic appearance. The windows were no more than twelve inches tall,
letting in very little light. The landlord of the make-shift apartment had chickens
running rampant in the backyard. A chicken is not a ferocious animal; a dog can
bite, a cat can scratch, but a chicken? Who would be afraid of a chicken? Me!

I was just a skinny little kid, a city girl, not familiar with the antics of chickens. I lived a life of fear of these fowl because they chased me and tapped at my
legs. In the pecking order of the flock, I was the lowest bird, and because of that,
when they saw me, they came a runnin'.

I would come home from kindergarten and look through the chain-link fence
to see if the flock of attackers was close. Perfect! No sign of them, but I still

needed to be careful. I opened the gate slowly enough that it would not squeak, and they would not hear me. With the gate ajar, all looked safe and appeared to be clear, so I walked confidently along the sidewalk. All too often, I would then hear the clucking. They had spotted me. It was a race to see who would win. I was sprinting for the stairs to our basement apartment, and they were running for my legs. Most of the time, they won, breaking my skin with their sharp beaks.

When I couldn't make it to our back basement stairs, I would run to the stairs that led up to our landlord's house and stand there crying. I'd remain there in my discontent until my gram would ascend from the basement with her broom in hand to chase away my attackers.

My gram always wore a crisply-ironed flowered cotton dress, lined with buttons down the front like well-spaced soldiers. She was a bit stocky, so the cloth fell snugly across her round hips, stopping just below her knees. Her twinkling green eyes softened her controlling exterior, implying that she was not as tough as she portrayed. Each morning, she would choose my clothes and line them up on the bed: a red and black plaid skirt, a white blouse with a peter pan collar, and a cardigan sweater. I always wore a dress or skirt, as pants were not an option. The school bent this rule on frigid winter days. Only then, we had permission to slip on slacks, never blue jeans, to keep our legs warm, but the skirt rule still applied. We then wore our skirts over our pants. Not an attractive style, but everyone did it, so that became the norm.

The no-pants rule continued through my high school years in the 60s, where skirts were still required and needed to be the proper length. The hem could not be higher than our knees, yet the style of the day was to wear our skirts to our mid-thighs. If the distance from our knees to our skirt was in question, we had to kneel on the hard concrete floor so the teacher could check to see if our hem touched the floor. If not, we had to walk home to change into more appropriate apparel. Even wearing culottes, that looked like a skirt, was forbidden.

When I first started in grammar school, after I had dressed, Gram placed one soft-boiled egg and grapefruit sections, served from a can, on the kitchen table. With our tummies filled, we would go out into the blustery wind to walk to school. The choice of clothing was not the only unreasonable demand put upon me on school days. There was also footwear.

Gram felt that a good pair of sturdy shoes would produce healthy and small feet, so wearing gym shoes, the day's style, was not allowed. My shoes were as reliable as hers. We clunked along the streets, her in heavy old lady black shoes, me in polished black and white saddle shoes. I am petite, yet now my feet top out at size eight and a half. Her plan, not previously tested, failed.

One school day in my odd life, when I was eight years old, my not-so-treasured saddle shoes were at the repair shop, and I had nothing else to cover my feet. Chain stores had not overtaken the market, so lining the commercial roadways were small family-run businesses owned by people from many different countries. The cobblers were abundant and busy because their skills stretched the family's dollars, making their business lucrative. I can still recall the aroma of leather and shoe polish at those stores.

So, without shoes, how would I be able to go to school? Staying home was never an option. Even when I was sick with a cold, Gram did not grant me a reprieve. The rule in our house was to listen to Gram and get to school. Certainly, bare feet were not a reason to stay home. Gram had a plan, but it did not do me any good.

My instruction that day was to don my tap shoes and click over to the school. I danced because, as a good mother, Mom used some of her hard-earned money to teach me poise through dancing. In the long run, I don't know how well that worked. I often recall having Band-Aids and scrapes on my knees from my unsteady gate. I began my tap-dancing career at three, it ended at five, but apparently, Mom was going to give me one more try to be graceful at eight. So, I owned a pair of tap shoes that fit my third-grade feet.

Gram figured those tap shoes should not go to waste, and by her standards, if they were good enough to wear to dance class at the park, they were good enough for school. Never mind that my steps echoed through the streets as I strode down the concrete sidewalk. They were shoes, and I was to wear them. I followed the directive enforced at home, but the school had rules that were going to create havoc that day. I maneuvered through the schoolyard without a hitch, shuffling along scattered gravel, which dampened the clicking tones from the metal plates; but once inside, things changed.

When the first bell rang, we lined up at the entrance of the school door. As the second bell chimed, we entered the halls, carefully passing the monitors who maintained the silence. We walked in an orderly fashion, heads facing forward, mouths shut, no eye contact. As I tip-toed in front of the monitors, one sentinel posted at each landing, making sure we were obedient, I made it past the first few. I appeared to be safe.

My school was three stories tall with twelve-foot ceilings, brightened by numerous ten-foot windows that lined the outside wall, corner to corner. Our teacher would pull out a nine-foot pole from the classroom's corner to open the windows on hot days. The stick had a brass hook with a ball on the end. She would place the hook into the hole at the top of the wooden window frame. It made a pleasing melodic sound from the chain clattering as it opened, bringing the fresh spring breeze to flow across our neatly aligned wooden desks, giving comfort to our class. One lucky child would be picked each week and given the job of closing the windows at the end of the day. I must say it was a tricky job for a four-foot-tall child to attempt to balance and direct the long pole into the tiny hole eleven feet above their head, but it was a privilege and a sought-after position.

The long staircases accommodated the tall walls in this massive structure, so I continued to trudge up to my appointed floor along with the other children. To move in silence with metal, not diamonds, on the soles of my shoes, was virtually impossible. I assumed I was doing just fine as I tried to be invisible. I thought perhaps no one noticed my loud clanking as I walked up the concrete stairs. But that was not the case.

A monitor with a commanding presence, towering over my elfin form, pulled me out of line and made me stand in the corner behind her. I was not embarrassed enough by making a racket with my patent leather shoes. She felt she needed to make an example of me. So, there I stood, as other students, each looking puzzled at me, quietly walked to their classrooms. I held my head down, looking at my shiny shoes, tied with the black grosgrain ribbons, wishing that the cold dark staircase would open and swallow me up. My teacher was notified of my whereabouts and rescued me from the corner of the stairs. She did not reprimand me, and I was allowed to go home at lunchtime. After lunch—I don't recall how or why, I only know I thanked God—I did not have to wear those noisy shoes when I returned to school. Perhaps a phone call to Gram from the principal encouraged her to find me another pair of shoes. From her own free will, I cannot imagine that she spared me from the embarrassment of wearing dancing shoes all day at school. It is no wonder I now rebel against conformity.

MOM AND GRAM had the same level of stress, expressed in different ways. Mom cowered from life. Gram felt she had no control over what happened in her life so, she attempted to control those around her, including family, neighbors, or anyone that attempted to change what she already had in mind. That was the way my mom and gram coped with the anxiety of being alone in the world. They had both lost their male partners, and neither had the strength or desire to find another.

We lived in a three-room attic apartment across from Portage Park Grammar School from my third to eighth grades. We had to cram ourselves into this tiny space, but I was not that tall, so it appeared spacious to me. I even had a private space where I shelved my toys under the sloped attic ceiling that followed the slanted roof, and though the nails protruded past the wood, they did not bother me. It made me happy to stand and marvel at my acquisitions, all neatly stacked. Here before me were Colorforms, Parcheesi, Monopoly, paper dolls, coloring books, and boxes of crayons that would melt in the intense heat of the summer. I could stand to be there only a few minutes, so I would quickly make my selection and return to sit by the fan in the living room. Aside from the temperature fluctuation from winter to summer, this place was comfortably my utopia.

My brother and I went to sleep at 8 o'clock in our only bedroom; and at 10 o'clock, we were shuffled into the living room, half-awake, to continue our slumber on the couch or the roll-out bed. It all seemed very reasonable to me; I knew no different.

On school days, Gram was delighted that she was close enough to keep her eyes on her grandchildren as we walked across the street into the schoolyard. For whatever reason, Jim and I were not allowed to go to school early and play. The bell rang at 8:50, and when the second bell tolled at 9:00, we were late. Gram did not permit us to leave for school until the first bell rang. Then we needed to race across the street, scamper the full city block of the graveled playground, and scurry into our place in line. We then stood silently in front of the school door, to wait for the second bell. After repeated begging, we convinced Gram we must be allowed to leave earlier because the rule stated we should be in line at the first bell.

Why did she object to our playing and having fun? There was no rationale for her behavior. We were only eight and nine years old, as were the children in the playground. Monitors and teachers were observing our conduct. Who was there to harm us?

Gram could hear the bell ringing at the end of the school day, and if we were not home promptly, less than five minutes, we would be grilled as to our whereabouts and instructed not to let it happen again. Mom and Gram's fear of us being harmed by someone had been fed by the news on television that posted stories of children murdered in the woods nearby. The event was not close enough to be a threat, but for women who dread what life might bring, they found it too close for comfort.

There was an incident when I was in fourth grade. Gram was angry with my brother and me for some silly thing kids do. She told us that when we came home for lunch, the orphanage lady would be there to pick us up and take us away. I walked to school, unable to focus my eyes, filled with tears. I returned at noon in trepidation, fearing this would be the last time I would be with my family. I came in for lunch, and to my astonishment, there were no authorities from the orphanage. Gram was in good humor and did not mention the morning's rift—just another one of her control tactics to keep my sibling and me in line. Later in life, I shared this story with my brother, and he as well holds this incident embedded in his memory. He shared, "I too cried at school and was afraid to come home." Because of our issue with our father's rejection, this punishment held an extreme emotional charge.

To my dismay, Gram's control did not stop with our family alone. Her wrath spread far and wide. She would turn the kitchen chair with the chrome metal legs and silvery vinyl seat to face the window to get a bird's-eye view of the children below as they walked home from school, eavesdropping on their chatter. If they swore, she would yell, "You stop that kind of talk and get going home."

I was mortified the day when a boy in my class realized, "That crazy lady who yells at me from the window is your grandmother?" Word had quickly spread throughout the school, and that was just another day I wanted to disappear into oblivion and never be heard from again.

ADVERTISING WAS DIFFERENT from what it is now. To our amazement, men would show up at our schoolyard, demonstrating yo-yos. Surely, we could learn what appeared to be easy skills: walk the dog, around the world, rock the baby, and the tricky stick spin. All we needed was to gather our pennies from our allowance, walk to the dime store and obtain a Duncan yo-yo, which I did with pride.

The advertising of lunch meats was the job of the man in the Oscar Meyer wiener wagon, which only showed up in the parking lot of the grocery store. Word spread throughout the neighborhood when it arrived, and we raced to meet it. There we stood in line waiting while the man in the white coat and butchers' hat handed us the coveted Oscar Meyer wiener whistle. I did not always get there on time. On those days, I sadly stood at the curb, with no treasure in my hand, as I watched the wiener wagon pull away.

But the man who got my attention and began my musical career was the one who was handing out tickets for free accordion lessons. I first attempted to play the piano, but all I received from the school was a sheet of music and a cardboard keyboard. Without the sound of notes, my enthusiasm to practice diminished rapidly.

Yes, I played the accordion. It was quite the fad in our Italian neighborhood. Three weeks of free accordion lessons was a price that fit Mom's budget, so she gave her approval. I must have impressed Mom with my talent because my classes continued after the free sessions. Mom was a trooper. She packed my rented accordion and Jim's guitar, for he too requested to be musically educated, into the red wagon, and we walked to our lessons. It was a mile or two away, but we ventured out in the cold and often in the snow. My music conservatory put together an accordion band to hold the interest of its students. We were all under the age of twelve and sat behind cardboard frames to hide the music stands, as we entertained our relatives. Being in a group has a way of putting me at ease, but one frightening afternoon, I shared my talents before all the parents and students of my entire grammar school.

The teacher had asked me to play my accordion at an assembly. I agreed, but on that day, I reluctantly walked onto the stage, all by myself, with my heavy, mother-of-pearl accordion strapped to my body, resting on my chest. As I gazed across the filled auditorium, every eye was upon me, making this seem like not a good plan. I took a breath, ready to play the song I had been practicing for weeks. I placed my right hand on the white keys and my left on the buttons. Oom-pah-pah, oom-pah-pah rang out the cords to "Lady of Spain," and I relaxed into the flow. I ended hearing the roar of applause.

I UNDERSTAND THAT Gram was working from her old programming, being a victim of her fears, and she did not know any other way to act. Thus, life with her was a battle from the start. Navigating around her control became a gift. It taught me to develop the art of negotiation. I carefully planned my conversations with her to sidestep her unrealistic demands—another silver lining from the clouds of my life that helped me as an adult. But there was one stormy day that still haunts me.

Kitty-corner from our apartment was what we called the school store with a soda fountain, school supplies, and my favorite, a glass cabinet that displayed candy. When I was younger, Gram permitted me to visit the store to purchase penny candy. One of my favorite candies was a flat string of black licorice wrapped around a pink sugar center called records. Occupying the lower shelf were red hot dollars, a chewy gummy candy in the form of a coin. Folded neatly were candy sugar buttons in graduated colors flowing down long strips of paper. The paper often stuck to the back of the candy, and though the paper wasn't flavorful, the boys found it made great spitballs. Also, to tie in with the Russian-orbiting satellite, were light blue, lumpy gum balls called sputniks. The case always had the one-inch tall, cream-colored wax coke bottles with sugary liquid inside. Only at Halloween could you buy wax red lips and the black wax mustache. I often visited this virtual candy land and had numerous cavities in my teeth to prove it.

All was fine for a time, but as I grwe older, I was forbidden to hang out at the soda counter, making the school store off-limits. Gram could not see the store from the window of the attic apartment, so she assumed there were questionable people there. Maybe that was true after school, but it was only benign grammar school kids during school hours.

Naturally, as I matured, I disregarded my gram's rule, and in eighth grade, I would pop over during lunch to visit my friends. One day, while we were squeezed together on the red upholstered bench, our hips touching, I was laughing with the girls, as they sipped their Cokes in the green bottles. Then I looked up and exclaimed, "Oh no, my gram! She is coming this way!" Her steps stomping towards the store, her green eyes focused upon me, she knew where she was going and who she was going to get. I crunched down, lying across the laps of my friends, but I was not hidden. "You get over here, young lady!" She grabbed my upper arm, squeezed tight, and dragged me out onto the sidewalk and down the street. To be handled in this manner, in front of my friends, I just wanted to die.

When I was thirteen, there was an episode with Mom that made me stand up for what I knew was right. It was dusk, and with permission, I was walking in the neighborhood with my girlfriends, laughing, being silly teenagers, and heading home. As we turned the corner, an image of a woman appeared before us on the sidewalk. It was my mother. I was shocked to see her condition—her eyes red, tears flowing down her face, she was wringing her hands as she frantically walked the street.

She probed, "Where were you? I have been so worried! I have been combing the streets! You should have been home sooner than this!" It was not dark, and she had not given me a curfew. I was as alarmed as she, but for a different reason. Again, I was so embarrassed in front of my friends. My response to her came from a place deep inside, one I rarely dared to access, but this time for once, I spoke my truth. "Mom, I will always be protected, and when it is time to go, I will die. This is not that time." There was no call back from her. She could not argue with the wise young woman who stood boldly before her; my words came from my heart, heated as they were. My friends went home to their respective families, and Mom and I walked back in silence, the subject stuffed away, never addressed again.

Later, I found that each bizarre occurrence from my youth had made me stronger. Mom did the best she could, but at some point, I wanted her to admit she had a hand in causing some parts of my screwed-up life. But that view of her changed one day when my opinion of her crumbled to the ground.

Each morning, she (Gram) would choose my clothes and line them up on the bed. I always wore a dress or skirt as pants were not an option.

Gram delighted that she could keep her eyes on her grandchildren as we walked a few yards into the schoolyard. For whatever reason, my sibling and I were not allowed to go to school early and play.

The teacher had asked me to play my accordion at an assembly.
I agreed and reluctantly walked onto the stage, all by myself, with my heavy, mother-of-pearl accordion strapped to my body, resting on my chest.

My music conservatory put together an accordion band to hold the interest of its students. (Marnie—1st row on the left.)

1950s memorabilia

1950s Memorabilia

THEY DID THE BEST THEY COULD

W HENEVER I QUESTIONED MOM ABOUT THE PAST, SHE WOULD always say, "I did the best I could," and then she dropped the subject. My body would tense up as my anger rose; her statement became my trigger. I viewed her phrase as, "I don't care about your feelings." Without any consideration for her position, I felt it was all about me. Her indifference activated my lifelong feelings of unworthiness.

My awakening came in the summer not long after reconciling with my father. It was late morning, the usual pleasant Colorado weather; warm, comforting, and bright. I brought Mom some marigolds to plant in the flower boxes that outlined the top of her redwood fence. After a short visit, I began to leave her condo, and without thinking, I turned to her and said, "Mom, even if you don't mean it, I need to hear you say you are sorry for what happened. I don't blame you. I just need to hear the words."

There was a long pause, and a blank look came over her face. She gazed at me as if I was not there. Time stood still. At last, she spoke, but it was not the reply I had wished. She said something utterly unrelated to my appeal. I was stunned when she offered no appropriate response. It was as if I had never presented my question. I just wanted her to acknowledge that she knew I still held pain from being abandoned by my father for all these years. I asked myself, "Didn't she hear me?" She looked like she had.

My whole being began to whirl. My mind was attempting to process as fast as Mom was struggling to understand and avoid my query. She had no clue why I would request such a thing. It was not because she was rude. It wasn't that she did not want to ease my pain. She just could not conceptualize that I had agonized about my father. Why would my heart ache? My father leaving was her story. It appeared to me she had no concept of how others had been affected, especially her children, whom she never wanted to hurt. She thought she was protecting us. All she could do was ignore my plea as I was attempting to fit the pieces together myself. Because I saw no hope for a resolution with Mom, apparently, I needed to readjust my thinking.

There was no way Mom was going to entertain this discussion. She seemed riddled with anxiety that her actions might have messed with my emotional health. I was so puzzled and confused by her lack of reply that I too was unable to speak. I said goodbye and walked towards my car in a daze. Sitting in the driver's seat, I began to back the car away. I could see Mom standing in the sunlight, framed by her tall redwood gate, as she waved goodbye. She stayed there until I was out of sight, as she so often did. I had forgiven her even before my car entered the street.

I did not consciously exonerate her. It came through, like a gift handed to me, from a place of love beyond my reach. I lived only a short distance from Mom's home, about a three-minute drive. Like Mom, nothing seemed to change. It was a pleasant day, and as I drove past the park, I noticed mothers with buggies, boys fishing in the pond, and teenagers playing baseball. All seemed right in the world, even though Mom had not given me the answer I was looking for, yet my world was overturned.

As I drove away, I tried comprehending what had just occurred. I then realized Mom did do the best she could, but she had used that phrase so often I had become numb to the words. Now, for the first time, I heard what she was saying.

By ignoring how I might have hurt, Mom had found a way to live with her pain. Any change to that course of action was so foreign that she could not react to my request. Instantaneously the push-pull of our relationship was gone. For the first time, I heard her words from my heart, and there was no longer a reason to hang onto being justified with my anger. I was relieved. I was free!

At last, I could let go of the judgment I harbored about how Mom and Gram had kept me from being with the man whom I hoped loved me, my father. Now I had seen there was no one to blame. It just happened. Oh my God! Again, it rang in my head, "She did the best she could!"

Looking back on our past interactions, when she had shown no concern for

me or how I felt, I saw it was not all about me; this was her issue. I was a prod-
uct of her relationship with my father, but her problem was with him, and her
confusion about her love for him was not about me and how I was loved. She
loved him, but he did not treat her in a way that she felt honored. Mom held to
her stand as the injured party. Did she ever imagine that her children also felt the
same pain and loss of love that she had kept hidden?

When Mom did not respond to my question in that split second, I had a realization: I had a choice; I could go on with my life, feeling victimized as my mom
did with my father and Aunt Mary, or I could choose to see things from a new
perspective. I could own the judgment I had for Mom and never entertain that
thought again, thus tearing down the wall around my heart, freeing it, and releasing the pain associated with abandonment. It was my choice. At that moment, it
was so easy. I let it go. What a gift! I did not forgive her for a wrong committed
because that would be judging her. There was nothing to forgive. There was no
wrong committed.

I drove away from Mom, lighter than I have ever felt before, infused with a
deep love for her. Not only I, but Mom was liberated as well. Even with no words
exchanged, our lives were still altered.

I know on a deeper level that Mom knew at that moment that I stopped
judging her and accepted her for who she was. That is all she truly wanted, not to
be changed or made wrong, just acknowledged for who she was and the choices
she had made. Therein lies freedom, and Mom could have it too, if she chose.

NOTHING CAN REPLACE the family is a principle that I saw in my father's family—and my father lived that truth. He did not know how he
could adjust his life without my brother, mom, and me. He left Chicago to con-
ceal his pain, creating a void in our family, leaving Mom with no alternative but
to take legal action. Thus his isolation began.

I don't know what he was thinking at that time. He could have easily mailed
the checks to Mom, but the longer he stayed away, the bigger his debt became
until it appeared to be an insurmountable debt to pay. Was he angry, and did his
fury create the separation? These were questions I never had a chance to ask him.
Our time together was so brief. We were with each other for only hours, not days.
But one day, I was able to understand him better.

After his death, Dolores, my father's second wife, called and asked, "Would you like your father's old watchmaker's cabinet?" "Absolutely," I emphatically responded. I jumped at the chance to have something of my father's. On a trip back to Chicago, Frank and I loaded the heavy cabinet into our van and escorted it back to Colorado. It was made up of small drawers with brass handles, chipped paint, and dinged wood. It did not look like a gem, but it was to me. I found that Dolores had no interest in its contents and had not emptied any of the drawers, not one. Inside were some treasures that revealed segments of my father's life journey and a few things that showed me how, in some ways, we were alike.

My father had kept the bill of sale from every new car he purchased, a habit I have adopted over the years as well. His autos were large sedans, while mine were fast little sports cars. Did he enjoy parading around the neighborhood with his classy vehicle as much as I relished speeding across intersections, beating out the cars next to me in my red Corvette? If he had known how many times the cops had stopped me, would he have reprimanded me?

If only I could have shared the story about when I was pulled over while delivering a German chocolate cake to my boyfriend Frank—yes, the one I married. The policeman looked down at me, as Corvettes are low to the ground, and said, "Are you going to a race?" "No, officer, I'm delivering a birthday cake. See? It's on the floor. Would you like a piece?" He could not help smiling and said, "Go on, get out of here. And slow down." I had a blast. I wonder what my father would have thought.

In my father's watchmaker's cabinet, my treasure hunt continued as I opened and looked to the back of each long drawer. I found foreign currency which showed that we both had traveled abroad. Another drawer revealed watch parts, springs, screws, and broken pieces. Curious that he, like me, spent time tinkering and discovering how things worked. He used his hobby to pass the time. My pursuits became a business, and I created my toy company.

Tucked in a corner, under paper clips and dust, was his little black book. Contained within were women's names, phone numbers, and details about how they responded to his affections. I may not have had a long relationship with him, but this gave me an insight that most children do not get to see. It made me chuckle to think of my father as a good-looking guy, sharing his time with ladies. After all, I had never known him as a father figure in my life; therefore, I had no emotion attached to his life as a single man.

Father's mental state began to unfold in the creased, thin paper that crinkled as I opened it. It was a legal document on the same type of paper as the divorce documents—the ones in Mom's safety deposit box. The report noted a court case where my father had had his license revoked from a drunk driving conviction. Again, he was making poor decisions, and though I do not know how extensive his drinking was over the years, in my eyes, it confirmed that Mom had made the correct decision to leave him. I suspect she was foreseeing alcohol abuse and was not going to allow us to be part of that kind of life. Thanks, Mom.

I began to see that my mom and father carried similar negative attributes from their upbringing. Unknown to them, those qualities created their magnetic attraction. Neither one of them had the strength to stand up to the ones who had raised them. It was more important to have family approval than to follow the dictates of their hearts. That directive was so instilled in my parents that it rendered them unable to recognize what they truly wanted. They hid their feelings for too long, and I too fell into that pattern.

When I was twenty, I did not go out to find my father, which I could have done. I was afraid of what my gram and mother would say. Deep down, I was living in fear. My subconscious concern was that if I searched for my father, my mother and gram would stop loving me, and there was a good chance the man I searched for would deny me his love as well. It was too much to risk. I had to hold onto what love I had obtained so far, even if it was not enough to feed my soul. It took me twenty more years to build enough self-worth to confront my greatest fear, abandonment.

I got married because of the pressure from my mom and gram. They insisted the only honorable way to move out of the house was marriage. I wanted to live alone, but I was afraid to stand up to my mother and say, "I'm moving out." I ignored the quest for freedom that was ringing out in the streets in the 1960s. Sadly, I had a deaf ear to those bells, and I fell into what I thought I should do, rather than what I wanted to do. If I could have looked at my situation independent of my family's opinions, perhaps I would have made better decisions in my life and not have married at twenty-one.

I was no different from my parents—what a paralyzing realization. I could no longer hold a grudge because I was like them. At that point, my judgment and sorrow began to disperse. If my mom and father had ignored their families' opinions, possibly they would have felt better about their decisions. Did they judge themselves for what might have been the wrong choice to divorce? Certainly, their love for each other haunted them for a lifetime.

On that summer day, when Mom had not understood my request for an apology nor acknowledged my childhood pain, a huge weight was lifted from me. I granted to myself the grace I was looking for from her. I later found that my mom and father's love for each other never waned, yet I wanted to understand what caused the crumbling of their relationship. So I looked for the reason why.

My father's autos were large sedans, while mine were fast little sports cars.

Don't compromise yourself.
You are all you got.
JANIS JOPLIN

THE LAST STRAW

M Y PARENTS' FAMILIES AT FIRST HAD A CORDIAL RELATION-ship, which enabled my mom and father to meet and fall for each other. Aunt Mary had reminisced, "They were so in love. When they would visit, your mom sat on your father's lap, and they asked for one cup of coffee that they would share." If they were so in love, why didn't their love last? Perhaps if I could understand their original attraction to each other, I might know my mom and father better.

Because Mom never talked about her time with my father, I received no clues from her and never felt the door was open to ask her questions. While speaking with my cousin Pam, I learned things about her mom JoAnn, which helped me see why my parents might have gotten together.

JoAnn and my father were the youngest and closest of the six siblings in their family. Interestingly, they took their exit from the earth within months of each other; JoAnn in June, my father in October. Could it have been that they did not want to be on earth without their close family connection? Pam's description of her mom mirrored the traits of my mom. Unfortunately, the main one was fear. Did my father fall in love with Mom because she reminded him of his sister, whom he had protected and cared for?

I observed how simple problems would upset my mom, and she rarely felt safe. Once I parked in a no-parking zone to run into a store quickly and drop off payment for a bill. I left the car running with Mom in it, but she was adamant.

"You can't do this. You must move the car, the police will see you, and you will be in trouble." I tried to console her to no avail, "This will take only a few minutes. I will be right back," but it didn't ease her apprehension.

Doctors were also authorities she did not question and followed their orders explicitly. In her late 60s, the doctor found curious cells in one breast and suggested a lumpectomy. Though the cells were not malignant, Mom so greatly feared cancer, she asked for a mastectomy. She even took it one step further and requested that both her breasts be removed. She told me, "I do not want to go under the knife a second time in case something else appears. My brother supported and agreed with her decision, and she had both breasts removed. It made me sad to see how her body became altered because of her worry.

Like my mom, Aunt JoAnn's nervous reactions kept her from driving. Pam recalled the day her father, my Uncle Mario, had attempted to teach his wife to drive. Pam, being small, was taken on the ride and sat in the back of the car. Things were going well until Mario screamed, "Brakes, brakes." Pam said, "My dad reached into the back seat and pushed me to the floor and said, 'Stay down.'" He quickly turned to face the windshield and shouted again, "Brakes, brakes." After that night, JoAnn never sat behind the wheel again. It took years before Pam heard what transpired that night.

Uncle Mario had seen a cat crossing the street. JoAnn did not. Even his shouting did not save the cat. Traumatized, JoAnn had no desire to master the skill of driving. Although, my mom never hit an animal, she was always extremely uncomfortable at the wheel. She learned how to drive when she was forty, but she stopped operating a vehicle a few years later.

Both these women shuddered at the most superficial problems finding them to be insurmountable. Luckily JoAnn had Uncle Mario. In the beginning, Mom had my father, but that was for only a short time. I now could see that perhaps my father had picked Mom so he could care for, nurture, and love her. It did not work out that way, but it consoles me to know that perhaps that was his intent. So, why was Mom drawn to him?

When I met my father, his life was at its end. The light had gone out of his eyes, so I had no clues to his personality. After he passed, Pam described my father as the sweetest man, with a smile that twinkled in his eyes, just like her mom's eyes. Oh, how I wish I could have seen him that way. Apparently, my mom had. Perhaps the tenderness she felt in my father reminded her of her gentle caring father. If my mom and father only could have held onto the good parts they first saw in each other and nurtured them, but alas, they did not.

ONE UGLY NIGHT, a fight began between my mom and father. Their rage overflowed, and it started a family feud. My parents retreated to their respective family camps where their resentment for each other, at the time, was supported and fed. Mom had recalled that she and my father attempted to mend their relationship by obtaining counseling from the parish priest. She said, "The priest gave us suggestions to reconcile our differences, but after repeated sessions, your father did not follow the guidelines set, and so I felt our marriage was not worth continuing." I heard little else from Mom about how they addressed their conflicts. After finding the court papers for his drunk driving in my father's watchmaker's cabinet, I wondered if alcohol was one of the reasons they did not reunite.

Uncle Nunzi saw the result of his family's interference in his brother Tony's marriage. Specifically, his family pointed out to my father that he would be better off without my mom. Nunzi knew if his marriage was to endure, he had to get away from their clutches and leave the city. He moved to the city's suburbs, which were just far enough away to build a clan of his own. His wisdom paid off. His marriage lasted for decades with daughters and grandchildren by his side.

Though Pam saw my father as sweet, my father had a hot Italian temper, which was different from my mom's experience living with her father. Grandpa Blake was quiet and never spoke a harsh word to his wife or anyone else. Therefore, life with my father was foreign to Mom. I suspect my father's family was a bit more boisterous. What Mom did not understand is that loud voices do not always mean danger, some families are more excitable, and that is how they converse. My parents came from very different backgrounds, and yet there were some similarities.

They were both raised by women who demanded obedience, my father's sister Mary and Mom's mother, Cecelia. I do not know why my father succumbed to Mary's reign, but he appeared to be weak and unable to speak his truth to those he deemed in authority.

Even though Grandma Palm was present in my father's home, Aunt Mary, ten years my father's senior, had a ruling hand in his upbringing. She guarded her youngest brother and took him on as her own. Much to my mom's dismay, Mary's influence colored my father's actions during his marital disagreements. I wondered if Aunt Mary even understood what it was like to be in love, but Aunt Rose told me a story that answered my question. She told me, "Mary once had a man in her life, and with her suitcase in hand, she bought a train ticket and followed him out West." When she arrived on the warm California soil, the land turned cold when she discovered he was already married. With a broken heart, she returned home and never ventured into another intimate relationship. Her heartbreak set a precedent for her entire life, as did my mom's.

Like all new brides, Mom must have held expectations of marital bliss, but her new life did not fit her dream. I sense she was more than discontent. My parents wanted to obtain freedom from their families in their new relationship but were unsure how to achieve it. My father's expressive personality frightened her. Mom was already very timid, and immediately getting pregnant after their nuptials made her even more emotional, so it did not take much to scare her.

After years of separation, I know my mom and father wanted to clear the air from their past because they both expressed the love they held deep in their hearts at the end of their lives. How sad they never had closure.

T HE FIGHT THAT ended my parent's marriage was not often a subject discussed in my childhood, at least not while I was in the room. My mom repeatedly said that during the disagreement, my father threatened her. He said, "I have a gun, and I am not afraid to use it." Those are words my mom had never forgotten, nor had I. She confessed, "I was alone, your brother was not yet one. I was pregnant with you and didn't know what your father might do. I didn't know whether there was a gun in the apartment or not." I imagine with trepidation, she ran for the phone, hoping my father would not follow, and called the police for help. But there was one more untold part of this frightening story that rattled me.

The first day I sat in Uncle Mario's living room, I heard about rumors they possessed about my brother and me, and I wondered how they could have known of our experiences, yet not of our whereabouts? I found that stories were passed between my parent's sisters who worked at the same telephone company, making our life not as private as my mom and father thought. When I decided to become a hairdresser, my mom told me, more than once, that I had a cousin on my father's side that also entered that vocation. How bizarre she would share with me details about my cousin Paul, yet she had never opened that door for me to meet him or my father. Still, she knew things about my cousins.

Now I understood we had been kept track of via a vague line of communication between Aunt Ceal and Aunt Mary, yet they did not speak to each other. Or did they? All I know for sure is neither our father's nor our whereabouts were ever revealed.

Back in the 1940s, technology was not what it is today. There was no direct line to the local authorities in an emergency as we have now by calling 911, nor could a person dial a call directly. The caller would pick up the receiver and request a number through the operator. The operator would then choose the correct pegs in the panel before her, and the board would light up as the operator connected the callers. In emergencies, the telephone operator's duty was to link the call to the proper authorities and stay on the line until help arrived, thus making sure the caller was safe. Though weak, the operator was the lifeline from the caller to the support requested. When Mom called the police on the night that changed our lives, she was scared and did not recognize the telephone operator's voice on the other end of the line. Who was the person who picked up the call on that ill-fated night? Aunt Mary!

Chicago is a big city. What were the odds that Aunt Mary would respond to this alarming call? I'd say slim. It was not until the day I met my father that Aunt Mary shared her recollection of that night. "At first, I did not recognize the voice on the other end as your mom's." Mary knew the protocol, she notified the police and they were on their way. When she realized it was her brother who was the one with a gun, she forgot her training, immediately overreacted, and the next thing Mom heard was a dial tone. Mary unplugged the cord from the switchboard, disconnecting the call, as well as Mom's safety net. When the police arrived, they found Mom shaken but unharmed. I know nothing more about that part of the story.

Sadly, Aunt Mary did not hear the fear in my mom's voice and keep the call connected to make sure her sister-in-law and baby nephew would be unharmed. Aunt Mary was also afraid. She did not know what her brother was capable of doing and was not thinking clearly. I believe she did not want my mom harmed.

From that point forward, the war raged with each family taking sides, which did not help the situation. My aunts recalled a day when my father drove over to my grandparent's apartment to pick up my young brother. That day my father brought his mom along. I was too small for my father to take me with him, but I was near, in the baby buggy, on the sidewalk. Grandma Palm walked over to my pram to take a peek. Upon her approach, Gram covered my face, so Grandma Palm could not see me.

Gram must have harbored deep pain to respond in such a disrespectful way to an older woman who never harmed us. How unkind. I suspect Gram was adjusting to losing her husband, upset about her daughter's divorce, and just trying to cope. Her demons lived inside her and controlled her, but she never realized it.

Mom and my father were trying to find their way through tough times. Aunt Mary and Gram urged them not to go back to each other, jeopardizing any reconciliation. My parents listened to these two emotionally damaged women who were not inclined to guide them towards an amicable relationship. Then communication between these young lovers was lost. Sadly, not only did they break up, but these families never spoke to each other after this unfortunate event. Gratefully, the contempt did not last forever, only four decades, for when I met my father's family, all healed in the blink of an eye.

L OVE HAS NO boundaries. Time and distance can't stop it. And when I met my Italian family, I was astonished by how the love in their hearts poured out to me. I hadn't received a lot of affection in my youth, yet there they stood, embracing me with their love, with tears in their eyes. They did not know me, yet that didn't matter. That day every person in that room shared how they had always wanted to meet me. I felt it was natural for my father to think of me over the years, but I never considered that my cousins and aunts would as well. The caring continued months later, proving that my brother and I were never forgotten, not even from the grave of my father's mother, Grandma Palm.

Before Grandma Palm's death, she told Aunt Mary, "I want to leave something for my grandchildren. After I pass, will you take money from my bank account and gift each of them." There were fourteen of us. Even though she did not know our whereabouts, Grandma Palm told Aunt Mary to place money in safekeeping for us as well. Aunt Mary once had said, "Grandma Palm always prayed for your mom and father to get back together." Though her desire for my parents to make amends never happened, her intuition told her that my brother and I might someday be back in the family's graces, or maybe it was just a dying mother's wish. Nonetheless, my brother and I reappeared to fulfill Grandma Palm's wish.

Grandma Palm lived a healthy life in the comforts of her home until she passed at one hundred and four years old. The women in my genetic line come from good stock, having longevity on their side. Aunt Mary passed away at eighty-six, Aunt Rose at ninety, my mom at ninety-one, and one of Grandpa Blake's relatives, Aunt Jess, stayed healthy until one hundred and eight.

Grandma Palm never spoke a word of English, but my cousins told me they always knew what she was saying. Carl reminisced, "Her eyes said it all, and if you didn't get the message, her hands would rise to complete her thought." I think it's an Italian trait to talk with your hands. I acted that way naturally without ever being exposed to this practice. When I was in my late teens, I had a boyfriend who suggested, "Why don't you sit on your hands and talk to me." I must say I had less to say without using those appendages.

After my mom passed, I did not talk about her often, but years later, while having lunch with a friend, our conversation turned to stories about our mothers. Our close friendship allowed us to be vulnerable and have an intimate discussion even though we were in a public place. I have heard it said, 'Women can accomplish as much over lunch, as an hour on a psychologist's sofa." That afternoon was such an occasion. So I reached into my past, opened my heart, and shared why I felt Mom completed her life's journey and tucked her memories away with dementia.

Tony (my father)—**Grandma Palm**
Gram—**Lorraine** (my mom)

My parents' families at first had a cordial relationship, which enabled my mom and father to meet and fall for each other. Aunt Mary had reminisced, "They were so in love."

THE FINAL CURTAIN

MOM FIGURED OUT HOW TO NAVIGATE THROUGH THE IN-stability of her life by closing off her painful memories and hiding her true feelings. The result became the inability to understand and process everyday tasks. Once old painful memories surfaced, her habit was to push them away, to avoid the recall, not realizing that turning away from her struggles did not diminish the agony. With her pain stuffed away, never being appeased or claimed, and with no validation for her hidden sentiments, those emotions eventually raised their ugly heads with a vengeance. Mom's memory diminished, making her incapable of caring for herself.

She could not admit that my brother and I were psychologically injured because she and Gram had made it challenging to see our father. She felt her actions were appropriate. After all, my father did not financially support us. In her mind, she acted accordingly. She was protecting her children from a man she felt could do them harm. Even when we were adults and able to make our own decisions, her concern continued to direct her actions, perhaps out of habit. Maybe she felt if we found our father, the meeting might cause us pain. All was fair in her mind, even though she did not offer us a chance to choose what was appropriate for us.

Mom justified why the measures she took were correct, but her body would not accept that reasoning. Her body reacted to her actions. With dementia, her mind shut down following the directive she lived with all her life: don't look at the past. Regrettably, that command overflowed, hindering her current-time thoughts. I wondered if other people with dementia have also closed off their recollections of unpleasant situations, so I did a little research.

During a fundraising event to raise awareness of Alzheimer's, I walked alongside adults whose loved ones had been affected by this disease. I asked one family at a time, "Did your parent have a major incident from their past that they did not face or talk about, yet you know it still deeply disturbed them?" From the handful of people I asked, their answers always came back in the affirmative, showing me that Mom's issues followed others with dementia. Mom's memory loss put her on a rocky path, but when I looked closely, I found the silver lining in the cloud that hung over her head.

Within that illumined light, I noticed divine order. Death will come to all of us; there is no way to avoid it. Once her disease took hold, I wanted my mom back. I was sorry I could not pop her in my car, as we did in the past, and take her for a ride while I ran errands. During those trips, she would often say, "Let's go to lunch, my treat." It saddened me to be only with her body and not her mind. As time passed, I could see that was my selfish desire.

Mom carried enormous stress, as many single moms do, but hers was compounded because she embodied a fear that began when she was small. My gram told me when my mom was five years old and attending kindergarten, she would be so scared of leaving her familiar surroundings that her digestion would go amuck. Gram would yell at her through the bathroom door, "Lorraine, get going. School is going to start!" Mom never felt safe in the world around her. She could not easily navigate the situations that all too often arose. Thus, life overwhelmed her, creating havoc in her body. As she grew older, her stress manifested in the form of migraine headaches and digestive issues long before her dementia began.

Her mind began to fail as she was getting to the finish line of life, but then she gained control. Living in an assisted care facility, she created what she could not obtain in her youth. Freedom from stress!

In care, Mom had no worries about finances, meals, laundry, or cleaning. She did not need to lift a finger. Mom created the relaxed lifestyle she yearned for, and who am I to say her way of accomplishing it was wrong. From one perspective, one could say, "Oh, the poor woman, she has lost her mind and can no longer live on her own. It is so sad." I felt that way at first, but I began to see it differently after a few years.

In care, I noticed Mom was more relaxed than I had ever seen her. If she wanted to play with dolls with other residents in the middle of the night, which she often did, no one stopped her. If she wanted to dance before eating her meals, the caretakers partnered with her as they glided across her imaginary dance floor. The woman I had known was not comfortable expressing her emotions, but in her new environment, her inhibitions of intimacy washed away, and she freely voiced, "I love you." She said it not only to me but to the ones who cared for her. I could have been jealous of the love she openly expressed to seeming strangers yet never to me in the past. Instead, I saw Mom taking a huge step forward. She may have had limited access to her mind, but she was letting her spirit joyfully take over.

W HEN I WAS first married, I thought, wouldn't it be nice if Mom and I went out to lunch, shared our stories, and were close? But that was not our relationship then. Our conversations on the phone, though often, were also distant. I desired to hear her give me compliments, adoration, or the simple sentiment of I love you, but I did not hear those words. Then I realized I was not verbalizing my heart's love either, so I decided to take the initiative to make a change. I started by saying, "I love you, Mom," as our phone conversation ended. On the other end of the line was silence as I heard the receiver click when Mom hung up.

Our chats continued every few days, as was our custom—me, expressing my love and receiving no response in return; Mom ignoring my heartfelt closing. Then one day, just as if it was always our adieu, Mom said, "I love you." I hung up the phone with tears of gratitude filling my eyes. My plan worked. Mom finally voiced what I knew was in her heart. It took only a month.

A few years after Mom retired, she wanted to spend more time with her grandchildren and me and thought her life would be better out west. We packed up her wares and found her a condo minutes from my home. We shared family activities with her for fifteen years until her memory loss changed her life.

In years past, her mind was sharp, and she held management positions during her forty-four-year career at Allstate Insurance Company. Her last assignment was in the call center, responding to benefit questions from retirees of the corporation. Five years before Mom's diagnosis, she asked me to organize her bills. With sad eyes, she told me, "I don't know why I need you to do this. In my job, I helped the seniors, and now I need the help." "It's okay, Mom," I told her, "I'm here for you. You have helped me during my life, and now it's time for me to repay the favor."

I did not see her dementia coming, for it crept in slowly. At one of her doctor's appointments, the doctor pulled me aside and said, "Your mom's memory is fading, and she will probably need care in about a year." I dismissed her observation. Dementia? Not my mom. But the doctor was right. In one year, Mom could no longer safely live alone.

TO DISCOVER WHY Mom's memory became challenged, I needed to look deeply into her life to understand what brought her to this situation. Then perhaps I would be better able to support her, so I looked into her past.

Mom wed in 1946, about one year after the end of World War II. My father was 27 years of age, my mom 25. One would think they knew how to manage their married life, but the war had a way of delaying their emotional growth. Death had been close at hand. As mentioned earlier, Mom had lost her high school love in the war, and my father, who served in the Navy, faced torpedoes that could take him down at any moment. Their fear was not imagined. It was real.

Once the war was over, couples wanted to put the past behind them and get their lives rolling. Falling in love and getting married was supposed to accomplish that purpose. My parents were both pampered siblings in their respective families. Their upbringing did not allow them the foundation to be empathetic with each other and foster a successful partnership.

Marriage is challenging at best and requires support, love, and compassion. Because of their tainted youth, both felt entitled to and righteous in their ways of doing things, leaving little room to resolve confrontations. The decade of the 1940s did not lend itself to self-reflection. That could have helped couples understand why they acted the way they did and how they could overcome their inner conflicts. Life moved too fast for my mom and father. They had their first child nine months after their wedding and a second pregnancy six months later, creating a financial strain that rocked their already unstable world. They could not handle what life placed before them, and their relationship became shaky.

Their split was not a healthy one; without the skills to nurture each other, their stress overflowed and caused their imminent divorce. Both were angry, resentful, and felt justified in their actions. They suffered from bitterness, and it tainted their connection with their children and reached into every aspect of their lives. Because they did not address their issues, their ill feelings lasted for years. My father reluctantly remarried fifteen years after the divorce and did not father any other children. Mom never dated or remarried.

Once Mom was diagnosed with dementia, I located a pleasant assisted-care home for her, tucked into the pine trees of Parker, Colorado. One warm day, Mom was sitting on the porch with Loretta, her caregiver, who uncovered a secret, indicating that Mom still cared for my father. It became a gift from her dementia. Loretta commented, "Lorraine, what a beautiful ring you are wearing." It was odd that Mom still possessed a diamond ring, small as it was because I thought her valuables did not accompany her when she moved into the home.

I have noticed in the beginning stages of dementia, those affected by this disease hide items. Even though family members repeatedly search for an object, it does not appear until the senior decides to bring it out from its concealed place. I believe Mom did not reveal her ring's presence until she wanted to voice this part of her past. Mom said, "Tony gave it to me." Through the wisdom of this brilliant caregiver, Loretta was able to draw the truth from Mom with this simple reply, "He must have loved you very much." Mom responded, "Yes, he did."

When Loretta told me how Mom acknowledged that my father loved her, I was shocked. I suspected the quick change in my parents' past relationship left Mom hurt and afraid. I imagined she was terrified to entertain the idea of stepping into a new relationship and allow her heart to be vulnerable once again. The thought never occurred to me that her reluctance to date other men was because she still thought about my father's love. Dementia had a way of breaking down the barriers she built in her memories. Her disease held not only troubling attributes but positive ones as well.

With her filters off, dementia allowed Mom to express the feelings she held deep in her heart. In the safety of her new surroundings, Mom revealed she still thought lovingly about my father. My parents never spoke after my father stopped paying her child support, and she died thinking his love for her ended when he left decades ago. It was so sad she never knew that my father confessed his love for her to his son Jim, the day they sat on the park bench, moments before my father's wife approached.

EVEN THOUGH MOM had no use for a purse while in her care facility, she carried one anyway. It was not until she passed that I discovered what was kept inside. There were a few tissues, her old driver's license, and something that surprised me. It was my father's funeral card listing his birth, date of death, and a prayer. It was worn and torn, so I suspected she had pulled it out of her wallet and looked at it often. She never told me she loved my father, but her actions gave me a reason to believe she did. My parents' lack of personal empowerment and the inability to work out their issues kept them apart, not the absence of love. Knowing they both loved each other touched my heart. How sad they lived a life of lost love, affection that they never regained.

As my mom neared the end of her life, she appeared peaceful, free from the cares she had had earlier when she raised me, and for that, I was grateful. For a time, I was sad to see how she was not what society calls normal. But Mom was living the life that was right for her, and each day she gifted me the opportunity to accept her in her current state. Now in a facility where she was safe, she no longer resisted intimacy. She would openly tell me she loved me. I lost the Mom I knew, but I gained, most of the time, a content woman, allowing me to let go of my ideas of how things should be and to accept how they were.

During the eleven years Mom was in care, she received the help she never manifested earlier in her life. Now she had no worries. She didn't need to cook, which was a culinary task she never adopted in her life anyway. She loved to clean, and even though that was also provided, I would often see her wiping off the counters in the community room when I visited. The nurse commented, "She is happy doing this chore, so we do not stop her."

Mom's agitations were usually due to a physical imbalance. Once discovered and remedied, she would be back to her old self, staying up late, taking shoes from other residents' closets, and dancing at will. Yes, Mom had times of anger and confusion, but it was short-lived. My son had told me when he visited her, if she was out of sorts, he would step out to the nurse's station, converse with them for a short time, and when he returned to Mom's room, she had switched back to his pleasant grandmother, who was happy to see him.

It may appear that people with dementia have lost their ability to think clearly, but another one of their senses may be opening. Verbal communication might be lost or inhibited, but telepathy is not. I have seen dementia open their minds to extrasensory perceptions.

I recall a day when I came to visit Mom. The community room was buzzing with activities: TV, art projects, and the serving of ice cream, but Mom said nothing when I approached her. She kept her eyes closed and pretended I was not there. "Hi Mom," I said, and there no response in return, but I saw she was tapping her feet to the music playing in the room. I said, "Mom, I know you can sense I am here, and you can hear me." She did not open her eyes, but a grin appeared on her face. In her unique way, she communicated, "Hello, I love you;

your presence makes me smile." I had to look closely to see how Mom conveyed her love. It happened in so many ways; the words were merely a small part of her expression. As the disease progressed, we would sit in silence, and yet I could feel her love more then than at any other time in our life together.

One Mother's Day, I saw how Mom joined another resident in this silent pattern of connecting. I entered her space with flowers in hand and a box of chocolates, but she was not in her room. She loved her chocolates, so I knew it would be a welcomed gift. Another time when I had brought her chocolates, I returned a few days later when she offered me some candy from that box. I found as I picked up a confection that enticed me, each had a small finger hole in the bottom, placed there when Mom had previously inspected them. If it did not suit her fancy, she neatly placed the bonbon upright, back in its designated spot, and proceeded to examine another chocolate. With the box of chocolates in my lap, she sat across from me, watching me attempt to locate an untouched truffle, smiling, knowing there was none to be found.

Still looking for Mom, I stepped into the community room, seeing small groups of relatives gathered around their family members, sharing their love, but my mom was not there. I asked for her whereabouts. The nurse smiled, pointing to a corner table filled with laughing voices. There was Mom with another family and their mother. Neither Mom nor the other resident verbally communicated. No words were exchanged between them, and yet they comforted each other. The other woman's family told me, "When we come to visit our mother, we often find your mother sitting with her." It consoled me to see how Mom connected with her friend without words. I also found that there were others in her unit who bonded to Mom.

Mom had the habit of entering the rooms of other women, slipping on their shoes, and wearing her newly acquired possessions all day. No one seemed to mind. The nurses told me, "Yes, your Mom does that often, and it doesn't hurt or anger anyone, so we let her be." There were times when Mom would visit another resident and stay in her room till three in the morning playing with dolls. She was allowed that freedom as well. As long as the residents were safe, no one told them what to do. They lived in a place where they could be themselves, without judgment, living their lives as they wanted, just as if they were still in their own homes.

THE YEAR MOM passed she had little desire to speak, yet she was active in the home, walking to the dining room for meals and sitting silently with her friends. Both the nurses and I observed that Mom began to sleep more, and it appeared she was getting ready to move on. The week of her passing, I sat with her each day as she lay in her bed, motionless and unresponsive. On the third day, Mom mysteriously became completely conscious and spoke clearly to me. Because of this change, I called Blake and Crystal. "If you want to see your grandmother before she passes, now is the time. She is coherent, and I do not know how long it will last." "I'll be right over," was each of their replies. It was as if she wanted to stay conscious as long as their visit lasted because once they left, she slipped back into a gentle sleep, not a coma, but a calm resting state.

Word spread throughout the facility; Lorraine was not going to be around much longer. Nurses, aides, and workers began to come to her room, some of whom I had never met before. These were the ones who touched her heart and she theirs, and they came to say goodbye. I was so blessed to be part of her in-body memorial. It showed me who loved her beyond our family. I should have known, but I never realized the close kinship between her and the people who cared for her for over a decade.

One morning two nurses tiptoed into her room. They told me, "We will miss your Mom. We are not always here on the day residents pass, so we come in before and give them our love. Do you know that they have been part of our lives as well? Your Mom liked it when we sang to her. May we sing to her now?" "Of course," I replied. Then their voices rang out with three of her favorite songs that warmed my heart and made me cry. With teary eyes, they took their leave to continue their day of serving others in the home. Not only did Mom receive their blessing that day, but I did as well.

That week, I know that even though her brain activity was slowing down, she was aware of what was happening around her. I felt my last act of kindness was to make sure she was not afraid to pass and help her let go of any remorse. I spoke softly, "Mom, you are going to a place where you will not be alone. Gram, Grandpa Blake, Aunt Ceal, Uncle Bill are waiting for you." She remained motionless, with no expression to let me know she heard me. I continued, "Tony is there too." At that point, she gently smiled, making it clear she saw him, and I sensed their love was still alive.

Because Mom and I were close to Loretta, Mom's first caretaker, I invited her to join me to support Mom's transition. Loretta and I did our form of prayer by placing our hands on Mom's body and transferring love from the Universe into her. Buddhists believe when we move to the light, our spirit exits out the top of our heads, so I placed my hands upon Mom's head and told her, "Mom, you lived a good life. You did the best you could under tough situations. I forgive you for the things that happened between us that caused us pain. I love you. You are worthy of receiving love. Your body is full of love and moving up to the light where there is only love."

I continued my dialogue and specifically named situations for which I felt she held regret. This process took more than a few passing moments. As I recalled the incidents, Loretta said, "I did not know those things happened to her." I revealed secrets the family held, things that had been swept under the carpet. I wanted Mom to let go of any judgment she still had for herself and others and be free from her burdens. I continued, "Mom, now is the time to let go of your bond to your body and this earth and step into your enlightened spirit. I am sorry for the things I did that caused you pain. Forgive me, Mom."

Loretta kissed her on the forehead and said, "I love you Lorraine, I am so grateful I came to know you. Thank you for staying at my home, you are a beautiful spirit. I will miss you," and with those words, Loretta quietly left. Mom's room was still and filled with light. Having Loretta join me in putting Mom at peace was a gift I have always cherished.

The exact moment of Mom's passing eluded me. Still, those who knew her best, the ones with memory challenges, had a direct line to when the passageway would open, and Mom would walk out of this realm. The day she passed, I was sitting quietly alongside her bed, and a resident walked into the room. She casually sauntered over to Mom's shoes, slipped them on as if they now belonged to her, and strode out of the room, quite pleased with herself. I laughed out loud. I watched as the baton passed to another. This woman knew Mom was starting on a new journey, and once Mom arrived at her destination, there was no need for shoes.

My son and younger daughter had said their adieus during that week, but Carmin, my eldest, lived in California, and it took time to rearrange her schedule so that she could bid her grandmother farewell. I was concerned Carmin would not make it in time. I had to let go and trust in divine order, and so it came to be. My husband, at the time, was with me but of little comfort. He did not understand metaphysical concepts, and it was a strain to hold a space for Mom to pass while being impinged on his disconnected energy. I sensed being alone with Mom would serve all involved to the highest order, so I told him he did not need to stay, and I released him into the night. With no resistance, he left before the sun set. Not long after his departure, strange things began to unfold before my eyes as the sky darkened.

The energy in Mom's room was changing, making way for her departure. Because she was so close to the other side, I could simply immerse myself in the tranquil space created, and the nurses did not disturb our peace. It was curious that I did not observe residents walking or visitors entering the hall outside her room for those hours. The entire unit became mysteriously still and quiet.

I sang Mom a song that had comforted her over the last few years, "Somewhere over the rainbow skies are blue, clouds high over the rainbow, make all your dreams come true." Then I stilled my thoughts and meditated with the intent to hold open the doorway, so without effort, she could move to her next form of existence. The room was serene, and my thoughts were quiet as I allowed the peace to ease over my body. My physical condition became weightless. I opened my eyes and looked out the window. I know I was not dreaming. I could hear Mom's gentle breath, and I knew I did not see a hallucination.

There was construction on the interstate at the edge of the facility's property. I could see the red taillights on the trucks as they drove to and fro, so I considered that the image I was seeing could be a mirage created from my night vision, just as I have experienced when driving at night when I'm tired. But I was alert and not tired at all. It took a few moments for my mind to process what was appearing before me. I questioned my vision more than once. I moved my head from side to side to see if the apparition changed, but it became clear what I saw was not a reflection off the trucks.

About fifty feet outside Mom's window, there appeared an image as tall as the semi-trucks, the face in profile was of a Native American man. He stayed there in my sight for about five minutes. I was being given a glimpse into my mom's passing, but I was not aware of it at the time. I did not question what I saw. I was drawn into the process and became an astonished observer. As his image dissolved, still dazed, I saw the physical presence of an animal come to escort Mom. A fox was walking on the grass below her window. My mind scrambled to put the pieces together and acquire a reason for these uncommon sights.

Loretta had insights into those who passed on and confirmed she would see deer, foxes, rabbits, birds, and other creatures appear outside the elders' rooms on the day they passed. Mom was being accompanied to her light body by the vision outside the window. The fox and the Native American were Mom's guides to the other side.

I returned my focus to Mom's face, and I saw something I had not noticed before. Her facial structure mimicked a Native American's. Like theirs, she had high cheekbones and a long prominent nose. In her aging, I could now see that her face was bearing this resemblance. I questioned myself, "Could Mom have been a Native American in a past life?" I have seen myself as a native living in nature during hypnosis sessions, but I never connected those lives to my genetic line with Mom. How egotistical and arrogant I have been, not making this connection and thinking I was the only one in our family who previously had a mystical life with a deep connection to the earth. I never saw Mom as having a spiritual side in this life, but perhaps that was not her role this time around. I felt so blessed to have seen her spiritual essence before she left.

Again, I wondered if my spiritual essence was tied to Mom's possible native life that flowed through her DNA. Mom was neither metaphysical nor showed signs of intuition, but she never judged or questioned my unusual approach to life. As I silenced my intellectual mind and let my intuitive awareness take over, I became aware of the intuitive gifts Mom unconsciously bestowed upon me. They were not always apparent, but now I was presented with a new way to see our relationship. However, this was not the time to go deeper into this investigation. I placed my thoughts aside, for this was Mom's time.

I heard someone enter the room, I first thought it was Mom's roommate, but I exhaled a sigh of relief when I saw who it was, "Carmin, you made it." With tears in my eyes, we embraced. "What a comfort to have you with your grandmother and me."

I wanted to let Carmin know what might happen at her grandmother's passing. "You know Carmin, when spirits pass, there are stories of mystical experiences that happen, and I observed one such event in a documentary about an enlightened being, surprisingly, a rock star, one of The Beatles, George Harrison. *George Harrison: Living in the Material World* highlights his journey through life: his musical career, his spiritual voyage, and how he encouraged the other Beatles to join him. You are too young to remember as I do, but I saw the band heartfully join Harrison on his quest to India. He was the kingpin and followed his path to enlightenment from that point forward. During the documentary, his wife, Olivia Harrison, recalled the day Harrison passed. She sat along with other family members, waiting for the moment he would cross over. Olivia emotionally shared, as Harrison left his body, "The entire room filled with light."'

I continued, "There are other stories I have known about people's passing. Not so dramatic, but equally telling, was a doctor, one of my clients, who shared how she had climbed into bed with her dying mother for comfort. As her mom passed, a hazy mist elevated from her dying mother's heart. Because of these accounts, let's watch for similar changes during your grandmother's transition." Carmin listened with no response.

Mom passed a few hours after Carmin arrived. She died with no grand fanfare, no misty spirit leaving her body, no light emanating throughout the room but also, no stress. Her breath just stopped for a few minutes. She took another breath and then was gone. Carmin inquired, "Are you disappointed, Mom? There was no light in the room; nothing special happened." I said, "No," but perhaps I was a bit. Then I recalled the vision outside Mom's window, and I knew I was part of Mom's mystical exit, and though I did not realize it at that moment, there was more to come.

It was almost midnight when Carmin and I walked out into the hall to tell the nurse Mom had passed. There before us was another baffling moment. I found the community room filled with residents. Not one of them was in their bed sleeping. Mom's roommate, who was blind and usually asleep by eight o'clock, was up with the others. This night she never once came into Mom's room, no one had asked her to stay away, she was just in tune with Mom's transition. Mom's community had held a silent vigil for her as she passed.

I was grateful to witness Mom's final curtain call, and I was blessed to receive so many other gifts throughout my life. Knowing my father and his family did not forget me, had always loved me, and had missed me more than I could have imagined lightened what I thought was my abandoned heart. I know Mom did the best she could, and she loved me as well. I know not everyone who has an estranged parent possesses a loving story like mine. I would never have guessed when Macy shared with my mom that prayers were requested for a man in her parish, that my life would change so dramatically. For that, I walk in grace.

Even though Mom had no use for a purse while in her care facility, she carried one anyway. It was not until she passed that I discovered what was kept inside…. It was my father's funeral card…It was worn and torn, so I suspected she had pulled it out of her wallet and looked at it often.

In Loving Memory of
Anthony J. Vincolisi
Born October 5, 1919
At Rest October 6, 1989
Funeral Mass
Monday, October 9, 1989
at 10:00 a.m.
Interment
All Saints Cemetery

— † —

I am the
'esurrection
'd the Life
he   believes in
me ev   if he die
shall Live
John XI - 26

8300 W. Lawrence Avenue
'orridge, Illinois
456-8300

Lorraine (my mom)
at 4 years-old

In the care facility, if Mom wanted to play with dolls in the middle of the night, which she often did with other residents, no one stopped her.

My mother and father's
wedding day.

**Friend—Aunt Rose—Aunt Ceal—My Mother—My Father
Uncle Nunzi—Macy—Uncle Mario
Flower Girl, Cousin RoseMary—Ring Bearer, Cousin Paul**

Gram

Aunt Mary—My Father—Grandma Palm

Part 2

Courses of Action

Techniques for Physical and Emotional Self-Healing

Introduction

Essential Steps for the Courses of Action

A few years after meeting my father, I started a new business, teaching meditation and personal empowerment that helped people find their intuitive gifts. For this business to be successful, I had to do my spiritual work, discover my value, and understand how I arrived at this juncture. The act of meeting my long-lost family catapulted me onto that path. Here I will share the accumulated wisdom I have acquired over decades.

The section that follows is called the Courses of Action. A course is defined as a path or learning experience while actions put the knowledge into motion in everyday situations. The following guidance will make life's pitfalls manageable and sometimes avoidable. By following my story and applying my examples to your experiences, you can find empathy for those who have caused you pain. Compassion becomes empowering by bringing renewed love for yourself and others.

The Courses of Action will guide you in being mindful, which is the act of keeping your thoughts in the present moment, not letting your mind wander into past struggles or worrying about what might happen in the future. Ellen J. Langer, the author of *Mindfulness, 25th edition,* states, "…mindfulness and mindlessness [not discussed here] are so common that few of us appreciate their importance…

[1] *Mindfulness, 25th edition*

or make use of their power to change our lives…"[1] Practicing mindfulness will not only keep you focused on the ever-present changes in your life but will expand your knowledge of how to cope with those changes and often improve the outcomes. In Langer's book, her one-year study describes how the simple act of caring for a plant made a difference in some seniors' lives. The test enlisted two groups of elders in a care facility. One group had a plant to care for; the other group did not. At the end of the year, the group with a plant had better memory and lived longer than their counter group. Merely caring for something other than themselves made the seniors more mindful and gave them a reason to live a better, longer life.

One way to increase mindfulness is to become aware of the energy in and around you through the hands-on healing modality of Reiki. An energy transfer from the Reiki master to the student opens awareness in the very first class. The student is shown how to become cognizant of the energy in their hands and then see how they can extend this energy into situations in their everyday life. When the practice is applied, it can ease pain, release stress, and open new perspectives. Reiki also helps build intuitive awareness and can change frustrating everyday occurrences such as blocked traffic, turbulence during airplane travel, emotional upsets, and anger. With continued practice, the Reiki student can see new perspectives to old situations with compassionate eyes. The transfer is energetic; therefore, it can be performed in-person, across the miles or online. In-depth information about Reiki can be found at http://www.lightinternal.com.

Qigong (chee-gong) is a practice associated with martial arts that focuses on the health of the body. The student learns to feel energy or chi (chee) in their hands and then sense how it feels to move that chi around themselves. It ties in nicely when applied with the personal empowerment found in Reiki or any time you would like to increase your awareness of the unseen energies in and around you.

Designed in each of the Courses of Action, you will find guided meditations and self-hypnosis scripts. Meditation can be beneficial in calming one's thoughts to create space for new ideas and answers to form. New perceptions and solutions do not always surface during the stillness of meditation. Thoughts may arise during the day while doing mindless acts, such as washing dishes, gardening, showering, or running. Often one might wake up in the middle of the night with an epiphany. Buddhists find four o'clock in the morning an auspicious time to reflect. The city is quiet while people are asleep, so higher energies can be tapped into more easily.

Self-hypnosis can also guide your worried mind in a better direction and help access your intuition. These practices are performed with closed eyes to filter out the outside world and diminish the amount of information taken in through our eyes. The darkness lessens the sensory input so that inner spiritual guidance can be accessed.

Begin the following practices by entering a quiet space free from distractions. Turn off all communication devices and let family members, even pets, know you do not want to be contacted for a designated time, anywhere from 10 to 30 minutes. Sit with your spine erect in a comfortable chair. This will allow your energy to flow freely from your head down your spine, thus opening the energy centers of your body. You may find it more relaxing to record the method in your voice and then play it while in contemplation. Keep your recording device close at hand to pause the guidance when you would like to work in-depth on a section. If your mind wanders, don't become frustrated thinking you have wasted your time, merely bring your thoughts back to the guidance and continue. You will find, it is all part of the process.

Energy Centers Called Chakras

Be aware that we process information through not only our eyes and ears but also through invisible energy centers called chakras. They respond to words, images, and thoughts, and there are seven major ones. Each has its unique way of communicating messages to the body. By tuning into these unseen etheric/ energy centers, one can acquire whole-body knowing, opening inner wisdom to aid in making decisions. Then one will not be confused, fooled, or tricked by so-called authorities trying to influence your choices. The body can signal a warning by a lump felt in the throat when emotions are sad, pain in the heart if love is lost, or tightness in the stomach when fear is present. The forehead may become tight or even painful for a short time when this intuitive center starts to open and increases your inner guidance.

Chakras can function like electrical transformers. A transformer steps down the electricity, so our home circuits will not overload and cause a fire. Similarly, as we view the world around us, our chakras protect us from sensory overload. Chakras interpret our experiences of the world and adjust our body systems physically and emotionally. The mind and body's chakras are the ones that are taking over when we walk or drive with no conscious thought.

Chakras are part of our nonphysical world and open and close depending on what is happening around us. They take note of what is occurring, not only physically but also mentally and emotionally. The best way to understand their function is to become aware of how you collect information from these etheric channels. Do not doubt what you cannot see. Have an open mind to discover how to pick up your body's messages. Activating this form of awareness will be beneficial in many aspects of your life. It will help you make better decisions by enhancing communication in intimate and business relationships.

The first chakra anchors at the base of the spine, where our bodies began to form in utero. Subsequent chakras align up from there. The last is at the top of the head. They are as follows:

1st Root Chakra—anchors at the tailbone. It holds our survival needs, such as obtaining nourishment, proper shelter, and financial supply.

2nd Sacral Chakra—rests below the navel. It feeds our sense of creativity. Women's ovaries and men's testes support the physical formation of life and feed artistic talents.

3rd Solar Plexus Chakra—sits in the area of the stomach just above the navel. It harbors our emotions and can be felt by the activation of butterflies when excited or tension when afraid.

4th Heart Chakra—is found in the chest's center. It balances emotions, holding love and hatred while overshadowing grief.

5th Throat Chakra—resides in the neck. It supports our expression of thoughts and feelings through words and writings. It is also the doorway to addictive behavior such as the overuse of drugs, alcohol, smoking, food, and rage.

6th Third Eye Chakra—rests at the forehead. As the name implies, it is another form of sight, opening intuition that reveals what is hidden behind the physical appearance.

7th Crown Chakra—is located at the top of the head. It is the portal to the infinite Universe which accesses divine or spiritual realms, supporting the body until the spirit exits through death.

These are the major chakras; there are minor chakras throughout the body, two of which are:

Hands and Feet Chakras—the hands and feet have direct lines to the heart. Their sensitivity can be developed by learning Reiki, practicing Qigong, or having the intent to feel these invisible fields through the following practice, *Tune Into Your Chakras.*

Chakras are anchored in the physical body, close to the spine, and radiate into the energy field or aura around our body that holds three etheric bodies; they host our emotional, mental, and spiritual understandings. The emotional body is closest to the skin, about four inches in depth; hence the customary hug or handshake feels comforting. Next is the mental body, about twelve inches in depth, and holds our thoughts. Depending on the individual's spiritual strength, the spiritual body can extend eighteen to thirty-six inches or even more out from the physical body. The stronger a person's spiritual growth, the farther out it will radiate. With practice, you can sense these fields.

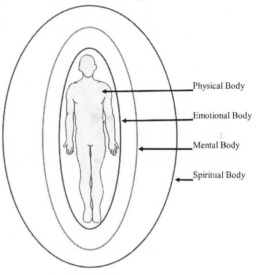

Physical Body

Emotional Body

Mental Body

Spiritual Body

Tune Into Your Chakras

1.   Begin this practice with a desire to sense the difference in each of your chakras.

2.   Imagine opening a door at the top of your head and invite the infinite love of the cosmos to enter.

3.   Give this love color and notice if it is warm, cool, buzzing, or something else.

4.   As the light fills your head, feel it move into your third eye at the center of your forehead. Hold your attention there until you can imagine seeing in all directions, past and future.

5. Let that color overflow and drain into your throat. Feel the light clarifying and empowering your spoken word. Think of how you can kindly express your truth to one who needs to hear it.

6. Allow the light from the stars to magnetically absorb into your heart, which then opens and expands. Notice if your breath deepens.

7. The light continues to flow into your solar plexus at your stomach and soothes the emotions held there. Can you feel any movement in this area?

8. The next center to open is your sacral chakra, where creativity resides. Allow the light to feed all the ideas you wish to manifest.

9. When the energy from the top of your head reaches your tailbone, you may feel pulled or weighted to the earth.

10. Simultaneously extend your focus from your head up to the Universe and think of your feet entering the core of the earth.

11. Take time to sense how your body and emotions link to the earth and sky.

12. You are now a radiant tube of light from your head to your toes.

13. Each time you repeat this exercise, pay attention to the subtleties and see how each practice feels different.

Connecting to Higher Frequencies on the Planet

Once aware of the chakras, you can become a vessel of light by opening your chakras and linking to the earth, the sky, and other people who are becoming mindful and sensitive. There is no need to search for these individuals online, for a web of pure light connects us all. The power of your intent will link you to their higher frequencies. In this way, you can increase your ability to help our planet.

Imagine there is an illuminated cloud above you that covers the entire planet. It has the support of deities, divine masters, and enlightened cosmic beings. They understand what is required to aid our planet and its inhabitants. Their evolutionary knowledge far exceeds ours, for they observe us from a higher vantage point and see how our actions affect the whole. Ask these light beings to support any goal you might have by merging your light into their web of light. There is no need to be proficient in a specific skill to achieve this connection. A clear intention is all that is required in order to tune into their web of light and feel the shift.

1. Follow the above exercise to *Tune Into Your Chakras* and once you have opened and felt your chakras, sense a tube of light from your head to your feet.

2. Extend this tube to connect to the north pole and then the south pole of the earth.

3. How different does it feel when your tube of light becomes this extended?

4. Now see the top and bottom of your tube of light as portals into the cosmos.

5. Imagine an hourglass over the earth. Your tube is in the center. The light beings of the Universe are filling the glass through your tube.

6. Your body is in the thin center of the hourglass where the sand flows.

7. Take time to notice if you can sense a shift.

8. Widen the middle of the hourglass to allow this gigantic flow of light into your body.

9. At this point, you should feel an expansion.

10. Blend your consciousness into the web of light over the planet.

11. Here you may ask for guidance or help. Trust that the connection is made, and your answer will come through, perhaps later.

12. Stay relaxed in this sensation for as long as you desire.

Sensing the Etheric Bodies

This practice requires two people and will acquaint the participants with the unseen but ever prevalent etheric bodies. Remember to be respectful of each other's energy fields and first ask permission to enter their field either in your mind or verbally. To become sensitive, begin by activating your own hand chakras and then continue to sense each other's etheric bodies individually. One person will sense the other's etheric field while that person stands still. All three bodies in the etheric field, spiritual, mental, and emotional, have a specific frequency, and though sometimes subtle, they will feel different.

1. Partners A and B shall sit across from each other, with knees not quite touching.

2. Each partner rubs their palms together for a minute to activate their hand chakras.

3. Continue the personal activation by separating your hands about one to two inches apart. Move your own hands in and out in micro-movements of ½ an inch.

4. With your eyes open or closed, notice what you feel in your hands. It could be heat, buzzing, resistance, a magnetic pull, or another sensation.

5. By activating your hand chakras, both partners will be more aware of the energies you both are sensing.

6. Next, partner A will feel partner B's emotional body a few inches off their skin.

7. Partner B, close your eyes and notice if you can feel where partner A's hand is over your arm.

8. Partner A, feel the emotional body of partner B by placing your hand two inches off their arm and moving your hand across the length of their arm a few times.

9. Partner A continues to sense their partner's emotional body by scanning their shoulder, heart, and head. Notice the subtle difference in each area. Ask partner B if they can feel where your hand moves.

10. Switch roles and repeat steps 6 to 9 before going to step 11.

11. Stand up and face each other, moving about nine or ten feet apart.

12. Partner B is standing still with their eyes closed. Partner A: Face your hands towards partner B slowly walk towards partner B, stopping when partner A feels the spiritual body of partner B.

13. Partner A, stop as soon as you feel a different sensation in your own hands. You have now touched the edge of the spiritual body. That edge

is about 6 inches thick, and as you move your hands back and forth through this field, you may feel a thick, rubbery sensation.

14. Partner B, open your eyes when you feel that partner A has entered your spiritual body. It could be 18 to 36 inches outside the physical body or even farther out.

15. Partner A, step closer to partner B's body and enter their mental body. This field may feel buzzy or more electrified than the spiritual body but always different from the spiritual body.

16. Partner A, continue closer to reach the emotional body that you felt on partner B's arm. It's a few inches from the physical body and sometimes feels warm.

17. Tell each other what you felt.

18. Switch partners and repeat steps 11 to 17.

Understanding Meditation

The body requires rest every day, but we often forget the mind does as well. Your reprieve from thinking and doing does not need to be a lengthy process, even ten minutes will suffice, but twenty minutes produces the best results. When you give your mind a respite, the silence created balances your right and left brain, relieves stress, calms your digestion, and opens your ability to hear intuitive guidance. People new to meditation often think they must eliminate all thoughts from their minds, but that is an almost impossible task. Try to have no ideas for thirty seconds, and you will see what I mean. Know that even though thoughts are running periodically during this quiet time, your meditation still has value because your mind will enter brief stillness, but you often do not notice it. Meditating five to seven times a week will build your intuition and rearrange daily challenges into new balanced perspectives. Remember, solutions may enter your mind when you least expect them. The ideas can come from words you hear in a song, a phrase in an ad, or a conversation overheard.

When you are stressed and allow life's irritations to direct your attention negatively, you can always ask for help from beings of higher vibrations than your own to stop this pattern. Present your request, and allow the answer to come to you in its own time. If you expect guidance, it will appear. The phrase, "The call compels the answer," means your intention holds power. All you need to do is ask and be open to receive help.

I had a concern that kept running in my thoughts. I used all the techniques I knew, but the chatter in my head persisted. I asked my guides for help and attempted to let go. They responded to my request while I was driving my car.

I pulled up to a red light, and the driver of the car to my left rolled down his windows. A little girl in the back seat inquired, "What does your license plate mean?" My plate says, IMLIGHT. A puzzled look came over her face as I told her, "I have light within me, and so do you." Her dad smiled back as he rolled up her window, and they drove away. My guides reminded me that there is no need to worry, I am light, but I was still agitated.

That day I heard my guide's message, but alas, that alone did not quiet my disturbing thoughts. Two days later, I was on the bench in my backyard, still upset, when my eyes observed movement in the evergreen tree. There was a small bird with a branch in its beak. I laughed out loud, which broke the negativity that I was holding. The message was, obviously, peace. I held onto the image of the bird carrying the symbol of peace, and my turmoil began to subside. Our guides do not stop challenges from happening, but they do show us how to learn from our experiences and manifest harmony in our hearts.

The Universe is continually sending messages to help and guide you. Your ability to access this information happens by observing the nuances placed before you. Here is how to do it:

1. Set a question or an intention for the day or a future time.

2. Sit still, focus on that intention and send it into the Universe.

3. Give your message form by seeing it as an image of written words, sound waves, or sparkles of light.

4. Meditate for five to twenty minutes each day to create a clear place for answers to surface.

5. When you notice your mind wandering, bring it back into the present moment.

6. Even in seeming silence, there can be information downloading to answer your question.

7. Don't dwell on your concern. Just go about your day.

8. Stay in the moment and observe your surroundings.

9. Notice the lyrics of music, words in ads, conversations overheard, and inner thoughts.

10. Affirm, you will acquire a solution, and it will happen.

> *"Change your thoughts, and you can change your world."*
> Norman Vincent Peale

Meditation Basics

When starting a new practice, such as stilling the mind, begin with small steps. Twenty minutes is the desired goal but, if that seems daunting, start with five minutes. Set a timer, and each day add one minute to the time allotted. After a few days, you may find you will want to stay in contemplation longer than your set time.

Meditating at the same time and in the same place has the advantage of building a focus to make meditating easier in that location. Before starting any of the following practices, place all communication devices in another room, turn off auditory notices on nearby computers, and ask not to be disturbed, even from your pets.

Guided meditations can silence stressful memories and clear your focus. Thoughts can be stilled by noticing your breath, thus giving your mind a different focus. Start by imagining light flowing into your muscles and tendons, causing them to relax. Follow the light as you direct it into every organ. If your mind wanders, which it will, just bring it back to your focused intent. Thoughts will flow during this time, do not let them upset you. Your mind is clearing. There are many guided imagery meditations throughout this section to help you achieve your goal to release stress.

Consider various locations for meditation. They can be inside your home, basking in the sunlight, sitting near the sound of water, or listening to the songs of birds. These sounds will fade away as your mind stills. Let your body temperature be comfortable, not too warm or cool. The desirable length of time to meditate is twenty minutes, but shorter times can also calm the mind. Remember to record lengthy meditations and listen to them rather than trying to recall the entire process.

Most importantly, do not judge or compare your sessions. Some sessions will be more relaxed than others, but they all have value. Consistency is what brings the best results. Be patient with yourself.

> *Don't blindly believe anything I have suggested in these processes.*
> *Prove their value to yourself.*
> *Apply them and note the results.*

Oxygen Meditation

1. Set a timer for five to twenty minutes.

2. Remove all communication devices.

3. Be alone, sit with an erect back, and keep your body temperature comfortable.

4. Close your eyes and slow your breath.

5. For the next few breaths, notice how your chest rises and gently falls.

6. Picture an oxygen molecule entering your lungs. Watch it move and see if you can feel it.

7. Observe how this tiny form gives your body energy, supports your organs, and sustains your mind.

8. Follow and feel the oxygen molecule moving through your blood, touching each organ.

9. Notice if your attention stops at one place. If so, let the image of the molecule stay there until it is ready to move.

10. See that eventually, the molecule will complete its journey back to the lungs.

11. Offer gratitude to all the oxygen in your blood and body.

12. Rest in this feeling.

13. When the timer goes off, slowly and gently open your eyes.

Meditation for a Healthy Body

Follow the guidance above from steps 1 to 5, then you may:

1. Bring a colored light into the top of your head.

2. Allow the light to enter your head and see it in the:
    a. Frontal lobe, the right and then the left
    b. Back quadrant, right and then left
    c. Pinal and pituitary glands in the center of your head
    d. Eyes, iris, and optic nerve
    e. Sinuses and nasal cavities
    f. Ear canal, drum, and cochlear
    g. Teeth, gums, and throat

3. The color of the light may change as it moves down and touches your organs.

4. Stay focused, and if your mind wanders, bring your attention back to your practice.

5. See the light glow as it flows into and balances your:
    a. Esophagus
    b. Lungs, right and left
    c. Heart, all four chambers
    d. Lymph nodes
    e. Liver
    f. Gall bladder
    g. Stomach
    h. Pancreas
    i. Small intestine
    j. Large intestine
    k. Appendix
    l. Kidneys
    m. Adrenals
    n. Ovaries or teste
    o. Rectum

6. Imagine your entire body radiating light and notice if you feel different from when your meditation began.

7. Think of three things that make you happy.

8. Take a deep breath and open your eyes.

Courses of Action
Chapter One

HIDDEN LOVE

When I heard a man was ill in Macy's parish, my instinct was to change my travel plans, leave Denver a day early and contact Macy to see if this man was indeed my father. I did not need to evaluate the pros and cons of visiting Macy. I made my decision at that moment because my instinct was so strong. My sense was this very well could be the man I sought. Following my intuition paid off.

Everyone possesses the ability to access their inner guidance. Our intuition appears as choices that we make daily, often on a hunch. Because this guidance happens naturally, this intuitive part of our being often goes unnoticed. When you decide to take a different road home from work only to find that your regular route had a significant traffic jam, you have tuned into the natural insight and listened to your inner voice. When you pay attention to sensory guidance, these messages will begin to increase. Indicators for advice comes through knowing, feeling, hearing, smelling, or sensing.

Becoming Aware of Your Intuition

Telepathic guidance can be as subtle as a whisper in your thoughts or actions

you take and do not even question. The five most common intuitive gifts are:
clairvoyance—seeing
clairaudience—hearing
clairsentience—feeling
claircognizance—knowing
clairessence—smelling

To build your intuition, take a moment and think about how you receive omens. Clairvoyant people will have a picture in their mind's eye. I had a student who saw words in light over two men stating, "Your next husband." If you can see a completed project in your mind, as an artist, designer, or photographer would, you may hold this gift. Those who hear the messages in their mind or outside of themselves are clairaudient. They often are musicians, singers, or writers and can distinctly hear a strong directive voice.

By sensing direction or feeling another's pain, you are clairsentient. The sensation to guide you can be goosebumps on your skin, butterflies in your stomach, or an uneasy feeling when you need to avoid a situation or person. You can also have sensations that show when there will be a positive outcome. People who hold this skill may be healthcare providers, therapists, or teachers.

Claircognizance may be difficult for people to trust because they don't see it, hear it or feel it. They just know it. These highly intuitive people could be scientists, religious and spiritual leaders, successful business and salespeople, and philosophers. Claircognizance comes through thoughts, intuitive ideas, or dreams. These perceptions embody an inner knowing so reliable that it needs no further questioning when received, yet sometimes we do. This guidance requires faith and trust because sometimes, there is no reasonable explanation for why the information is known. I find it to be the most accurate of the senses. When the mind's eye sees an image, it could be real or a projection from another person and not the truth. On the other hand, when you know the answer, there is no denying its certainty. In that state, you own your inner guidance, and it empowers you.

A less common telepathic gift is clairessence or clairalience, where subtle aromas portray the messages. I know of a man who could smell every time his wife was pregnant and detected scents when there was a problem at home or work. I asked him to describe the smell. He could not, but he knew what each odor was telling him.

These fragrances often arrive unsolicited and take you by surprise. When I am doing house clearings, I will notice a foul smell in the location of an entity or adverse deceased person. I then will communicate with them to see why they are there and release them to the light. Not all smells require clearing. One day, a client and I were walking in my yard when she recognized the aroma of the perfume her departed mother wore, yet our conversation was not about her mom. It pleased her to know her deceased mom was with us. Once in a church, I detected the attar of roses and distinctly knew it was the presence of Mother Mary. So can any of these intuitive gifts be activated at will? At times, yes.

We possess all forms of intuitive gifts, but one is usually dominant. Knowing your specific skill is as simple as noticing, listening, and becoming aware of your surroundings. By being tuned in, you can perceive the information that is waiting for you to discover.

The words we hear are not our most reliable form of communication. There are unspoken messages naturally perceived and sensed by people's body movements, facial expressions, and eyes, indicating the hidden meaning behind the words. But you can take your natural awareness one step deeper.

Look for your form of guidance in your heart—green heart chakra, your stomach—yellow solar plexus chakra, or somewhere else in your body or etheric energy field—the aura. As described earlier, contained in the aura are three unseen bodies: emotional body, mental body, and spiritual body. Your inner knowing is felt through these unseen bodies. The phrase gut feeling is not only in the stomach but registers throughout the entire body and mind.

Discovering Your Telepathic Nature

1. Sit quietly alone in a room. Observe for a few moments the arrangement of items in the space and how they make you feel.

2. Close your eyes and recall what you saw.

3. What comes to mind?
    a. Does it appear as a picture? Clairvoyant.
    b. Do you recall sounds that were apparent at the time of your observation? Clairaudient.
    c. Can you elicit a feeling from the room? Clairsentient.
    d. Do you know what is in the room, yet you are not seeing, hearing, or feeling it? Claircognizance.
    e. Do you remember a scent? Clairessence.

4. You will unveil your dominant sense from this test, but you may notice picking up guidance with several different telepathic gifts throughout time.

5. Strengthen this awareness, not by practicing, but by paying attention and noting in a journal how you pick up telepathic guidance in your daily activities. Do this for about thirty days.

Courses of Action
Chapter Two

If the Truth Be Known

Acts of Kindness

My father did not realize when we first walked together to his sister's house and he reached for my hand, that it made a lasting imprint in my psyche. I never had an opportunity to tell him what it meant to me. That memory has stayed with me, along with the recollection of holding my children's hands on that warm summer day, both these experiences warm my heart. There were no words spoken, no eye contact, yet the connection made carried a memory of love. Metaphysically our hands link to our hearts, making a circuit that gives us a loving charge. Also, when we hug, our chests touch and aid in opening our hearts.

So often, we are unaware of how our kind acts can instill a positive memory for someone. When you smile at a stranger, that kind-hearted gesture may have changed their outlook on life. Carolyn Myss is an inspiring author, and while I attended her lecture, she addressed how our kind acts may have made someone's life better, and we didn't even know it. Ms. Myss was looking for input to a new book, *Invisible Acts of Power*, and wanted to glean from her readers their experiences when they helped a stranger, unaware of its impact on their lives. A man wrote about a woman who saved his life with just her smile. It was on a day when he was deeply depressed and felt life was not worth living. He was walking home, ready to stop his pain by committing suicide. He paused at a corner because of traffic. The driver in the car motioned for him to proceed across the street. No, he gestured back, "You go." She smiled at him and again indicated, "No, you go."

He hesitated, processing what had occurred, and then preceded across the street, impacted by her action. Her small token of kindness made him realize he did matter, someone did care, and even though she was just a stranger, it touched him in a way that changed his intention for that day. Her polite act let him know he was seen and of value. Think about taking a moment today and physically touching someone you love or smiling at a stranger. It may become a memory that will stay with them for a lifetime.

A Smile is Worth a Thousand Words

Smiling benefits the giver and the receiver. When you smile, neurotransmitters turn on in your brain, which releases endorphins and serotonin. Feeling happy as you smile is not necessary to produce these effects. Your grin will activate good vibes in your brain, relax your body and also help reduce pain.

1. With a brief thought or in meditation, have the intention to bring joy to someone that day.

2. Smile at someone you see in passing, offer a driver the right of way, or open a door for another.

3. If you don't feel happy, follow steps 1 and 2 to lighten your outlook for the day. The response received from the people you connected with will assist you to be more positive.

4. At the close of the day, recall what occurred and see if it makes you smile.

5. In a small journal, note your experiences to remind yourself that kind acts create positive results.

For forty years, my apprehension, not my mom, held me back from venturing out to find my father. I cannot blame her because I was the one who was not honoring my heart's desire. I saw her and my gram as the authority figures that I had to obey, even into my adult life. I knew what I could expect from them, but not from my father. Fear took hold and created my resistance to venture into the unknown.

I had heard some stories about my father earlier in my life, but those tales had a unique spin once I met him. I had a completely different perspective. Enlightened with a new image of him, I had an opportunity to understand the motives of my parent's actions, right or wrong. I had a choice. I could hold onto reasons that justified my pain or let go of how things turned out. I chose not to forgive them because forgiveness would still contain blame. There were no wrongs committed, just unfortunate circumstances from the decisions they made. I put myself in their place, which allowed me to realize their dilemma, and move forward.

There are ways to avoid being under the control of another, but first, you must look at their ideas and how they affect you. We are the ones who give away our power to those we see as authorities. They could be parents, older siblings, religious figures, or ones you deem wiser, more experienced, and intelligent than yourself, but the truth is, they do not always know what is best for you.

Realize Your Best Direction

Your inner guidance comes by clearing concepts that are not yours to make a space for your wisdom. There is a simple way to see issues free from others' opinions. First, you must remove any distractions and be alone. Then, clear your thoughts and beliefs from the media, the collective consciousness, and others involved. The collective consciousness holds subtle energies, ideas, and opinions recorded from humanity for eons of time. This unaddressed aspect of the psyche is quite strong and reflected in fashion, media, and customs. Placing this acquired yet unsolicited information outside your emotional, mental, and spiritual bodies will allow the best solution to emerge, unencumbered by the interference of others' opinions. In this clear state, you will feel the correct answer in your body.

To break a habitual pattern of allowing others to influence your actions, apply this practice until it becomes automatic. You will know when this occurs when you can decide what's right and not waver. That assurance is sensed in your heart. Always make decisions from this center, not from your mind. The mind can offer solutions, but your heart will hold the final decision, revealing a clear, correct path.

Using the Bubble to Attain Clear Answers

1. Still your thoughts and relax your body with three deep breaths.

2. Imagine a 12-inch bubble in front of you, outside your aura, and fill it with love from your heart.

3. Imagine the decision you need to make and see it as an image in this circle.

4. This picture should be in the future, holding the outcome you desire.

5. Now is not the time to decide how to make it happen; simply visualize the outcome.

6. Within this form, add the ideas and opinions that have been influencing you from others.

7. Imagine their thoughts crowding your intended outcome.

8. These directions could come from:
    a. Your significant other, parents, or friends
    b. Employer, co-workers, or business associates
    c. Society, media, religious doctrines, politics, or family ethics

9. Give each opinion you have heard a color.

10. Through silent intention, ask for ideas that do not resonate with your highest good to dissolve away.

11. Drain off the colors representing alternative beliefs other than yours so you may look at your desire uncluttered from outside influences.

12. Observe what idea remains in the bubble and how your body responds to the uncluttered image.

13. The right decision will resonate in your heart, not in your head.
    a. If you see your direction in your mind's eye, move the image to your heart and notice how it feels.
    b. Is your body stimulated positively or negatively?
    c. Is it foreign to your energy?
    d. Comfortable?
    e. Does it need some tweaking?

f.   If it does not feel right, repeat this exercise until the answer resonates joyously.

Hearing Clear Answers

1.   Define your question and see it as an image before you.

2.   Notice if you hear voices from ones who are trying to influence or disempower you. They could be voices from:
     a.   A significant other, parents, or friends
     b.   Employer, co-workers, or business associates
     c.   Society, media, or religious, political, or family beliefs

3.   Focus on the loudest voice and decide if it resonates with you. If not, turn down that volume.

4.   Listen to the other voices one at a time and quiet the opinions that do not fit.

5.   Continue silencing the voices that don't feel right, even your own, until there is only the voice of wisdom playing.

6.   Move that voice from your chattering mind into your emotional heart.

7.   If it is the best decision, it will resonate in your heart and remove all doubt.

Courses of Action
Chapter Three

SUPPRESSED LOVE

It took courage to follow my heart and venture into the unknown and locate my father, but it took even more nerve to share my actions with my family. They were the ones who judged my father, and I was afraid to face them, fearing they would no longer love me. I needed to stand in my power and tell them I had searched for him. But this was not an easy task because I held a pattern from my youth of not speaking my truth, just like my mom and father had held their tongues and allowed their family members to influence their decisions. They, as I, were locked in their patterns. Addressing personal growth was an uncommon practice in the 1950s, so they allowed others' opinions to control them. Yet, there is a way to avoid this pitfall in life.

Connect to Your Divine Essence – Know Who You Are

Too often, we forget that we are creators and that we hold the ability to manifest our heart's desires. It all begins with acknowledging our higher essence while visualizing and feeling that presence. Before starting this exercise, search the internet for images of stars and nebulae. Pick a color that appeals to you and imagine it as the color of your divine essence. In this practice, you will learn how to be aware of your divine essence and then expand it so no one can drain your energy, make you angry, or diminish your light. When you are present in this expanded state, nothing negative can attach to you.

1. When you stop moving, your thoughts will still; therefore, sit, have an erect spine, and focus on your breath.

2. Is your breath fast? Slow it down by taking longer breaths.

3. Is your breath shallow? Deepen it by allowing your lungs to expand.

4. Notice how each breath offers an opportunity to receive light into your body.

5. Relax with your breath for as long as you are guided, and then move to the next step.

6. Think of the Universe and recall the images from space, ones of the stars and nebulae.

7. Choose one color and imagine it as the essence of you, sparkling and bright.

8. Imagine this hue dropping from the Universe into the top of your head—crown chakra.

9. Take a moment to sense if this color creates a texture, temperature, or tingling in your body.

10. Allow it to emanate into your brain, firing your neurons and making new connections.

11. This light moves and balances your memory, hearing, sight, and speech.

12. The color of your divine essence runs down your spine and into your nerves, electrifying your body with energy.

13. Sense the strength in your muscles.

14. Your light fills you from head to toe.

15. Relax in this sensation and then begin to expand your light.

16. Allow your essence to fill:
    a. the room
    b. your home

    c.   the neighborhood

    d.   your city

    e.   your state or province

    f.   the continent

    g.   the earth and atmosphere of earth

    h.   the infinite Universe

17. In this state, no one can upset you or steal your energy.

18. You are one with all that is.

19. In the future, this expansive light can be activated in seconds.

Finding Your Truth

Take the next step to discover the best solution to a conflict. Once you have connected to your divine essence, your inner sight is open so that you will know your next move.

1. Feel your expanded light, then ask your question.

2. Breathe in your divine color, exhale it into the room. See it sparkle.

3. Appearing before you are three different ways you can approach the issue. Some may hold the ideas of someone else.

4. Let each idea play out as a video on a screen.

5. Each outcome concludes with your desired result.

6. While holding your divine light and power around yourself, step into each scene where the process will be cloaked with its essence.

7. Each will feel different. Notice if:

    a.   your power and light increases

    b.   your light diminishes

    c.   you are confused

    d.   you feel uneasy in your stomach—solar plexus

    e.   your heart is light or heavy

8. Let go of what you think and notice what resonates in your body, spirit, or chakras.

9.   Your choice should now be clear.

Speaking Your Truth

Visualizing a positive outcome to difficult conversations will provide for a positive result. In this process, you will see how to support that vision. When we are sleeping, we are in a receptive state, and our subconscious mind is open. Imagine your dialogue with the other person while they are sleeping. They will subconsciously hear your side, preparing them for a harmonious discussion when you talk face to face.

When you think the other person is sleeping:
- o   Talk to them silently.
- o   Tell them how you feel.
- o   Mention what is important to you.
- o   Show them how you would like your relationship to be.
- o   Ask them to respond to you with kindness.
- o   Express that you are open to hearing their perspective.
- o   Imagine a harmonious outcome. It may turn out different from what you had imagined.

When you meet with them, make your conversation cordial. Remember, their perception does not need to diminish your power, and their comments are merely information. That day, whether your conversation is in person or not, wear the color of your divine essence to remind yourself of who you are beyond your assumed physical and emotional limitations.

Practicing Empathy, Put Yourself in Their Place

When I shared my excitement in finding my father with my cousin, brother, and mom, they did not share my joy. I was frustrated and judged them for not seeing the value of this reunion. Their reaction threw me off-kilter, and I felt they did not care. To rise above my pain, I needed to reframe how I saw this impasse. Defending myself would only bring more confrontations; so, as difficult as it was, I needed to honor what I was feeling without their approval and honor their resistant feelings. I obtained empathy for them by releasing my judgment and imagining myself in their place. There I found their core of discontent was not necessarily with me but had begun earlier in their childhood.

Issues can be defused with family, friends, and even co-workers when you apply this technique to locate their buried issues. It will take more research to uncover the core issues for those you are not close to because you may not know their history. Therefore, recall conversations you have had with them, looking for stories they mentioned about how their parents, siblings, or intimate partners have treated them. And if they have never spoken about people close to them, could they be lonely, afraid to reach out to someone, and locked in their pain? Look at their triggers and follow that thread back through their life, to practice empathy. A clue will arise to help you understand who or what has hurt them in the past.

Fostering Compassion for Those You Resent

- o   Recall a story you have heard about this person's young life.
- o   Imagine what their life was like as a child.
- o   What were the customs at that time?
- o   Where did they live: a city, a farm, or a place that was not safe?
- o   Were they shown love?
- o   What demands were upon them as a youngster?
- o   Were they abused either physically or verbally?
- o   Did they think no one cared about them?
- o   What did they have to do to survive?
- o   How is that reflected in their life today?
- o   What memory do you mimic to them that makes them want to treat you unkindly?

By creating a story of how their life was when they were small, you can better imagine the emotions they held then and still have now. By observing them as an injured child, crying out for help, not the adult that hurts you, can put an end to your resentment that holds you back and keeps you from being the loving person you are. Contact these sentiments and notice the feelings that arise. Allow compassion to be your salvation.

When you imagine a scenario in their childhood, it is easier to forgive a youngster who is just learning how to live harmoniously in a turbulent world rather than the adult you judge. Let go of how their adult self acts and see them as the little one who is hurt, sad, and feeling unloved. Even if you fabricate the wrong story, it does not matter because you intend to see them from a new perspective. It will represent a person that you can understand, who doesn't aggravate you.

Practice Compassion

1. Close your eyes, deepen your breath, to see a challenging person in a new light.

2. Allow your intuition to open and uncover the story that reveals how you can build empathy and compassion.

3. In your mind's eye, imagine them younger, troubled, and confused.

4. Look to see who is hurting them, either physically or emotionally.

5. Talk to them and give them the compassion and understanding that you are seeking from them.

6. Allow a loving feeling to envelop both of you.

7. Once established, continue your meditation until an awareness surfaces that softens your heart and activates a sensation in your body.

8. Test the result by bringing the present-time hurtful situation to mind and notice if the negative charge has lessened.

9. Repeat this process until you can be neutral to their behaviors.

10. Now you are set free, as are they if they choose.

Developing Patience

I was agitated when my brother did not jump at the chance to meet our father. I needed patience, but it's not my strong suit. When you push for things to happen according to your time frame, it inhibits the process and restricts the flow, possibly slowing things down to a crawl. To stop this controlling pattern, take time to still your mind in meditation before you say or do something you wish you had not.

Follow the steps in *Connect to Your Divine Essence – Know Who You Are* at the start of this chapter to adapt to this skill. The mind does not recognize words as well as it does images. The brain interprets thoughts as pictures, so starting your meditation with a visual will be more productive. When your mind is still, picture the one who tries your patience and notice how you play into this scenario and how you might be restricting them. A mild situation could look like strings or spider webs, spun to envelop you or them for control.

If one is more attached to the outcome, there could be chains or ropes pulling them, or you, in the direction each of you desires. Mild or firm, these restrictions limit the harmonious outcome you both desire. If you think the other person does not feel your influence or impatience, think again. Thoughts and feelings have a vibrational frequency, like radio or sound waves. Others can sense your control, which may halt the movement for which you are impatiently waiting.

See the following activity as an exploration rather than another task to do and enter it with child-like wonder. It will take only a few minutes to rearrange your thoughts and adjust your feelings. When you approach this task with a lightness of heart, it opens the space, relaxing both parties. The results are often pleasantly surprising.

How does resistance appear?

o Follow the steps for *Connect to Your Divine Essence – Know Who You Are* earlier in this chapter.

o Relax and recall the issue which makes you impatient.

o See the person or situation before you outside your aura.

o Play with your imagination. There are no wrong ways to see the situation.

o Feel the resistance, impatience, and control coming from both of you.

o   Imagine these feelings as images. For example:
- ▷   Feet in sticky tar—melt the tar with sunlight to free each of you.
- ▷   Spider webbing hiding a better outcome—dust it away.
- ▷   Ropes that bind people or structures—untie the line that attaches.
- ▷   Doors closed and locked—find the key.
- ▷   End by seeing each of you standing in your respective light as free individuals.

Courses of Action
Chapter Four

IN THE STILL OF THE NIGHT

Why was my grandfather so reluctant to allow Nunzi to have a paper route? Why did he insist on being with his boys on their venture through the city streets? Subconsciously did he know the boys would need protection? My answer was an emphatic yes.

Grandfather, like all of us, had a natural ability to foresee the future. Our society has become so sophisticated, it negates that our inner vision and intuitive knowing exist, yet we all possess these gifts.

Inner sight needs to be nurtured to develop. When parents disallow their children's imagination, it stifles their natural instinct. When little ones talk about their imaginary friends, family members sometimes find it amusing, stating, "Oh, we let him pretend, but it is not real." Even if this invalidation is not voiced in their presence, children still sense their parent's doubt. Don't doubt what you cannot see. Children will know what you're thinking, and it will suppress their intuition.

When we follow our inner guidance, and it turns out to be a correct decision, it is often considered a coincidence, but what is this knowledge? Where does it originate?

o   It comes from our greater wisdom. Own it; it is yours.
o   It is a divine spark that enlightens us.
o   It is the aha that gives us an electrical charge.
o   Its sensation ignites a flame within that generates excitement.

o   It is the energy that drives us.
o   It is our divinity in action, and we should not ignore it but
     rather claim these gifts.

In days past, intuition was necessary to stay alive. When living in the wild, people needed to follow their instincts to find food, shelter, and safety. Though our lives no longer depend on this type of insight, it behooves us to familiarize ourselves with how our inner knowing appears and follow that lead.

The first step is to discover where you sense intuition. This guidance does not always originate in our thoughts. It is a whole-body knowing, referred to as a gut feeling. There lies the mark of genuine psychic ability, but I suggest you look beyond the stomach area. As mentioned earlier, in esoteric teachings, the stomach's energy field, called the solar plexus chakra, houses our emotions. Yet when danger is near, you may feel fear in other parts of your body. Full-body knowing comes in many forms. The fun begins in discovering how your insights feel.

Become familiar with your chakras' qualities in order to acquire insight from your body rather than from your intellectual mind. Guidance can come through a feeling of excitement that assures you are making the correct decision. If you waiver and do not act on the guidance, doubting its factual content, you have stepped away from full-body knowing, thus giving your mind time to invalidate what could be your best option.

Body Awareness

With a curious mind and firm intention, you can find how your body channels unspoken messages. Intuition is our innate instinct; it keeps us from harm, guides us in the correct direction, and is most reliable in our youth. Yet, it often goes unnurtured, making one unsure of its existence as we grow older. One can reclaim this ability by acknowledging the sensations felt when heading in the right direction or when you should cease an action.

When contemplating the best action, give your mind time to analyze the pros and cons and then allow your body to direct you towards the correct path. Full-body knowing comes from silencing your thoughts and sensing what your body is telling you. Try the following exercise to relax and to become familiar with the subtle difference in each part of your body. Focusing your attention on your body and away from disturbing situations will also calm you. You can stay focused on the process by recording the steps in your voice and playing them back as you proceed.

Sensing Intuitive Guidance in Your Body

By fully sensing your body, you will gain the ability to receive clear directions. In this state, you will not question your decisions.

1. Sit erect in a chair. Close your eyes to shut out distractions.

2. Notice the weight of your body on the seat of the chair.

3. Place your attention on your head. Feel its weight resting on your neck and shoulders.

4. Observe the space your head takes up in the room.

5. Feel the air on your face, then compare it to the air in the room. This can be a sensation that is difficult to describe. Notice the difference.

6. Feel how your spine holds some of the weight of your head.

7. Feel how the vertebrae are stacked while bearing the weight of your head.

8. Your shoulders support your head differently from how your spine cradles this mass. See if you can identify the subtle difference.

9. Feel the heaviness of your arms hanging off your shoulders. Your forearms carry some of this weight by resting on your lap or the components of the chair.

10. Notice what part of your forearm is taking most of this weight. Move your attention to your wrists and hands.

11. What part of your hand is resting on your body?

12. Does your skin exposed to the air feel different from the part that rests on your body?

13. Let your attention move slowly down your spine. Visualize how the vertebrae stack from the base of your head down to your tailbone.
    a. Feel the space between each vertebra.

     b.   Scan each vertebra from your neck to your tailbone.

     c.   How are they the same? How are they different?

14. Can you feel your buttocks touching the chair? Is the weight even on both sides?

15. Notice the large bones in your thighs. Do they sit fully or partly on the chair? How are your knees supported?

16. Scan your lower anatomy and see if it feels different from your upper body?

17. Feel how your femur connects to your hips, down to your knees.

18. Tune into the bones in your knees and sense the weight from your knees down to your ankles.

19. Can you imagine the tiny bones in your feet? Even though you are sitting, is there some weight distributed to your feet? How much?

20. Is the weight on the inside or the outside of your feet? Where do you feel your feet touch the surface?

21. Scan back through your body and see if any part calls for your attention. If so, move into that part and notice if it holds tension from a muscle or tendon. Relax that part of your body.

22. Bring your awareness into the entire structure of your body. Do you feel light or heavy?

23. Now that you are tuned into your body, recall a question you have or a decision you need to make.

24. Take that thought and see how it resonates in your body, not in your mind.

25. Once you receive clarity, take a long slow deep breath, slowly open your eyes and move on with your day.

Steps to Build Intuition

Once you are familiar with tuning into your body, you will be prepared to pick up intuitive messages in your body's field of consciousness. When asking a question, always expect a response; then you will be more likely to receive guidance. Insights may come from outside sources. The answer may show up on the radio, in an advertisement, or a movie or television show. Listen for comments you overhear from a person passing by. Messages appear when you are open, receptive, and listening.

To increase your intuition, make a list of the times you followed a hunch that turned out to be a good lead. Did a gut feeling lead you to a gathering where you met a valuable contact? If you were not there, the chance would have been lost. So many times, we ignore our natural ability to tune into this innate sixth sense. By acknowledging your insights, you honor your telepathy, and that will increase its frequency.

How Do You Receive Insights?

Think of your question and be assured an answer will surface. Pay attention to your surroundings and your dreams. The way to access the guidance is to be aware, stay in the present moment, and not negate what you see, hear and sense. The following are various ways to receive information. You may not always receive it in the same way.

1. Recall how intuition registers in your body.
    a. Do you get a gut feeling?
    b. Does it feel like a download of information?
    c. Do you feel energy charging through your body?
    d. Do you feel drained when the direction is wrong?

2. Notice how you are receiving guided information.
    a. Do you hear it on the radio, television, or in the movies?
    b. Is it coming from overheard or casual conversations?
    c. Are your dreams showing you something?

3. Journal every intuitive thought for one week.
    a. Did you remember items needed while at the store that were not on your grocery list?
    b. Was the quickest way home found without a GPS?

    c.   When you called a friend, did they say, "I was just thinking about you?"

    d.   When you followed your guidance, did it put you in the right place at the right time?

    e.   Write down every hunch, even ones that did not manifest, because they may later.

4.   Keep track of when you have followed simple inner guidance to increase its frequency.

Who They Were

No guidance for this chapter.

Courses of Action
Chapter Six

BURIED MEMORIES

Relieve Stress by Staying in the Moment

When my mom was in labor with me, the nurses pulled on her cervix each time she had a contraction. I assume to speed things along. It seems coincidental and may not be connected, but I have always felt the urgency to get things accomplished quicker than necessary—often creating more problems. When I do not give myself time to think things through, I make mistakes and wrong decisions. Could this be a trait I took on because my birth was hurried and not allowed to flow naturally? Real or imagined, my quest to move fast needed adjusting. I do this by slowing myself down by placing my thoughts in the moment and paying attention to what's happening around me.

Staying in the present time completes projects faster, eases stress, and keeps your body trim. When you sense your mind is racing, trying to complete an activity, notice if you are in the moment or thinking about the next task. If you are not fully absorbed in your current endeavor, it takes longer to complete, mistakes happen, and stress occurs. To stop this habit, refocus your attention. Concentrate on what you are doing and watch the movement of your body and hands. Imagine you are mentally racing on the road ahead of you and walk back into the present moment.

Clear your thoughts by making a list of the activities you desire to accomplish. Then your mind will clear, releasing any tension. When you apply this practice, you may find that you can finish all of the things on your list with time to spare. This present-time technique will also help maintain a healthy weight. By not diverting your attention while eating, you will eat less, digest your food better and enjoy the taste.

Being in the Present Moment

o   When your mind is racing, treat it like a child and tell it to STOP.

o   Bring your thoughts back to the present time by looking at three things in your sight. It does not matter what they are.

o   Do not focus on what needs doing next; put that task on a list and think only about what you are doing at the moment.

o   Pay attention to precisely what you are doing to stop your mind from wondering.

o   To maintain a healthy weight, do not multitask when eating; be present and only eat.

     ▷   Do not read, watch tv, answer emails, or search the web.

     ▷   Chew your food slowly, observing the texture, temperature, taste, and smell.

     ▷   Stop eating when you first begin to feel satisfied.

Courses of Action
Chapter Seven

HIDDEN AGENDAS

Words have power. Even our mind's unspoken chatter collects in our thoughts, drains our energy, and, if not addressed, can make us ill. This behavior is so unnecessary, yet we all do it.

I can't help wondering what my mom and gram perceived as a positive attribute for telling a lie about my father's existence. I don't understand how they assumed the facts would stay secret. I imagine my mom did not want to face what she perhaps held in her heart, that my father was a man who hurt her deeply, yet she always loved and missed him. Or is that my childhood fantasy?

Mom and Gram's made-up stories were not as hidden as they thought. Words are energy and are recorded on devices as waves. Once these sound waves move from our lips, they continue to vibrate into the air and can be picked up by others as intuition or gut feelings.

Tales about others can be positive or negative, but the person discussed will often sense the conversation's vibrational frequency in their bodies. The phrase, "My ears are ringing," describes that body-felt awareness that you are the subject of a discussion. How does this happen? It comes from the intuitive gifts that we all possess and our connection to others through a web of light. Just recall a time when you mentioned a person to someone else, and then that person walked by or called you. It is curious when it happens.

My brother was the one who picked up on the lie that was told to us. Brave soul that he was, he presented the question to Mom and Gram. "How could my father have died in the war when I was born after the war ended?" At that point, Mom and Gram had to tell the truth. I assume they lied to control us so we would never search for my father. My brother, at least, halted one of their dominating actions, but there were others.

When I was young, I wanted my father to be in my life, to talk to him, and to have him close. The teachings in Sunday school professed God is in heaven and will hear your requests. Therefore I surmised by my father's passing, he was there as well, so I could talk to him in the same way as I talked to God, so I prayed to my father. Even after I met him, I did not share my little girl's wishes with my father. I was too embarrassed. How foolish I was to believe the stories professed by my mom and gram. I was so naïve.

When people lie to us, it brings an opportunity for personal growth. We have a choice about how we respond and how long we carry our pain. We cannot change what people have done to us, but we can adjust our perspective to disperse our anger, release our discontent, and form a positive slant to the event. Then we are the ones holding the reins. We are in charge, and at that point, no one can anger or hurt us.

Every lie offers an opportunity to look within and search for the part of us that can love unconditionally. Look to your heart, for love starts at home. The psyche wants answers, but the answers are not always available. To understand why my mom and gram acted the way they did, I had to look at their lives to find the answer, a journey that led me to imagine the insecurities and fears that they held.

To satisfy my inquisitive mind, I gathered fragments of stories I had heard, pointing to their upbringing, and I looked into those tales in order to speculate who withheld love from them. From there, I put together my fictional account to allow me to understand how their personalities formed as adults. Next was to imagine why they acted the way they did. To acquire this knowledge, I had to touch the pain they emotionally still held. Taking on their pain was not required, only being aware of it, and then I found compassion for them.

Even though I thought I knew why they treated me poorly, I still could not let go of my regret. My psyche wanted to hang onto the injustice. That is where my personal growth began. I had to let go of the negative feelings gnawing at me, thinking they kept me from having a fulfilled life. It did not always appear obvious, but these old, buried, unkind thoughts affected every aspect of my life:

business, personal, and family. These thoughts reflected the insecurities that started in my youth and the unfairness I chose to hold.

There is a way to make peace with our childhood pain, but it requires patience and inner searching. By delving into the subconscious mind, with the use of hypnosis, one can answer questions addressing physical and emotional struggles. Once you uncover a new perception, it needs time to integrate. In that way, you begin to heal.

Self-Hypnosis Guidelines

Self-hypnosis can uncover the triggers hidden deep in your subconscious mind. Begin with a query, then still your thoughts, follow the script below, and see what transpires. Search for one answer at a time. If your question is too broad, you may not receive the guidance you desire. Narrow it down to precisely what you want to know.

If health is your concern:
- o   Name what part of your body is in distress.
- o   List how it inhibits you.
- o   Ask to see if there is an emotional component causing your illness.
- o   Ask for a divine being to appear to heal you.

Searching for a new job or vocation, list the important factors:
- o   How far are you willing to drive, if at all?
- o   Does your job need to fulfill a purpose? What is that?
- o   How important is the financial aspect? What is that number?
- o   Is your co-working community important?
- o   Ask to be guided to your next step.

Are you looking for a balanced, healthy, loving relationship?
- o   Describe your heart's desire, be clear and precise.
- o   Ask for a scene to appear from the past that has held you back.
- o   Ask to be shown what it feels like to be in a new relationship.

Enter this practice with no expectations. Hold an intention that something will appear to give you clarity, do not doubt your abilities and be playful. When you feel uncertainty and doubt, your mood will color the procedure, making it seem complicated. Thoughts have power, and when you approach an unfamiliar method with excitement and wonder, you will have better results. Recording the script in your voice is an excellent way to receive the full impact.

Hypnosis Relaxation

1. Devise a question to help you understand why things happened as they did. Perhaps ask, "Why did they lie to me."

2. Sit erect in a comfortable place—by a fireplace, in the sun, or beneath a cozy blanket.

3. Turn off all communication devices.

4. Be assured you will receive an answer.

5. Close your eyes.

6. Slow down your breath, feel your chest rise and fall.

7. Allow the relaxation to flow throughout your body, beginning with your eyes.
    a. Your eyelids are lightly closed and slowly begin to get heavy.
    b. A relaxed feeling moves to the muscles around your eyes.
    c. This calmness turns into a warm liquid that penetrates your forehead and then flows down to your cheeks.
    d. The soothing warmth extends down to your
        i.   lips
        ii. tongue
        iii. neck
        iv. your entire body

8. Be aware of a still feeling in your body. It feels good.

9. There is a black screen before you and a table by your side. Upon the table are white numbers from one to ten.

10. Place the numbers in sequence, one by one, on the screen, removing the existing number before placing the next one up.

11. Each time a new number appears, you feel more relaxed.

12. By the time you reach number ten, you are deeply relaxed.

Deepening the Process and Accessing the Subconscious Mind

1. In the calm state you just created, see an elevator before you. Push the button, and hear the door opening.

2. Step inside. On the wall are four buttons marking each level—A to D.

3. Move down, one level at a time. Feel the elevator descending, stopping, and the door opening. When the door closes, your relaxation will double.

4. Press letter B, feel yourself descending, the elevator stops, and hear the door open. Push the button for the next level. As the door closes, your relaxation doubles.

5. Repeat the process until you reach level D. The door opens.

6. At level D, step into the hall before you and walk to the library.

7. Look at the books. One will draw your attention. Take the book off the shelf and sit on a chair.

8. Read the title and look through the entire book. The pages will give you information.

9. Place it back on the shelf.

10. Continue to reach for books that answer to your question.

11. You may also receive knowledge from the items you view in the room.

12. When you are satisfied with the knowledge attained, move back to the hall and into the elevator. Press the button and ascend to level A.

13. Walk out of the elevator door and into a soft white light.

14. There is a staircase before you with seven stairs.

15. Slowly climb to the top. Feel your foot on each step.

16. As you ascend, you will feel lighter, happier, better than you have felt in days, weeks, even months.

17. At the top, open your eyes and feel completely refreshed.

Banish Grudges, Resentment, and Lies

How many times have you believed something to be true, only to find out that you have been duped, betrayed, tricked? These lies show up in all aspects of our lives, with friends, family, politics, religion, and the work environment. Once the truth becomes apparent, the invalidation runs through your whole body. Irritation and resentment build, accompanied by sadness, followed by the question, "Why"?

Looking back at my childhood, I could choose to hold resentment towards my mom and gram for keeping the truth hidden about my father, but it does not serve me to harbor ill feelings towards them. The only one it would harm is me. I know their actions were inappropriate, and it deeply affected me, but once I was out from under their rule, I was free to express my emotions. Unfortunately, anger was one of them. It oozed out to those around me, and I did not realize where those negative feelings originated.

Once I had met my father, I could begin to understand the temper that festered within me and let it go. It took only a year from meeting my father to adopt the changes needed in my life and begin to balance what was off-center within me for decades. I released the people who harmed me, which set me free and allowed me to reclaim my power. But in reality, no one invalidated or denied me anything. These effects I made up in my head; therefore, I could change my perspective and diminish my anguish.

How can you move beyond the pain of deception? What does life look like under the umbrella of this newly discovered knowledge? Follow the guidelines outlined in the Courses of Action - Chapter 4, *How to Foster Compassion for Those You Resent.*

Taking the First Step Towards Resolution

My mother held resentment for her unkind sister-in-law, and as they grew older, Mom never envisioned Mary maturing and dropping her aggression. Mom did not want to address these issues, so she stuffed those thoughts away, but things changed once Mary and Mom met.

About a year after my father passed, Mom nervously walked with me to Mary's door on a cool fall night, and when Mary did not answer, Mom walked away, relieved. The next day, we once again appeared at Mary's door, but Mom was relaxed and ready to face whatever would happen this time. By preempting their meeting with the non-meeting, Mom liberated herself from her fear. You can enact a similar scene without being present with your nemesis.

Is there a story you have held in your mind over the years? That memory may not still be valid, yet you hold onto the pain, telling yourself:

o   They don't care about me.

o   No one loves me.

o   They don't miss me.

o   Of course, my story is true.

o   They must still be angry at me.

Think of the grief you could release if you let go of the unresolved problem. You have two choices, contact the alleged party for clarification, and if that is not possible, conjure up in your mind what other reasons there could be for this troubling situation.

Questions to ask yourself about painful stories from alienated people:

o   Are the stories you have told yourself over the years still true?

o   Could the parties involved have remorse?

o   What is the worst thing that could happen if you met again?

o   Could you reconcile, with no need to create a long-term relationship?

o   Can you see how resolving your misunderstanding could serve both of you?

Reacquaint with an Estranged Individual

One of my family members has isolated me for some time, so I decided to follow my advice and reach out. On their birthday, I called them and sent a text. They did not respond to either, but the Universe showed me that my efforts were not in vain the next day. My daughter called, unaware of my actions the previous day. She said to me, "You're a good person; you did not do anything wrong, sometimes as people mature, there are things that happen, but know you are not to blame." Her words brought tears to my eyes and made me think the heart of my angry family member was beginning to soften. In my heart, I know, in some way, they feel the love I send them.

Another confirmation of love came later that night. It was 8 o'clock, and my cell phone rang, I looked at the screen, and the name of my estranged family member appeared. I answered with joy, but there was no voice on the other end. I could hear footsteps but no voice. I whistled and called their name, but this was a pocket call. They were not aware they called me, we never spoke, but I breathed a sigh of relief because we made a small connection. Even if it appeared as a mistake, I accepted this action to be our heart's connection, one that I know we have even in our absence.

Don't expect divine messages to come in flashes of light, words in living color, or profound images. They could appear that way, but the responses are often subtle, quiet, and take a bit of detective work to recognize. Be assured you are not alone. The Universe is listening and responding to your request.

Suppose you wish to reconnect with the estranged person physically. In that case, each practice will give your mind a tangible focus to release your fear of what might happen. It all occurs in your thoughts by picturing an event, giving it structure and color. This way, your mind will have something substantial to release rather than a reaction that has no form. Remember, in *Speaking Your Truth* in Chapter 4, you can also talk to them as they sleep and see them listening and kindly responding when you meet.

Images to Clear Your Resistance of Meeting an Estranged Person

While in meditation or during a self-hypnosis session, envision one of these scenarios to remove resistance between you and the estranged person.

1. A dark brown door is closed tight.
    a. Hanging on it is a rusty heavy padlock with a chain.
    b. At your feet appears a key. Pick up the cold metal key and open the lock.
    c. The chain clangs as it falls to the ground.
    d. The door squeaks as it swings open, and you step through to meet your nemesis with a loving embrace.

2. A red brick wall has some bricks removed, making it weak.
   a. The structure is dusty, dark, and covered with cobwebs.
   b. Each brick holds a useless emotion. Pull out the bricks and drop them to the ground. Watch them crumble as your emotions calm.
   c. With a slight push, the wall tumbles down with little effort.
   d. You step over the rubble into the light to greet your old friend.

3. A computer reflects the stories from the past with your distant person. They are titled in yellow folders.
   a. Drag each file into the trash.
   b. If one will not delete, open it and forgive the situation.
   c. One by one, you hear the click as you place the old programs into the trash.
   d. Once the desktop is clear, empty the trash.
   e. Create a new file that holds the way you desire your relationship to be.
   f. The screensaver on your computer shows the image of both of you, embracing and happy.

Invoking the Strength to Reconnect

To clear the issue from deep within the subconscious mind, begin with the script, *Hypnosis Relaxation* earlier in this chapter and then proceed.

1. For a few moments, take some deep breaths to quiet your mind and let your body become still.

2. See the estranged person standing before you. Envision their reaction, surprise, or discontent.

3. Contact your expectations and fears.

4. Feel your anxiety, misgivings, or apprehension and give those emotions an image so the mind can release them. It could be in the form of a red face, a black dagger, or a person with their back to you.

    a.   Do not avoid disturbing feelings. Allow them to surface and take form while you turn to face them.

    b..   When you address your fears, the hold they have upon you will diminish.

    c.   Stay in this meditative state while you release the effect of unresolved sentiments. Notice that you begin to feel lighter.

5.   Picture your separation as a physical object you design or the dark brown door, wall, or computer screen, as described in the exercise above.

6.   Allow that separation to change to a welcoming vision.

7.   Ask for and receive help from higher beings with one of these suggestions:

    a.   Ask wise beings to make the necessary adjustments here on earth to ease the strained energy between both of you.

    b.   Hand the disturbing images of your emotions to a divine being, and ask them for assistance. Trust that they know what to do.

    c.   Imagine help from unknown sources who whisper to your alienated friend words that soften their feelings towards you.

8.   Your fear of what might happen is more significant than what will happen. Let go of that fear and trust good will come from your efforts.

9.   Even if you believe they will not respond, contact them in a way you feel is appropriate: text, email, or phone call.

    a.   Contacting them will free up your energy.

    b.   The action alone will make a difference, even if you do not talk to them.

    c.   If they do not respond, don't fret, adjustments occur in their energy field, and they will think of you differently.

    d.   Divine beings have more power than we think, and when you ask for their assistance, they act upon your request.

10. Ground the process by calling someone who is supportive and share your experience.

When there is no response, know your action to connect kindly is not lost.

Every loving act is stored in our etheric fields. Kindness sent to others will always, in some way, return to you. It is the law of the Universe. Circles are its pattern. Our planet circles around the sun, moons travel around planets, and our Universe moves in a spiral as well. What we send out, good or bad, will cycle back.

Uncover celestial help by starting to dialogue with the powers in the Universe, the divine, or a guide.

o   Ask the Universe to remove your pain, see what happens in a day or two.

o   Present a question to the divine and expect an answer. Then watch for the response.

o   Imagine someone in the love of the cosmos and notice how they are the next time you meet.

o   Sit in meditation and ask your guides to give you a sign that they are here. Notice what sensation occurs in your body.

WORKING ON THE RAILROAD

Did Grandpa Blake cause the trains to delay Gram's funeral procession? Did he also make sure his last resting place, the red chair in the railroad office, would remain as a whisper of his energy until his grandson, my brother Jim, found the chair, creating a moment where they could once again, in some distant way, connect? Similarly, was Aunt JoAnn's passing tied to my finding my father? My father's family thought she was an element that brought us together, for she died the same week Macy called my mom with the news of my father's illness.

These could have been just coincidences. Yet, I have seen messages filter down from those who have passed. I do not dismiss these as happenstance because one way to discover for yourself if the deceased can contact the living is to begin a conversation with a family member or friend on the other side. Do not fear being harmed, for ghosts cannot hurt you. They don't have a body.

Connecting to Spirits on the Other Side

When my grandfathers passed, the loss was devasting to their spouses, Gram and Grandma Palm. If someone could have contacted their husbands on the other side and found they were at peace, it may have eased these widows' pain.

Applying this skill can become a beautiful gift to give to friends and family when their loved ones exit this earthly plane. It is a method you can quickly become proficient in with a little practice.

The perfect place to greet the deceased is at their memorial service. They are almost always in attendance. After all, this is their last worldly party. It's interesting to watch how they respond to the ceremony. Some are aloof to the pomp and circumstance, others sit quietly as people pay their respects, but at some point, there could be an activity that arouses their attention. I have seen it happen many times. You may share the vision you receive with their loved ones, which is often well-received.

Do not be afraid that a spirit will connect to your energy and attach to you. When you work from a place of love, holding the intention to assist the deceased, you are safe. Fear acts like Velcro, and it can change the outcome. If you like, you may ask for a divine being to shield you, but this is also a form of fear. If you feel you need protection, you are not standing in your power.

At one service, I noticed the passing spirit sitting in a chair and observing the goings-on, and then she followed the procession to the gravesite. I saw her watching us from a tree branch, but I noticed she was not alone. Her husband, who had passed years before, was in the same tree on another limb. I informed her adult children what I envisioned. They were quite pleased to know their mom was not alone and their father was there to escort her into the next realm.

One spirit did not show up until after the service began and stood as an on-looker at the stained glass window outside the sanctuary. She did not step in until the priest gave communion. At that point, she expanded her spirit, joined the ceremony, and spread her light over the people kneeling at the altar. Her loving presence radiated to everyone in attendance, and later many remarked about the intense light and calmness they felt at the alter. It was beautiful.

A man who left his body appeared bored as he watched the proceedings that honored his accomplishments. He had been active in three organizations: The Sons of the American Revolution, The Veterans of Foreign Wars, and The Volunteers of America. The representatives of these groups marched through the church carrying flags that rippled over their heads. The aisle filled with the flag's colors of red, white, blue, and green. The deceased sat unmoved, but what brought him to attention was the melodic notes of "Amazing Grace." At that moment, he rose from his chair, stood erect, and I could see he was honoring his spirit, not what he had done in his life, but reverence to his soul. It moved me as I observed this in my mind's eye. Don't expect the spirit to contact anyone in the ceremony. They are usually there only to watch.

I do not see spirits floating in the air when I call to them. They come to me in my thoughts. I sense their presence and then an image forms in my mind. By trusting and not doubting the process, I let the story continue to unfold. Sometimes, a family member would confirm my apparitions. One time, learning of my client's passing, I looked in to see how her spirit was doing. I saw a dog pacing with her. Later I found that this yellow dog was her dog which had died the previous year.

Observing the Deceased at Their Memorial Service

1. Begin this process while sitting quietly at their memorial service.

2. Close your eyes and let the sound of the music still your thoughts.

3. Imagine the deceased in your mind's eye, noticing if they are above, behind, or outside the room.

4. Do not force the apparition, pay attention to the service, and look for the spirit during the proceedings.

5. Something will happen that you did not expect. If nothing comes to mind, prime the pump of your imagination by making up a story.

6. Pretend that they are in the room and notice what part of the room calls your attention.

7. You may not always see the spirit, but you might feel a shift in your energy.

8. If nothing occurs in the room, see if they will travel with their mourners to their gravesite or the reception following. Trust that your imagination is connecting you to the passing spirit.

Courses of Action
Chapter Nine

STRUGGLES

Though Mom did not physically abuse me often, the memory is locked in my subconscious mind, and I still adjust my behavior. So, where do you go after you have been abused? I don't remember where I hid after the day she almost suffocated me, but I can see where I went as an adult. I retreated into my shell. I started to close my heart, little by little. I locked my feelings away to protect myself because I did not feel safe around those I loved. My mom and gram were not respecting or protecting me from harm. To do so, they would have to protect me from themselves, which was impossible.

How and when do you release your pain? How do you let it go? By building a new perspective that will open the door into your own heart, thus creating self-love.

Peace lies within your heart. No one can give it to you. You must provide it to yourself. Those who have abused you live in their own private hell; there is no need for you to join them. One cannot know the thoughts of another unless they tell us. I have seen through my clients and my personal experiences; abusers have been mistreated themselves. They are injured, stuck in their childhood, and don't know how to act otherwise or change their behavior. It is not an excuse, for there is no justification for the mistreatment of any living being, but having a different perception, you are free.

Do you hold anger and sadness because of an abusive incident? Do you still give your power away to that person or other people in your life? Know you have the key to set yourself free, there is no jailer, no locks, and all you need to do is open the door and walk through into peace.

Clearing Abusive Memories

1. Follow this process after a restful night and feeling good.

2. Give yourself time after the process to nurture yourself.

3. Close your eyes, and be assured you will come through this victorious.

4. Breathe deeply, and be aware of oxygen flowing into your bloodstream.
    a. Soon your muscles will respond to the oxygen, loosen and relax.
    b. Let your mind absorb the oxygen and still your thoughts.

5. Place your abusive memory into your heart with your inner child.
    a. The heart represents love so allow this love to envelop you.
    b. If you need assistance, imagine an angel by your side, radiating a pink light of love.

6. Recall the first time you were abused and see yourself at that age.

7. See your abuser as a small child rather than the one who disempowered you.

8. Feel how at this moment, they are not a threat to you.

9. Look into their life when they were small.
    a. See them with their father and how he treated them?
    b. Did they have a loving connection?
    c. Imagine them with their mom, and notice if she was nurturing.
    d. See them in school. How did their siblings, peers, and teachers treat them?

10. Imagine an angel or a guide coming to them to protect and hold them.

11. See them relax into the angel's embrace and receive love.
    a. What you do for another, you do for yourself.
    b. As you give love to your abuser, love will return to you tenfold.
    c. If you are unable to give love to this person, ask the angel to do it for you.

12. Let this new information move from your intellect and anchor in your heart.

13. Turn and face your inner child.

14. Hold them in your arms and tell them they are safe.
    a. Tell them they did not deserve the treatment they received.
    b. They have done nothing wrong, and they are perfect as they are.

15. See them receiving your love, which is self-love.

16. Hold them so close you can sense them melting into your heart.

17. Check on your inner child from time to time, do not forget they are in your heart.

18. When your memory goes back to the abusive incident, you will know your inner child requires your love, so repeat steps 13 -17.

19. Smile as you open your eyes.

There is no magic approach to clearing old childhood traumas. It takes time and willingness to let go to see things in a new light. The magic lies within you. It is a lifelong journey that I have learned to walk. Hidden in the abuse is an opportunity for greater understandings and opportunities to grow. If I had even one loving parent to nurture and protect me, I would never have had the chance to see how I could be empowered to go it alone. By looking within myself, I discovered my love of self. As a child and as an adult I had to look to a higher essence for love and support. Call it God, Spirit, angels, the wisdom of the Universe; it is all the same, and turning my attention inward and upward has been my savior.

There were strong beliefs in the 1950s: one must not make waves, don't talk about what disturbs you, and above all, your faults and shortcomings must be kept hidden. My family followed those dictates and therefore, many of us back then never understood who we really were. This pattern of not talking about what upsets us followed many children of the 50s throughout their life. Avoiding what had been bothering us for decades has its liabilities. The results are long-term stress from tucking away our true selves. The medical field understands that stress is a significant contributor to disease; and in my practice, I have seen the effects of holding stress. It takes the form of cancers that eat away at the body or Alzheimer's and dementia, which inhibit people's ability to focus in the present moment. When you don't express what's bothers you—when you don't live your truth—the mind forgets and thinks traumas, even small ones, never happened. However, the body remembers, and the old issues fester in the organs, blood, mind, and bones. But it is never too late to change this behavior and reap the rewards of a healthy, balanced life.

Releasing Repressed Feelings and Stating Your Truth

Gram's disdain for my father seemed to affect my mom, and whatever love mom had for him, she never allowed herself to feel. I lived under the umbrella of my guardians' animosity toward my father until that memorable day in July when I met him. Even though Gram had passed away fifteen years previously, Mom was still stuck in her old program, living in fear of her mother's wrath even though she would do nothing to provoke it. Mom marched to the drum Gram had played for so long, it made me question, did Mom even understand why? And, if given a chance, would she have wanted to reconcile with my father?

Did Mom consistently use good judgment during her life? Do any of us? Was it her fault I did not have a father figure in my life? I could ponder these questions and blame her, my gram, my aunts, and my father, but it would do me no good. Still, these thoughts persisted until I chose to release them on that day at Mom's gate when she could not acknowledge that my father's absence had hurt me.

Any judgment held towards another, even if it is justified, does not serve you. It delays your spiritual growth, keeps you locked in the disturbing time frame, and limits the potential to manifest your heart's desires. Releasing blame will clear that pattern in your DNA, which will also help your family and descendants move forward.

Follow *Step into Your Divine Essence* in The Courses of Action, Chapter 10, then invite the wisdom of higher beings to uncover the ways to dissolve your invalidation and pain.

Consider these questions:
o   What are the words I never felt safe expressing to this person?
o   What did they hold in their heart that they never had the strength to say to me?
o   What do I need to say to this person?
o   What would I like to hear from them?

Steps to Speak Your Truth

1. Alone in a quiet room, set up two chairs facing each other.

2. Sit in one chair and imagine the person you have judged sitting in the other.

3. Present your questions and imagine them talking. You may move and sit in their chair, as if you were them.

4. Make up the conversation in your mind.

5. It may feel pointless, but pretending primes the pump of your imagination and uncovers a path of discoveries.

6. There could be a moment when you hear a phrase that will elicit emotions.

7. It may make you angry or cry, and then you can see the situation in a new way.

8. Let go of how you think the exercise should happen, and it will free your mind to birth new perceptions.

9. Give this process time as it may not fully finish in one session. You may need to repeat it.

Another way to remove bitterness is to write how you feel in a letter, fill it with your emotions, then burn it. While looking at the flames, affirm this person no longer has a hold on you. Send their words and actions into the light. See the golden flames turn to violet flames of love that consume pain, abandonment, misgivings, distrust, or the terms that apply to your situation. The painful memories will subside and will not return to haunt you because you consumed them with love.

Reframing Stressful Situations

Stressful situations can be adjusted and calmed by creating a new perspective. With a little practice, you will find your ideas will surface without long deliberation. I was working with a young boy who was starting middle school. To protect his privacy, I will call him Trey. His trepidation came from leaving the safety of his grammar school, where he was the oldest, and moving to an unfamiliar territory where he would be among the youngest. He felt intimidated by the older children, anxious, afraid, and wanting to go home after the second day. His struggle needed to be perceived differently to change how he felt about school. His mother called me for help.

Trey was in school during our session, so I used his mom as a surrogate so that she would be able to sense any changes in him and guide me along the way. When working in this way, I have my client affirm, "I am a surrogate for …" and at the end of the treatment, they repeat, "I am no longer a surrogate for…" Then, the client does not carry the energy of the other person, once the session concludes.

Trey's angst came from walking through crowded halls with more students and louder voices than he experienced in grammar school. I felt his anxiety was not only from his present-time experience but also from another time, triggered by his DNA. Our tendencies can stem from our genetic coding, which reflects the experiences and fears of our ancestors. That coding can affect us physically, mentally, and emotionally, as seen in Trey.

My first guidance was to have Trey immerse himself in the sounds surrounding him in the halls, but I sensed that was too big a step for him. Then another thought arose. By reframing his situation, he will see his school differently, devoid of fear. I told his mom to find a program on the computer that shows sound waves. Have Trey speak into the computer to find out how his voice looks—loud, soft, and regular. I instructed her to make it a game and tell him this is a science experiment. Have him use whatever technique will hold his interest as he watches the waves change from soft curves to spikes, and be aware of the sound that makes them change. By tracking these vibrations online, he will see how sound looks. By relating to the form of sound, it may no longer scare him.

The sound became a solid form he could place in his mind while walking in the school halls. To support the process, I cleared him of past lives that had similar feelings. Later, when he applied my suggestions, he became empowered and saw things differently as the exercise sank in. His thoughts diminished from the idea that someone would hurt him to knowing the sound for what it is—merely waves of energy.

But Trey needed to do more than shut off the loud voices in the hall. He needed to feel he was safe. I approached this dilemma by showing his mom how he could be energetically invisible. When we are fearful or angry, our energy contracts around our body, where others' emotions can attach to our dense form.

If we see ourselves as the infinite beings that we are, fear and negativity would not connect because our etheric bodies would expand and not be a solid piece of sticky energy. In fear, we are flypaper, allowing the thoughts and feelings of those around us to attach and stay in our personal space. I recall a child's rhyme we would say to the kids that were being unkind, "I am rubber, you are glue, everything you say bounces off of me and sticks to you." That was an excellent way to deflect bullying.

The following exercise is similar to *Connect to Your Divine Essence* in Chapter 3 but made simpler for children. I told Trey's mom to give Trey the following imagery, pause after each picture and give him time to feel and focus on each design.

Guide for Children to be Empowered

1. Think about how your body feels when you run.

2. Now recall how it feels when you are tired and need to sleep.

3. Imagine the powerful energy of running, give it a color, and expand this color through your entire body, not just your legs.

4. Pretend you can extend that color and energy outside and around your body.

5. See if you can extend this color and energy into the room around you.

6. You have the power to push this energy into an entire building, so do it.

7. Imagine this energy as a balloon that is growing.

8. Expand it into the:
   a. entire city
   b. state or region
   c. your continent
   d. across the oceans
   e. around the globe

9. Does your body feel the same or different from when you first began? If you cannot explain the difference, it does not matter; it only matters that you sense a change.

10. Your body contains molecules. These particles have the same minerals as the stars, making you are part of the gigantic Universe.

11. You are now big, tall, invincible, and no one can harm you because you are no longer a solid form. That makes you invisible.

12. No one notices you in the hall in this expanded state unless you want them to see you.

13. Feel strong and safe.

Trey's mom informed me a few days later that the process was a success. Trey liked seeing the sound waves on the computer and being invisible. He then felt relaxed and began to enjoy school.

Another client felt negative things were always happening to him. Every time a good thing appeared, he negated it because of an adverse situation that soon followed. He said, "I was having a beautiful day, enjoying nature, while walking in the sunlight, and I was happy. Then I stepped into dog dirt, and I was wearing my favorite shoes. These are ones I cherished and kept immaculately clean, and now they are ruined because I cannot remove the dirt." Once again, he had proven to himself that good feelings don't last.

Rather than seeing his situation as a negative, I suggested he should tell himself, "Stop, change, new direction." This simple statement comes from a well-known author and speaker, Joe Dispenza. When you find yourself entering old patterns or obsessive thoughts, tell yourself, "STOP." That phrase alone halts the disturbing thought in its tracks. Saying "Change" asks your mind to adjust your thinking. Demanding a new direction tells you to reframe the situation immediately and not follow the familiar path, where old patterns reside.

I asked how old his shoes were. He told me about one year. I asked him, "Can you afford a new pair of shoes?" His reply, "Well, yes." I informed him the Universe is gifting him with a shopping spree to purchase a new pair of shoes, even cooler than those he had. With this mental image, he chuckled, and with that laughter, I knew he was breaking up and letting go of the old pattern. The common phrase, laughter is the best medicine, is especially true with emotional issues. When you bring joy into a situation, even if for just a moment, it changes the energy and redirects your thoughts.

Courses of Action

Chapter Ten

A Strange Way to Live

In this Course of Action, you will be moving forward on a path of discovery to uncover your unconscious patterns triggered by childhood experiences.

I question what drove my gram to be so controlling. Where did this tendency originate? And why could she not let it go? If I could answer these questions, my compassion for her would release my judgment and free our energies, even though she has since passed.

I believe her control came from fear. I saw her worry about the looming dangers that came with living in a large metropolis. Some of her concerns were: what if my mom, brother, and I associated with the wrong people, could we live unharmed in our city, and what might happen if my father reappeared in our lives. Keeping a tight rein was her way of loving us, but it did not serve anyone. It brought undue stress upon her and unnecessary restraint for my mom, brother, and me.

Life's traumas and experiences influence how we respond to situations. When we bump heads, argue, become angry, and act irrationally, we are usually reacting to past negative experiences. Through meditation, we can understand our adverse reactions and connect to the wisdom of our spirit. That will bring peace and allow new perceptions to form. There is no need to sit in a long contemplation to make this connection. All it requires is a shift of consciousness by directing the mind to see our irrational fears. Gram did not understand this concept.

Gram held to what she thought was right, which clouded her vision to see only her limited perspective. If she had known how to still her mind through meditation, she could have seen what was happening from a higher realm and benefited from her new perspective.

Gram never looked for the reasons why my father acted the way he did. She may have been more compassionate and understanding if she considered the following:

o   How his father's death from rabies affected him as a young boy.

o   How his growth became stifled from the effect of being raised by a controlling sister, rather than his mother.

o   How he was rarely given a chance to make his own decisions as a child, so he remained immature.

o   How the emotional trauma from fighting in WWII haunted him.

o   How his lack of self-confidence limited his ability to obtain a decent job after the war.

o   How he thought less of himself because he could not support his wife and family.

What Gram did not see and understand about herself and her family:

o   Spiritual guides reside around and support her and her grandchildren.

o   The power of the divine always protects her and her family.

o   The light around them never diminishes.

o   A difference could be made by envisioning a bright future for all their growth and advancement.

o   Her daughter had the wisdom to manifest a successful future on her own.

o   Both women could find the wisdom that could bring them happiness.

o   There was never a reason to worry.

Realizing these things could have helped Gram relax and let things happen naturally, rather than in her prescribed order. But Gram never knew how to access her divine wisdom or that she had the power to make what she desired to happen without force. This was a concept she did not grasp. Stepping into her divinity was not part of her religious training. The priests never taught her that being spiritually empowered was not moving away from God's love but closer to that divine spark.

Stepping into Your Divine Essence

1. Set your intention to feel, see, or sense your higher self—your divine essence.

2. Still your mind and body by sitting with an erect spine and taking three long, slow, deep breaths.

3. Release any concerns of the day by washing your body with light, following *Connect to Your Divine Essence* in The Courses of Action, Chapter 3.

4. Open your crown chakra and allow light to wash over you. Wait for a sensation.

5. Imagine your crown chakra connecting to the crown of the earth—a portal from where the robust love of the Universe flows.

6. Stay still, let the light fill your physical form; when your mind wanders, recall these subtle sensations.

7. You are now part of the power and love that comprise the Universe.

8. Reside in this space for as long as you are guided, knowing you are the light you seek.

9. From this place, you will make your best decisions.

10. Focus on a question and see if, in this stillness, an answer comes through.

When you judge someone else's decision, ask yourself if you are controlling or helpful. When you are close to that person or primarily affected by their actions, you could have expectations that may cloud your vision. To avoid this pitfall, call in light beings who will point out if you are the controlling one. Because guides view an individual's situation from a higher vantage point, they can see the past, present, and future timeline. They then hold the wisdom to lead us in the correct direction. Stilling your thoughts in meditation will allow their guidance to come through and wash your actions with light, showing you the right path.

Set the Stage to Transform

Children adapt to their circumstances, not questioning what is happening at the time. Their life appears normal because it is all they know. A client once shared her experience of being raised by parents who gambled. It seemed quite reasonable to be in a casino late at night and receive $20 to play video games while her parents played the slots. Abandonment has many faces. Even though she was with her parents during the night, she still had issues of being forgotten. So how do we process the loneliness of our childhood? By re-writing the script in our memory.

When our life experiences anchor a negative feeling within us, we will either follow what we have seen or do the opposite. Mom and Gram lived in fear. I could see how life's simple challenges distressed and bound them. I saw them held as prisoners in their self-designed, skewed world. As a young adult, I made a different choice. I decided to trust life. I opted that I was not going to be a part of the scene they portrayed. I was going to build a different world for myself. I was the writer, director, and star in my play; and over the years, I have designed a plan, though not perfect, which has served me well.

Gram thought she could mold us into accountable adults with her constant directions. She was doing what she supposed was right. It worked for her but not for us. I found I could release my fear of abandonment and reevaluate the burdensome circumstances of my life. I continually worked on this process, and my issues cleared, piece by piece. The feeling of loss is always there in my mind, but its frequency and intensity have reduced over time. It is uncomfortable to gaze into the past, but the gift I found by looking at my old wounds is that they scare me less each time I review them. With practice, I reframed these incidents, turning the old stories into something that no longer upset me.

Like a song that runs in your head, unable to be silenced, negative situations can do the same without the harmony found in music. I could have held onto my heartache when my father's wife did not allow him to meet my children. I was disappointed, angry, and confused. I was not there to cause anyone harm. I was not asking for money. I only wanted the attention and time, now as an adult, I was denied in my youth.

When I tried to talk to my mom about my father, she never responded with compassion. Her continued retort was, "I did the best I could." Grrrr. Her words cut into my heart like a knife, but my suffering was self-imposed. She never felt my anguish. She was merely speaking her truth. So how did I move on and stop the hurt so it would not affect me for the remainder of my life? I stepped away from the drama.

Know that you are always in control, and you write all the stories in your life. Some scripts guide us, while others hold us back from being our true selves as joyful, enlightened beings. Anytime you find yourself in a stressful situation, you may become the observer by moving off the stage and joining the audience instead of participating. By removing yourself from the limelight, you step away from the other participant's control. Drop your attachment to the struggle, and in letting go, you win.

The stories that run in your life are not new, they repeat with different characters in various locations, but the underlying triggers are often the same. In this exercise, you will not only clear the current emotions but make permanent changes by moving back in time to find the original cause of the disturbance. In the past, the old scenes occupied many of your memories. By dropping the attachment to the old scenarios, you will create a space for balanced ways to live your life. Begin by getting a clear understanding of what feeds your emotions in one situation at a time. The process that follows can be repeated as necessary.

To alleviate disturbing imagery from times gone by, see the story as a reoccurring drama that runs on a regular schedule. It is a performance that requires practice by the actors. At the start of the exercise, you are one of the performers, interacting with the people who hurt you. You will then remove yourself from the stage and become the writer and director, which lets you change the story.

To obtain a greater understanding, take a broader view of the story. Know that each disturbing memory in your life has been affected by characters that are not visible in the scene. This exercise will show you how to find these people and the triggers that repeat in your life.

o   Look at the situation. See the people in the scene as actors in a play.
o   Notice the people in the wings of the theater that are giving directions. Are those people happy?
o   How do their orders affect those in the scene?
o   Notice who else is influenced by their demands.
o   How far do the ripples of control and demands extend into your life?
o   Do you need to allow the ones you found off stage to still dictate your life?
o   From your expanded view, see if you feel empowered and hold a compassionate perspective.

Set the Stage to Silence Negative Stories

1. Tell yourself, "I will discover, access, and obtain a different understanding."

2. Sit in a quiet place, light a candle to illuminate your inner guidance.

3. Inhale deeply three times and affirm, "I am my own best guide."

4. Take a few breaths as your chest expands and your heart opens.

5. Breathe in your color of love and exhale its light around you.

6. Take time to notice how your physical, emotional, mental, and spiritual bodies respond as you breathe deeper and relax.

7. Recall the disturbing scenario you want to clear and balance.

8. Imagine everyone involved, including yourself, as actors on a stage.

9. Note your reactions as the scene plays out.

10. Who is off-stage controlling the scene? Are they helpful or a hindrance? Send them away if you want.

11. Step off the stage and become the director. Take charge of what is happening.

12. Compare how your power shifts when you are on stage while interacting with the characters and off-stage directing the scene.

13. Take time to feel the shift.

14. Become the writer and change the scene to an earlier time.

15. Once again, become the actor on stage, watch the new scene play out. Don't force anything. Open your imagination, pretend, and let new ideas flow.

16. While watching the play, can you see the original trigger that angers you today? An incident may appear that you did not recall.

17. Clear the trigger by rewriting the original core script. Change the outcome, people, and location if necessary.

18. See the performers acting out the new scene according to your direction.

19. Go over the new scene until you can bring the old story to mind and have no negative emotions.

20. Watch from the audience, and see if you feel neutral to what is happening on stage.

This practice can clear situations from the past so they no longer upset you. Continue to write and release earlier disturbances when they arise. My life journey has taught me how to reframe unhappy times from my past by looking back and shining a light upon those situations, thus supporting rather than hindering me.

Rewrite Childhood Disturbances with Self-Hypnosis

As we look back upon our childhood, we may be disappointed. Dark memories can haunt us for a lifetime, triggering old emotions that replay today. We can redirect these thoughts and alleviate our pain through self-hypnosis. Hypnosis is a deeper form of meditation that relaxes the participant so profoundly that the subconscious mind is accessed and will diminish the embedded emotional pain. Hypnotherapists are skilled in this endeavor, but as outlined in The Courses of Action Chapter 7, you can also hypnotize yourself.

Hypnotizing oneself is not difficult to learn. It starts by asking the mind to create a new memory that does not hold trauma or stress. Hypnosis will diminish the negative effect of the distressing memory, while changing the account registered in the psyche. Psychologists tell us that our recollections of an alarming situation are often inaccurate; it is called "memory distortion." The mind processes suffering and adjusts the story differently from how it might have occurred. Because the mind has changed how the situation happened, turning the memory into a new, more acceptable one is possible.

To change the experience in your memory, run through the incident numerous times until you see it the way you wish it had been. For example, to change the fear and pain associated with an auto accident, follow these steps and change the words to match what occurred for you. Remember, you are the observer and do not need to experience the pain from the past. From a higher level, your only role is to look down on the story and change it. Each time, begin moments earlier and extend the time afterward until you see the alarming incident never occurring.

1. Picture yourself driving minutes before the accident occurred.
2. See the other car heading towards you.
3. Feel your body relax and sense the impact.
4. Imagine you can exit your car unharmed.
5. Repeat the scene. This time, see yourself earlier, opening the car door and hearing the engine start.
6. As you drive, notice the sounds around you. Do you hear the radio, a voice, or something outside the car?
7. See the car approaching. It curves and does not hit you.
8. You are shaken but can continue to your destination.
9. Repeat the scene. Now imagine waking up in the morning.
10. Think about where you need to drive. Walk out of your home and into your car.
11. Hear the click as you close the car door, feel your seat belt around your body, and hear the engine start.
12. Drive down the road, recall the weather, the smell in the air, and sounds prevalent in the car.
13. See a car approaching. You swerve and miss it. You are safe.
14. See yourself arriving at your destination on time and relaxed.

Another possible traumatic memory might be that someone harmed you. Reenact that scene. Each time, see your abuser farther away from you until you envision that they have never approached you at all. Another disturbing memory might be when you made a wrong decision. See yourself doing what you wish you had. Each time you replay the scene, begin a few minutes before and end a few minutes after. Then extend that time to a few hours before and a few hours after your decision. Continue to run the story until you are neutral about what happened. You will then have erased the old memory and anchored a new one.

Hypnosis Script for a New Memory

1. Recall the disturbing incident. See yourself above the scene looking down.

2. Have the intention to register a new story in your psyche.

3. Do not influence the outcome by having expectations other than releasing anxiety. The process will evolve on its own.

4. Sit upright to allow energy to flow unobstructed through your spine. Be comfortable, warm, and alone.

5. Breathe consciously, slowly, and deeply for three to five breaths.

6. Focus on the calmness this elicits in your body.

7. Imagine a black screen before you.

8. There is a table at your side with white numbers lying on it.

9. Follow the next steps and tell yourself you will be more relaxed when you reach #10.

10. Place the #1 upon the screen, look at it for a few seconds. Let it dissolve.

11. Then place # 2 upon the screen. Let it dissolve before your eyes.

12. Continue this sequence, becoming more and more relaxed, until you have reached #10.

13. You are now deeply relaxed but will allow each proceeding step to deepen your relaxation.

14. Imagine yourself at the top of a winding staircase.

15. Slowly move down the stairs. Feel your foot touching each stair as your body descends.

16. There are seven stairs, and each takes you deeper and deeper.

17. When you reach the bottom of the stairs, a mist forms. Within the haze, a scene unfolds, revealing the memory you want to change.

18. You are not reliving this memory. You are merely the observer.

19. Change the scene to be how you wished it had played out.

20. You are in control. Make the adjustments that make you feel safe.

21. Each time the scene replays, begin the memory a few minutes earlier and extend it a few minutes later. Do this until the story starts hours earlier and ends hours later.

22. Recall the incident three to five times, each time change what happened to a more harmonious scene.

23. Run through the scene repeatedly until you feel no charge from the incident.

Remember, you are in total control. You have now registered a new story in your mind, thus alleviating the painful memory. If the incident should come to mind sometime later, remember the new, rewritten script you created in this exercise. You have the power, the strength, and the wisdom to do this. You are an enlightened being.

They Did the Best They Could

I do not believe my mom was able to acknowledge the damage my brother and I suffered because of the absence of our father. I wonder if she buried it away deep in her psyche because she did not know how to repair that schism. I know Mom loved us, and didn't realize how we felt when she kept our father from us. She was unable to understand that perhaps she had a hand in what went askew in our lives. She held to her truth, "I did the best I could," which to me at the time meant, too bad, deal with it, it's not my fault. That was not what she was saying but is what I heard, and every time she said it, I was triggered. Her words sent me back in time, and I was no longer responding to the situation at the moment and thinking logically. Our communication dropped out, I didn't want to hear her, and I created scenarios in my mind that were not necessarily true.

I held onto the idea that Mom was not taking responsibility for her past actions, and that was confirmed when I asked her to say I'm sorry for what happened, and she could not respond. Then I understood that she could not process my father's disappearance, and I stopped blaming her. It was me who had harbored resentment; therefore, I was the one who needed to release that opinion, not Mom. Forgiveness is a form of judgment because something needs to be perceived as wrong in order to be forgiven.

Even though my father left long ago, my internal dialogue of blame still ran in my head, but I had an opportunity to stop it. To respond to my request, Mom would have to face the role she played in my child-rearing, which would be painful, and I assume that's why she couldn't answer me. That day, at her redwood gate, we were locked and justified in our stories. Once I stopped judging Mom, my critical nature changed. I did it by seeing her as a woman scorned. I visualized her hiding behind a wall that she built around her heart.

Once I saw that Mom could not respond to my request, I stepped into the sun to live my life, free from the unspoken struggle of our relationship. Later I saw Mom more relaxed in my presence because I know she no longer felt I resented her. The beauty of facing my emotional pain was that it eliminated the misery my mom carried as well. Having the desire to overcome the anxiety held by the family heals all parties. It happens with clear intent, love, and maintaining a heart connection.

My mom and father closed their hearts after their divorce, and it left them feeling, like me, abandoned. When a relationship ends, the pain from the loss of love can be as devastating as death. When love is lost, one moves on but may feel that there is a part missing. How often do we shut down our hearts and close people out for fear of being hurt again? After meeting my father, I found out how he had felt and how he had carried his pain. He had lost all that he loved, his wife and the children that were so important to him. He had to go on somehow to live his life without us. Running away was not the best choice, but it was the one he chose.

I began to look at the pain families endure after a divorce. Children often become possessions, used as pawns, for parents to bargain with and use to get their way. These actions have lasting emotional effects, injuring the children and all involved throughout their lifetime. Some people are reluctant to show their emotions, but their hurt feelings are still there. When divorced couples show more compassion for each other, the children profit, but we all work from our injured upbringing. Once again, I recall my mom saying, "I did the best I could."

The heart is a muscle, and each time it is hurt, it tightens, making it challenging to be vulnerable in a new relationship. This pattern can become a habit, lodging in the subconscious, where it begins to repeat. When entering a new love relationship, one might instinctively draw in a partner who will act similar to one from the past. These people play into our old programming. Triggers become activated, and it feels familiar, thus comfortable. Then we are replaying and strengthening the past destructive patterns. Once we acknowledge that we are the love we seek, the void from a broken relationship will not fill with another unbalanced one. Self-love will break this old pattern as we see ourselves in a new light as a loving being who attracts love.

Create Self-Love with the Violet Light

Loving ourselves will attract a loving partner, but the mind requires an image of self-love before creating the same. The following exercise will describe how to do this. The body maintains a temperature of about 98.6, yet at death, this heat immediately fades. The question is, what is the source of this heat? Esoterically, let's see it reflected as a flame. Rather than a red and yellow glow, see this fire as violet to represent love. In a rainbow, violet resides at the top, giving it hierarchy over the other colors in the spectrum. Because love stands above all other emotions, tying love to the color violet makes sense. The mind now will have an image to reference when calling in self-love.

Not only will this picture activate a loving feeling, but you can imagine the flame encompassing your entire body to alleviate pain, disease, and discomfort. Once felt in the body, love can be directed to a specific body part, place, or person. Sharing this essence does not diminish its power within you because the more love we share, the more is available. The following daily practice will build self-love.

Activating Self-Love with the Violet Flame

1. Quite your mind, sit comfortably, be warm, and stop all outside communication.

2. Consciously listen to and feel your breath and notice your sensations as they change.

3. You may feel a mild vibration, the air around you lifting, or sense energy expanding out from your body.

4. Maintain this awareness for a few minutes before moving on.

5. Focus your attention on the center of your chest. Envision the violet flame in your heart and notice if it is warm or cool.

6. Allow the flame to grow into the four chambers of your heart.

7. Expand the light into the pericardium sac around your heart.

8. Continue moving the flame into your lungs.

9. Ask yourself how did each expansion feel? Did the flame pulse, undulate, or move in some way?

10. Make the flame grow and rise to your neck—throat chakra—and then drop to your stomach—solar plexus chakra. Look for a shift in your body.

11. Widen the flame to extend around your arms and back.

12. Let the violet flame descend past your navel —the sacral chakra—while simultaneously rising to touch your forehead—third eye chakra.

13. Expand the flame to reach the top of your head—crown chakra, at the same time, it drops past the tailbone—base chakra—and out your feet.

14. Give yourself time to notice how your body feels wrapped in love.

15. When you are ready, direct the flame to spin around your body. Place physical or emotional distress in this flame for healing.

16. Take all the time you need. Do not rush the process.

17. Relax by imagining you are lighter and free from distress and pain.

18. Slow down the spinning movement of the flame.

19. Send the flame of love to a person or place that needs help.

20. Picture the flame transforming and calming their situation.

21. Focus back on your body, allow the flame to diminish to the size of your heart while the color grows in intensity.

22. Observe if you feel different from when you began the process.

23. Stay in this space until you become aware of sounds in the room.

24. Repeat this practice daily. You have now activated and felt self-love.

Connecting to Light Beings

Our astronauts are lucky to spend time in the infinite cosmos. What they see changes their world. Many return with a different life focus. Back on earth, they seek knowledge to explain what they had felt and sensed on their journey in outer space. Some move deeper into organized religions, others research spirituality, and a few run from what they experienced with alcohol and drugs. Whatever their path, they all came back altered. If you would like to touch the infinite Universe, follow the next exercise.

Beyond our earth lies a place so vast that its existence is hard to fathom. It is the source of unconditional love. When your life appears to be falling apart, look at pictures of the cosmos to calm your senses. Search for photos taken by the Hubble Telescope on NASA's website. Make the image as large as you can and meditate upon these pictures. Tell yourself this is the look of love. Wash your mind and body with its cleansing colors. It just may clear the thoughts that have been dragging you down.

Light beings—deities, angels, and guides—can also direct you to an uplifting thought when you feel sorrow, guilt, or blame. Once you find these beings, you can easily connect to them. To make it easy, pretend the beings are by your side, and you will sense a shift that tells you they are with you. On the other hand, if you think this will be a difficult task, your mind will follow your thoughts.

You can practice alleviating pain, either physical or emotional, by handing your discomfort to a light being for transformation. By feeling the subtle differences throughout your body, you will begin to raise your consciousness. If you have been applying the exercises, you will find, by now, that you can enter a deep state of relaxation with only three deep breaths. Try it and see what happens.

Enlist Help from a Light Being

1. Begin this practice by knowing that light beings are available and ready to help you.

2. Walk away from the distractions of people and communication devices.

3. Sit comfortably with an erect spine and become present in your body.

4. Take three slow deep breaths to still your mind and body.

5. Ask for a light being to come and stand by your side.

6. Imagine their presence by sensing a soft brush on your cheek, hands resting on your shoulders, or a temperature change.

7. If you feel nothing, create a sensation to tell your doubting mind the unseen being is real.

8. Share your feeling of pain and sadness with this presence.

9. Describe your disturbing emotion or pain; give it a shape, color, and texture. Hand the image to the light being.

10. See the being dissolving that image and removing any of its residue from your energy field.

11. Feel the shift in your body.

12. Watch the being as it fills your body with light and builds a new light grid where the discomfort had been.

13. Ask the being to whisper positive thoughts to you daily. Remind yourself to look for their message.

14. Each day ask them to give you a sign to show that they are with you.

15. Once you have addressed all your needs, thank the light being for their help.

Expand Your Energy to Avoid Feeling Drained

By expanding your divine essence, you can access the high-energy field of the Universe. In that state, not only will you feel your power, but you will not be affected by the negativity of people or an adverse situation. If you feel a person or situation is draining you, this exercise will alleviate that problem.

When you are stressed, angry, confused, or agitated, it could be from taking on another person's struggles. To clear that sensation, even if it's negativity you created, try this quick release. Negative emotions contract your energy, and positive feelings expand it. Think of something that brings you joy. In that happy state, you will feel light and expanded. Then recall an upsetting person or event. Notice if your body feels tight, dense, or uncomfortable.

When you are criticized and judged, you could unconsciously constrict and tighten your energy to protect your heart. This creates a solid form where the disparaging concepts can attach, aggravate, and stay in your thoughts. By expanding your energy, the molecules around your etheric bodies spread out, and negativity flows through you rather than attaching. In this expanded state, people's actions don't upset you.

One way to expand your energy field is by imagining your entire body portrayed on a computer screen. Enlarge the picture by pretending to tap the + key on the keyboard until you see your form only as pixels. Continue your experiment and move the pixels farther apart until the distance from one pixel to the next is the vast space between the stars. Feel the space created in your body. Does it feel light, cool, or another sensation you can sense but can't quite describe? You have now become part of the infinite Universe, and nothing can attach to you—no angry words, judgments, fear, disease, remorse, or sadness. You are free from anything projected at you or old beliefs that you no longer need to follow. This may include information from the media, dogmas, education, intimate partners, family members, co-workers, or those you feel are wiser than yourself.

Use the following exercise to free yourself from the negativity of others—fast. Expand your energy and then recall an upsetting person or incident and see if your energy stays expanded. If not, repeat the expanding process. After you have once touched the Universe, you can then accelerate the process, and it will only take seconds to be in this powerful mode.

Free Yourself from Negativity

1. Run through this exercise a few times to lock in full-body awareness. Then you will be able to expand in seconds.

2. No need to sit. Just stop moving and still your thoughts.

3. Notice how the air feels around your body. Does it buzz, feel solid, or something else?

4. As earlier in The Courses of Action, Chapter 3, follow *Connect to Your Divine Essence* and expand your energy into the cosmos. Once you have applied this practice, your expansion will take only a few seconds.

5. Recall a disturbing incident while in this expanded state.

6. Does your energy contract? If so, repeat the process until you can keep expanded while thinking of the adverse incident.

7. Always use this expanding exercise before entering a difficult conversation, starting a creative project, or needing to feel empowered.

Courses of Action
Chapter Twelve

THE LAST STRAW

My parents did not handle confrontations well. Because their parents were strict, they followed the beliefs and religious doctrines set before them without question. No one rocked the boat, and they blindly abided by the unrealistic demands presented, leaving them to struggle through life. The stress from the Great Depression and World War II, depleted their emotional strength, leaving them unable to recognize their hearts' desires and, if known, how to follow them. They had no self-help books or psychologists to guide and instruct them towards healthy encounters with the people in their lives. Today, many publications, counselors, and coaches have found ways to awaken the unconscious mind of seekers, uncovering the path into mindfulness. Still, one needs to search for this knowledge, it may not come knocking on your door, and if it does, you must invite it in.

After my parents' blow-up, I assume they lacked the communication skills to sit down and talk calmly. They allotted no time to explore and accept their differences. My mom or father did not apologize for their fiery actions, thus creating resistance to resolve their conflicts. The art of patience and timing was a practice they had not learned, sadly making their time together brief.

Why Communication Drops Out

In the heat of an argument, old triggers appear, coloring the present situation. The words expressed are interpreted wrong, diminishing communication. Both parties begin to talk at the same time, neither listening to the other nor communicating clearly. They have disconnected from the current conflict, acting out old patterns that have nothing to do with their present situation. The ability to hear what their partner is expressing and feeling is gone.

No one is listening to the other person because each party is busy thinking about what they want to say next, not what is being expressed at the time. At the same time, their minds have taken a sabbatical from the current conflict, which stops any new information from filtering in.

Arguments with significant people in life often fall back to previous conflicts. The words may be different, but the underlying aggravation is still the same. It is a pattern that activates the same emotions, creating the same reactions, leaving the typical unresolved feelings.

Can you stop this behavior? You bet. It takes only one party to change the direction of the conversation. If one party does not react, the heated confrontation will cool down. Compare this action to the children's game tug of war, where both sides hold a rope and attempt to pull the other group over a designated line. The only reason the game continues is that each team is creating resistance. Once the cord is dropped, the struggle is over, and the game ends. Apply this tactic to a conflict by not resisting your partner. Stop the push-pull, drop the rope, and look at the argument from a new vantage point. Without opposition, there is an opportunity for solutions to surface and come to light.

During the acceleration of an argument, there is not enough vital life force to make proper adjustments. It becomes difficult to stop your automatic responses and act differently. There are ways to analyze the matter, free from past emotions, thus eliminating your unbalanced reactions. It becomes best to stop talking and agree to address the issue at a later time. Retreat and look at the problem from a neutral place where you are the observer and no longer engaged. The information gathered in this way will come in handy. When couples discuss what transpired, they can find a new perspective that can clear the air at a calmer time. Then each party may express feelings devoid of anger. Practicing being the viewer stops fueling reactive behaviors and opens the door to hear what your partner is feeling and why.

Identifying the core incident does not happen in the moment of a heated discussion, rarely are you addressing the matter at hand. So, what is feeding this disturbance? Trust me; it is coming from your past experiences. The illusion is that the other party is taking your power, but no one can take anything from you; you give it to them. You create the reality you perceive; therefore, you can change it.

After an argument, ask yourself:
- o What were my unconscious thoughts that were running?
- o How many times did I automatically react to their words without understanding why?
- o Did I let my emotions run me?
- o Could I possibly be running old patterns so profoundly rooted that I'm are unaware of how unbalanced my behavior has become?
- o Are my childhood incidents affecting this relationship?

Conversing From a Neutral Place

When involved in controlling interpersonal relationships, when people criticize your choices and make you feel wrong, you can regain your power by releasing their judgment. In arguments, whether between intimate partners, business associates, friends, or family, triggers are activated from our memories, patterns, and even from our ancestors via our DNA. Other than what we see and hear, an underlying network picks up nuances beyond what is said through our chakras and etheric bodies in the aura. As discussed previously, there are three unseen etheric forms. They are, as aforementioned, the emotional body close to our skin, the mental body next, and the spiritual body eighteen to thirty-six inches out from the physical body. In a dispute, not only are the chakras fired up—emotions are activated in the solar plexus chakra, memories in the mind or third eye chakra, and sadness in the heart chakra—but know the etheric bodies become unbalanced as well. We receive information through our emotions, thoughts, and even from higher planes of spirituality. To calm the situation, set angry or controlling words outside these etheric forms so that you can respond free from the past. Let's look at how you can place discussions outside the chakras and aura, so neither individual will be triggered.

Anger and judgment can stir and feed negative patterns. You might not realize it, but by arguing, you are pushing your ideas into the other person's personal energy field, negating what they are presenting. The result is noncommunication exactly when communication is most needed.

As you present your ideas neutrally by imagining words typed on a virtual computer screen, outside your spiritual bodies, the agitation will start to diminish. Allow the other individual's comments to appear on the screen along with yours. In this way, the other person's beliefs can be seen free from their past conflicts that might be clouding the current situation. The process of visualizing the confrontation as words on a screen may appear too simple to work, but it does.

This procedure can be used to clear the air after a disagreement, allowing space for reconciliation. Once you have grasped this idea and have seen how it works, you may share your experience with your partner, and they can also use this technique. You will be better able to follow these steps after mastering the concept by visualizing the practice. Then merely seeing the computer screen during the discussion will diffuse the heat of the argument. It is a simple act of not allowing your frustration to be held in the body. Keep the emotions and frustration at arm's length from your body and theirs. Then the words spoken will not spark old issues.

The process enacted at the moment creates the best results, but, if not possible, addressing the issues hours or days later will rebalance your feelings. If no solution arises during the confrontation, suggest returning at a designated time to resolve the problem. Visualize a computer, fill it with compassion and love, and place the issue into the computer. Here it resides in a respectful space where you and the other's ideas can blend. A new approach will form over time, fostered by the combination of your positive energies and love, even when you are not thinking about it. Love transforms the struggle into an answer that will anchor your relationship in harmony.

Eliminate Control and Anger

1.   During a disagreement, take a moment and deepen your breath.

2. Hold your tongue and do not respond immediately.

3. Create a calm place in your mind by imagining a computer screen filled with your heart's love and their words stopping at that screen.

4. Do not allow their control or anger to enter your body's energy field.

5. Place onto the screen what they are presenting, void of any emotions that could cloud your vision.

6. Imagine words, feelings, and emotions expressed by each of you registering on the screen rather than in your bodies, where emotions can get triggered.

7. Make sure when you respond back to them, your words are on the screen and not pushed into their mental or emotional body.

8. Allow the words to remain in the computer's field of love when the issue is not resolved. Revisit the issue together at a later agreed-upon date.

9. Apply this process at the moment for the best results. If not cleared, revisit the practice to remove remaining anger, resentment, or judgment.

I know a man who used this process in business at his Monday morning staff meetings. Before the meeting, he would enter the room and imagine a computer, filled with compassion and love, in the center of the conference table. Once the employees arrived, he imagined their ideas and concerns on the screen and not directed at one group or individual. The meeting always went well.

After a heated discussion, take time to be by yourself and invite nature to come in and calm you. If it is cold outside, bundle up and take a walk. Notice how the brisk air feels on your face. Look at what surrounds you where there is no turmoil. This will bring you back into the present time and away from the memory of the fight. Be aware of nature—plants, trees, water, clouds, and sky. Each time your mind wanders back to the disturbance, tell it to stop! Then redirect your attention to what you see around you.

Mend a Broken Heart

Aunt Mary and Mom lost what they deemed to be the love of their life, and they never dated after that. Sometimes people fool themselves into thinking they will never find love again and that love happens only once. Love does not have an expiration date. People protect their broken hearts and fear they will never manifest a new intimate partner. So it was for these two women. I wonder if their renewed friendship was because they realized how their lives had mirrored each other.

The relationships we have, and they do not need to be intimate, allow us not to judge our differences and accept each other as we are. Each association shows us how we can be compassionate, kind, and loving to others. There is not just one person who can fulfill our desires. There could be many. Love can be found by venturing out into new horizons, but those steps take courage. Life experiences give us the chance to acquire knowledge, avoid our past misgivings, and adopt a loving partner if we choose. We have an opportunity to grow through these new, yet-to-be-discovered, relationships. The heart is a muscle that needs exercise, just like all muscles. Intimate relationships fill this need.

Find the Love of Your Life

Affirm:
- o   I was born to give and receive love.
- o   Who I am is more than enough to be worthy of love.
- o   I am perfect the way I am and can have great love in my life.

Though not a new concept, loving yourself is the first step in attracting a balanced partner, but how can you create self-love. First, be aware of limiting ideas that might have been running throughout your life:
- o   I am not good enough.
- o   I am not loveable.
- o   I ask for too much in a relationship.
- o   I need to lower my standards so I will not end up alone.
- o   There is no one out there that will fit my needs.
- o   All the right people are taken.
- o   There is no one in my age bracket.
- o   Why try anymore?

These thoughts, contrary to your heart's desire, may not be only your creation. They could come from a projected idea in the collective consciousness, stories in the media, or ancestral beliefs. You can stop this kind of thinking by familiarizing yourself with the power you hold inside, where there is no room for negative thoughts. By seeing and feeling the source of love within, you build self-respect and self-worth that attracts loving people to you. As in *Create Self-Love with the Violet Light* in The Courses of Action, Chapter 11, self-love is seen as an image to allow your mind to manifest the same. Once you can feel the love you hold inside, recall:

o   What are your actions that make people smile?
o   What do you like about yourself?
o   What have people told you they like about you?
o   What do you know you do better than others?
o   Where do you excel?
o   When did you make someone happy?

Creating Self-Love

1.   See each of your positive qualities as an image. It could be a heart, smiley face, sun, star, flower, or whatever comes to mind.

2.   Imagine holding all of these icons in your arms.

3.   There are many times you have demonstrated these qualities, so allow the images to replicate.

4.   As they replicate, your arms are unable to hold them all.

5.   They overflow onto the ground and bless the earth.

6.   Feel the love you have given out, and know that love will always return to you.

7.   How do you feel now—happy, satisfied, or something better?

Acquiring Your Heart's Desire

Your emotions feed the manifestation of your dreams. Without this fuel, dreams stay as illusions, suspended in your mind, and never happen. In this practice, you will imagine moving through everyday routines with the knowledge you have accomplished your wish. Feeling and visualizing that you already have what you desire will make it happen sooner. You will not focus on the steps to achieve your goal, only on the sensation of the joy of living your heart's desire.

1. Think of the thing you would like to create in your life.

2. Take a few moments to feel what it will be like when you have accomplished your desire.

3. See how your life has transformed.

4. Imagine driving, walking, or riding to the grocery store.

5. Because you are happily living your dream, smile at the people passing by.

6. Enter the store and move to the produce section. While picking up an item, your eyes meet another person. Being content, you are more social and begin a friendly conversation.

7. Continue shopping, and because your heart is open, you continue to interact with others when appropriate.

8. At the checkout stand, smile as you pay your bill, noticing you have more than enough money for your purchase.

9. Walk back to your form of transportation and head home. What time of the year is it? The season could be a clue to when your manifestation will occur.

10. While putting away your groceries, sense a warmth around you because you have achieved your heart's desire.

Healing from a Broken Relationship

When a relationship dissolves, it helps to establish a new way of recalling the past, free from judgment, anger, sadness, and hurtful memories. In an alliance, whether intimate, family, or business, there are three entities involved; you, the other person, and the formation of the relationship, which is an entity as well, one which binds to your souls. Your combined experiences create this form, and it endures until you release it. After a break-up, emotions can continue to run when this entity is not removed, making your heart hurt. Strong feelings may make you want to return to the old broken relationship, even though you know it is not wise. Here you are out-of-control and addicted to the memories.

To reclaim your power and move on, you need to release the relationship entity. Once it has been addressed and nurtured, the dissolving of the entanglement can take place. Follow these steps.

Becoming Free From a Past Relationship

1. In the quiet of your mind, think of your past partner and all their positive qualities.

2. Imagine the entity of your relationship.
    a. Give it a color, shape, and form that holds the energy you created together.
    b. Make it real, because it is.

3. List your good times together. It is important to feel gratitude for those times.

4. How to practice gratitude and being in oneness
    a. Sense the love you embody by using *Activating Self-Love with the Violet Flame* in The Courses of Action, Chapter 11.
    b. Imagine yourself in nature on a beautiful sunny day, sitting by a lake. The sun is sparkling on the water, and there is a gentle breeze.
    c. In this space, picture yourself in the water, floating on the warm surface, relaxed and calm.
    d. Reduce yourself into a tiny drop of water in the lake.
    e. Imagine your drop expanding into the entire lake
        i.   You are in the center and the edge of the lake at the same time.
        ii. You are one with the water.

    f.   Notice the sunlight glistening on the surface of the lake. It is sparkling on you.

        i.   As you did with the water drop, expand to be one with the sun and the Universe.

        ii.   Feel this for a moment.

    g.   Return your attention to the surface of the water.

    h.   Look around at what surrounds the lake. It could be trees, plants, or flowers.

    i.   Picture yourself at one with what you see.

    j.   From the sensation of oneness you felt in the sky and nature, allow that sensation to move into gratitude for the beauty you have observed.

5.   Hold onto this feeling of gratitude while thinking about when you first met your former partner and how you were attracted to each other.

    a.   What positive qualities drew you to them?

    b.   Even if it's a business relationship, there was something you considered valuable.

    c.   Take time to recall this thoroughly.

6.   Thank the relationship entity for all that it has given you.

7.   Tell this form you are releasing it back into the love of the Universe and see it begin to expand.

8.   Allow the entity to change from a solid form into tiny particles that join the oneness you felt in nature.

9.   You are no longer bound to the entity of the relationship because it no longer exists.

10.   Feel released from any angst that this relationship caused you in the past.

11.   Visualize what it feels like to be in a balanced, loving relationship using the previous exercise, *Acquiring Your Heart's Desire*.

12.   Know you have put the past behind you and are moving forward on a new enlightened path.

Courses of Action
Chapter Thirteen

THE FINAL CURTAIN

In care, Mom always had loving caretakers, doctors, and nurses, but the day I first heard the doctor confirm she had dementia, I did not find the staff sensitive to my needs. I did not expect their findings, and I was shocked. The nurse told me, "Your mom's case is so severe we suggest you do not take her to her home but place her in care immediately." "I can't do that," I told her. "I need to think this through." Again the nurse reiterated, "No, you need to do it today!" I broke down and cried, and the nurse's uncompassionate response was, "Would you like me to give you something for that?"

That was her solution? To drug me so that I couldn't feel my emotions. I was not there to make this nurse feel comfortable. I had a right to how I felt, and I would not mask it with medication. I thanked her for the offer, left her office, and went to find my mom.

Mom and I left the building; Mom being unaware of her fate, and me scrambling for what to do next. I thought there was time to think this through, but Mom made it clear exactly what she needed within a few days. While visiting Mom, I was in her kitchen and found a burned-out cigarette that she had forgotten and had left sitting on the edge of the cabinet. I knew then, Mom was not safe living alone. I often traveled for my business; therefore, I could not care for her. My only option was to find her a safe place to stay, immediately.

My quest began by first envisioning the perfect place for my mom, whom I loved. I kept a positive mental attitude, and I never doubted I could manifest a place that would suit her to make her transition smooth. I visited a few elder homes in my neighborhood; though close, they did not seem quite right. Then, I recalled my friend Loretta whom I knew from the metaphysical community with which I associated. She had recently opened an assisted-care facility in a small home in Parker, Colorado.

Loretta is a soft-spoken, compassionate, intelligent woman who is well versed in caring for those who have Alzheimer's and dementia. At one time, she was the president of the Colorado Assisted Living Association. I trusted that Loretta would love, protect, and understand Mom and help her move to her next phase. Throughout our lives, we gravitate towards people in our age bracket with similar interests and intelligence. At this point, it seemed only natural for Mom to be in a facility with her peers. It became clear that placing Mom in Loretta's loving care was the best approach, yet it was not an easy choice for me to make.

Because of Mom's mental state, she was not capable of understanding that she had dementia. She was in denial. Therefore, to ease her stress, I did not tell her of my plan to bring her to Loretta's. I decided to take Mom by myself, feeling I did not need any support. My good friend at the time, Shirley, persuaded me to allow her to join us. In hindsight, I am so glad she did.

I told Mom I had errands in the nearby town of Parker, Colorado, and asked if she would like to come along. Mom never refused. We picked up Shirley and drove through the pine trees, ranches, and open space in Parker. It was a sunny day, we could see the entire mountain range, and I was glad to see that Mom was calm. I told Mom we were close to another friend, and we were going to say hello. Loretta's assisted-care home was in a small ranch home and looked like many other houses in the area, so Mom did not suspect anything. We sat in Loretta's living room and talked for a while so that Mom could become familiar with Loretta. I told Mom I would be traveling for business and she could stay with Loretta for a few days. Mom said, "Oh, I'll be fine alone." We bantered back and forth for a short time, and then Loretta motioned that I should leave. I tried to hold back my tears as I rose to leave. Then Mom shouted out to me, "You are not going to leave me here, young lady."

It took only a second for her words to register. Her tone and the words "young lady" took me back in time to my childhood. She would call me that when she was most angry with me. It always disempowered me. That day as an adult, her words had the opposite effect. Now, I was empowered. I saw myself as the wise adult I had grown to be. I looked back, and Loretta's compassionate eyes again directed me to leave. I walked out the door, knowing I made the right and only choice for Mom. I was so grateful to have Shirley with me as I drove away. Shirley's support that day was invaluable.

I called Loretta later that day to see how Mom was adjusting to her new surroundings. Loretta said. "Your Mom is very angry with you, but it won't last more than a week or two. Your Mom does not know the difference between days or weeks, so she will not realize how long you have been gone. There is no reason for you to feel her wrath." The next day I met Loretta at a restaurant to give her Mom's clothing and personal items. Every few days, I would call to see if Mom's anger had subsided. The answer was always, "Not yet." Two weeks turned into a month; the month turned into two, and Loretta finally said, "It does not appear that your Mom is going to change. Perhaps you should just come to see her."

I prepared to face Mom's animosity by meditating before I drove to her new home in Parker. Then I recalled the Tonglen Buddhist practice I learned from Pema Chödrön, a Buddhist monk. The practice embraces the idea that one can breathe in the suffering of another to release their pain. I knew I would not take on Mom's anger because I often had used *Connect to Your Divine Essence* in The Courses of Action, Chapter 3, and I knew in my expanded state that negativity would have no place to attach to me.

The practice of Tonglen begins by clearing the mind while listening to the calming sound of a gong or Tibetan Tingsha Bells. As the sound diminishes, the mind becomes still. When the mind and heart are open, there is no place for anything to become stuck. Therefore begin by breathing in suffering which has the quality of claustrophobia which is tight, thick, heavy, dark, and hot. Then breathe out the quality and texture of spaciousness and let it move out in all directions into the entire room. The out-breath is experienced as light, cool, open, and radiating from every pore of the body. Continue breathing in this way, allowing the in- and out-breath to become the same length.

With an expanded heart, your in-breath becomes the compassionate action of breathing in pain and suffering. You may bring to mind a specific concern. The out-breath expands, wishing to be free of suffering and happy. This out-breath is filled with peace, love, joy, and kindness. Once you have fully realized suffering, you can then switch to include the pain and suffering of all sentient beings of the world. Your out-breath brings peace and love to all who suffer, including you.

Before I left to visit Mom, I applied the Tonglen practice. I breathed in Mom's anger and suffering, and I breathed out peace and love. I continued breathing in this way for a few minutes. Then I extended my compassion out to the world by breathing in the anger and suffering from anyone in the world that was feeling the same as Mom, and I breathed out peace and love. I didn't measure the time as I was so deep into the process. When I stopped, I felt utterly calm and at peace. Just before I walked out the door, the phone rang—this was before cell phones. It was Loretta. "Loretta, I was just leaving to come to visit Mom." "Marnie, I don't know what happened, but your Mom is so calm, and she is not angry with you anymore." Relieved, I drove to Mom and found her happy to see me, and so it was from that day forward.

One day I was at Mom's place, and she was upset about something. Loretta suggested that I go into the other room, and she would talk with Mom and meet me there in a few minutes. Loretta came into the room and said, "Your mom is okay now." After talking a bit with Loretta, I left to bid Mom goodbye. I found her quietly listening to a meditation CD that Loretta had played for her to calm Mom's nerves. Mom looked at me and said, "I love listening to this." "Mom, that's me. That is my CD." "No," she said. "Yes, Mom," and I opened the cover and showed her my face. She stared at my picture in disbelief and looked up at me, speechless and confused. I kissed her on the forehead and departed. All the way home, I had a smile on my face.

Tonglen Practice

1.   Calm your mind by using one of these techniques:
     a.   Take three deep breaths
     b.   Listen to the sound of a gong or Tibetan Tingsha Bells until the sound is almost gone
     c.   Follow the guidance used in *Connect to Your Divine Essence* in The Courses of Action, Chapter 3

2.   In this peaceful state, breathe in the quality and texture of claustrophobia. It is constricted, thick, dark, heavy, and hot.

3.   Feel your heart expand to receive these qualities. Then they will not adhere to you.

4.   Breathe out cool, light, open, spacious energy in 360° from every pore of your body.

5. Continue breathing in this way until your breath becomes synchronized, making the in-and-out breaths equal in length.

6. Focus on the suffering you would like to relieve from another or yourself.

7. Breathe in their suffering. It is hot, constricted, and dark.

8. Breathe out peace and love. It is cool, open, and bright.

9. Continue breathing and visualizing for a few more minutes.

10. Change your focus and breathe in the same type of suffering of every being on earth, including yourself.

11. Breathe out peace and love to all of those beings, including yourself.

12. Continue until you feel deep peace. Then your practice is complete.

Loretta's home was perfect for about a year, but then Mom became confused and difficult to manage as her disease advanced. She did not understand why young women were giving her directions and medication. Other times, Mom felt this was her home and would awaken in the night, not knowing why other people were in what she thought was her house. Once again, to locate a new place for Mom, I kept my thoughts positive, knowing a more suitable location would manifest.

Mom usually seemed happy in her surroundings, but one day at Loretta's, Mom had a moment of lucidity and expressed how she felt. Loretta told her one of the residents passed in the night. Mom said, "We would not want to wish her back to live like this." It made me sad to see that sometimes, not often, she was aware of her condition.

I kept seeing Mom in an appropriate facility, and my positive focus paid off when one of my students mentioned Garden Terrace, a home that is part of the Life Care Centers of America. These centers are designed by a doctor who created a place with a philosophy where he would be comfortable leaving his grandmother. Upon my visit, I was pleased with what I found. I walked through well-maintained gardens, sat in the ice cream parlor, observed the activities in each wing and saw caregivers interacting with the residents. It appeared to be a good place.

I was concerned that Mom would be agitated by this move. Much to my surprise, she adjusted to her new surroundings immediately. The staff were in uniforms and wore name tags, so Mom felt she was in a hospital. The length of her stay was never an issue because her short-term memory had diminished to a point where she never questioned when it was time to go home. Mom often commented, "The doctors and nurses are so nice here."

Mom spent the last eleven years of her life free from the responsibilities that had riddled her with anxiety. She had worked when women did not receive the same pay as their male counterparts who held the same jobs. She was always afraid the company would fire her if she let her needs to be known. Other fears kept her from driving. Traveling to work became a challenge as the city grew and her employer moved into the suburbs, where public transportation was less accessible. Going to work on public transit would take Mom two hours, yet she hardly missed a day. She carried the financial burden of our household for over twenty years. The pressure she was under often manifested in her body as migraine headaches and digestive disorders. Strange as it seems, being afflicted with dementia gave her the peace she longed for her entire life.

Mom's new home became a place where people cared about her, from the residents to the nurses and aids. Even the lady who cleaned her room was fond of her. One day I saw a new purple plant in Mom's room. I inquired as to its origin. The cleaning lady admitted, "Your mom said she likes violets, so I bought her one." Her caring action brought tears to my eyes; I know her income was meager, yet she spent her hard-earned dollars on my mom. All is not lost when our loved ones are in care. Something special is happening. Keep your eyes open to recognize it.

There are times when finances dictate that we need to care for our loved ones ourselves, but when money is available for assisted care, do not let guilt keep you from making that choice. If you keep them at home when you know they need additional care, you can create undue stress on them and yourself. That can hinder the one you are trying to protect. Advanced care allows your elder to process their earthly lives with peace while they prepare for the next stage. Sometimes people are concerned that they are doing them an injustice. Au contraire, my friend, you are doing them an excellent service, and in time you will reap the joy of seeing how they fit into their new environment.

The first few years with Mom in care were sad for me. I missed my mom. I wanted her to be part of our family's life, join in my children's weddings, know her great-grandchildren, and have conversations with me. It took some time but, eventually, I saw I was only thinking of my needs. In assisted care, Mom was relaxed and free from worries. She was living the life that was right for her. Every day, she allowed me the opportunity to accept her as she was and relinquish my opinions that, in her situation, she should be living her life any differently. When I stopped making her disease about how it affected me, my sadness diminished.

When you decide that your loved one needs more care than you can provide, your positive mental attitude will make the transition easier. Recall the guidance in Understanding Meditation and Basic Meditation at the beginning of Part II, Courses of Action, and then meditate on the best situation for your loved one. Don't doubt the power of positive thought. Having a clear intention will make things go smoothly. Envision and feel your family member being relaxed and in their new place. The key to success is to sense your choice manifesting. In meditation, you don't need to focus on the steps to take. That will appear later.

Manifest the Best Care for Your Loved One

o   Know and feel, in every fiber of your being, that you will find the right place.
o   Imagine your loved one in a harmonious and caring place.
o   Never let your focus diminish.
o   Be still and see yourself walking out of the facility with joy.
o   See yourself talking to a kind and compassionate staff.
o   See your loved one making friends and interacting with other residents

Once you have decided on a facility, acquaint yourself with the staff. They can give you a clear perspective on your loved one's situation. Just sitting alone with your loved one provides limited information. I found my conversations with Mom decreasing over the years, but her caretakers, who were with her daily, observed a side of Mom that only they could see. The time I took to be with the nurses and inquire about what they saw was invaluable.

We think we know how our loved ones should be cared for, but their needs have changed. They are now with trained staff who know how to best support them. We remember the parent or spouse that we knew before their dementia. That is not who they have become. They are evolving and are not who they once were—but this is not always bad.

Caregivers carry the burden and responsibility of nurturing the elders. Let them know you understand they have a difficult job. Thank them for helping all of the residents, not merely yours. I found many nurses and aids in my mom's unit to be angels walking on earth, sweet beings dedicated to assisting aging seniors. They require our love, not our dictates and judgment. When talking to them in this way, that kindness will flow back to your family member by creating this personal touch. How we treat people is reflected in how they respond to us and others.

I was curious about how the staff handled seeing people decline and die, so I asked. The head nurse responded, "We are blessed to see people in transition, it is a process we all go through, and it is beautiful to observe." I was touched by her compassion. The nurse then shared a story of some residents who held a private vigil for one they knew was passing on. Late one morning, she noticed five men from the unit, standing in silence around a man's bed. They stayed there for a short time and then left and went about their day. That afternoon the man in the bed passed on. How did these elders, who had lost their sense of direction, know when a person was crossing? When the mind closes one part, another opens. For dementia patients, often, that part is their sixth sense. Look for it.

The night my mom passed, I had a beautiful vision of a Native American who came to escort her to the other side. Strange that her escort did not reflect her religious practices nor the urban areas where she had always lived. Yet, this was the image that appeared to me. I wondered if my memory of my past life as a Native American filtered in from Mom's DNA.

Years before, while guided in hypnosis, I envisioned myself as a wise and honored Native American woman living in a teepee wearing a white buffalo dress. I can clearly call this image to mind. In our tribe, I had gathered herbs and used my knowledge and intuitive skills to heal those in need. One day a young scout found a woman lying injured in the dirt out on the plains. He brought her to my teepee. She was not from our community and had fallen from a horse and been dragged for some distance. There was dirt lodged in her eyes, inhibiting her sight. I was able to help her regain her vision. This story of being a healer seems like it was fed by my ego, but, in my 40's, a woman entered my life having a similar issue which, for me, gave credence to this tale.

Katherine was a woman who was part of the religious community where my children attended school. She was from Germany and had been in America only a month when she lost her sight and was understandingly frightened. Being blind, she could not care for herself or her boy. Katherine needed to know she was not alone, and there was someone who cared.

I respect my privacy, and other than my children, I did not allow others to live in my home. Still, I could not, with good conscience, ignore her predicament. I was familiar with her plight as a woman raising children alone, for at the time, I too was a single mom, and I knew what a tough road that could be. I had to step forward and help her.

I invited her and her son to stay with me. Being trained in various healing modalities, I gave her more than just a place to rest and recover. For one month, I radiated the healing love of Reiki to her without any expectations, not knowing what the results might be. Within a month, her sight came back. I do not know for sure, not being a doctor, but I assume her impaired vision was psychological. Did I help her recover her sight? I never claim that I alone can make change happen. I was the gatekeeper. I held the key to the door. She chose to enter and return to health. Recovery comes from the individual who accepts they can shift their lives and move past the effect of injury or disease. Both the event with Katherine and the vision while Mom was passing I felt confirmed my connection to a past Native American life.

Helping Loved Ones Pass

There are numerous books by authors who have died and come back to life, confirming that light and peace are to be found as we pass. Therefore, the one who is passing is in good hands. When losing a loved one, you are often the one who needs help. You are the one left behind, missing their hugs, touch, and conversations. They will be fine. To lift your spirit as they move on, ask to be shown how they are transitioning.

When your loved one is ready to pass, you can help them evolve by asking for guidance from a divine being; but know, if you look, these light beings often show up all on their own without your request. So was the case for me with my mom.

Or did I make up the story on a subconscious level, affirming I was making it easy for Mom to pass? It does not matter which is true. The fact remains I visualized it, it comforted me, and now I can share it with others to help them feel peace as their loved ones move on. None of us knows for sure what lies ahead after death, but feeling the serenity of my mom's passage was real and valuable for me.

1. Intend to see their passing as a time when you can express the words you never were able to say.

2. Place your hands on them and bring in love for yourself and them in one of these ways.
    a. Fill yourself with loving, pink light and overflow that light of love into their heart and body.
    b. Depending on their belief, love can be from God, Buddha, Jesus, or deities close to their heart.
    c. If they do not have a strong spiritual belief, imagine light from the stars in the infinite Universe filling their body.

3. When you verbalize all the things you were unable to say before, it does not matter if they respond to your words; even if they are in a coma, they will hear you on some level.

4. If you can, speak softly and tell them you love them.
    a. Name the incidents that have hurt you or someone else.
    b. Share how you were affected, and then allow compassion to fill the room.
    c. Mention the incidents you know they have harbored in their heart.
    d. Tell them to forgive themselves for things that may have hurt them or others.

5. Whatever occurs, do not let their reaction deter you from continuing your dialogue.

6. Then place your hands on their head and tell them to exit their body through their head—the crown chakra.

7. If you feel sad, ask a light being to lift your pain.

8. If you cannot physically be with the one who is transitioning, perform this practice from a distance.

You can also create a connection to your loved one, even if they moved on years ago. Envision them before you and follow the above steps. The process will benefit both of you. Your actions will affect your entire genetic line, forward and backward.

Helping People Who Have Already Passed

When a person passes suddenly, they can be confused as to where they are. Some souls may feel they are still on earth and try to communicate with people who are alive. These spirits often don't realize they are stuck in a transitional plane and need assistance. If you desire, you can help them move through this self-imposed limitation. Your job is to invoke clarity and connect them to a being on the other side—one who will move them forward, acquainting them with their new surroundings.

Some individuals have an idea of how they will experience the afterlife. Once deceased, their spirit steps into that story. The movie *What Dreams May Come*, shows how this could happen. Robin Williams plays a husband who dies and finds the other side as beautiful as his wife's paintings. But when his depressed wife, played by Annabella Sciorra, passes, her regrets place her in her own form of hell. In the movie, *The Sixth Sense*, a psychologist, Bruce Willis, is killed yet stays connected to the earth by talking to a young boy who sees dead people, thus showing how a spirit is stuck on earth. We can help the deceased move on by introducing their soul to those on the other side, referred to as helpers, who understand how to guide them so they can progress.

You can connect to the dead by recalling what they enjoyed doing while here on earth and then creating that scenario. If you don't know them well, ask for this information from those close to them. Imagine the deceased enjoying this activity with people they knew on earth with one extra person. That being is the helper. A helper is a spirit on the other side whose only job is to move confused souls onto their new light path. The helpers are not necessarily angels or divine beings, but they are good to call in if you desire assistance. When the helper appears, your job is just to introduce them to the deceased. In the helper's care, the one who passed will move forward and not need to look for a connection from those still on earth.

In one session, a client asked me to check on her mom, who had passed years ago. The image came to mind of a woman shopping, standing near a wood showcase with a glass top. The clerk was showing her gloves. I asked my client, "Did your mom like to shop?" My client affirmed this was her favorite pastime. "Did she like a sale?" "Always," she responded.

I pretended that a woman stood next to her mom looking at the same gloves; this was the helper I called. The clerk walked away, and the onlooker/helper told her mom the same gloves were on sale across the street. They both left the counter and proceeded to the store across the street. As they entered the shop, it turned into a blaze of light, and they both gently ascended as my client's mom moved onto a higher level.

Another time I looked in on a deceased man who had been an alcoholic. I envisioned him at a bar, knowing this was his familiar place. The bartender/helper served him a drink and made a casual conversation. The bartender then asked if the man would help him carry a few cases of liquor. He agreed, and they both walked into the back room where the light enveloped them. He followed the helper out the back door and walked on a road that led to his resting place.

Some family members desire a continued connection to their deceased loved ones, but doing this keeps both the spirit and the one on earth in limbo where no one is moving forward. Later the ghost may contact their loved ones on earth, but this will take time. Letting them go is an act of compassion but sometimes difficult for the family left on earth.

Steps for Helping the Deceased Move On

1. Envision the deceased in your mind.

2. Talk to them as you would anyone. Imagine that they respond to you.

3. If they seem confused, calmly explain how they passed, that they are no longer in a body, and you are here to help.

4. Pretend to see them in a scene with their friends or relatives in an activity they enjoyed, with one additional person—the helper.

5. Introduce them to the helper, make up a story about why they have joined the group.

6. The helper is now in charge. You are free to watch what happens as the helper moves the spirit to a new scene.

7.   This place is where the spirit is free from the earth and all that has held them
     back.

So, what happens when we leave our body and pass from the earth? Do we
create what will happen then while we are living? Can we control what occurs
once we pass out of our body? There is only one way to find out the answers
to these questions, but currently, I am not willing to go down that path. For one
reason, I do not know how I would get the answers back to earth.

I found one man who made it clear what heaven would be for him. Gene understands spiritual and metaphysical concepts about death and dying, but his father held contrary beliefs. He did not think an afterlife, or an ultimate power, was
directing his life. Days before Gene's father passed, Gene proposed this question
to his father. "If there were life after death, what would you like that to be?" His
father had been an avid tennis player his entire life, so it was not difficult for him
to form a response. The old man decided to play along with his son and quickly
replied, "Playing tennis for eternity."

Gene and I are part of a group of eight who checks in on spirits who have
passed. After his father's death, Gene requested we look in on his father to see if
he was at peace or required assistance. As a group, we closed our eyes and entered
meditation, each in our prescribed way, in order to meet his father. His father
appeared to the group dressed in white tennis shorts and seemed quite happy and
content. Gene asked, "What does this mean? Do we need to direct my father to
the light where his spirit can continue to grow and advance?"

I think not. Gene's father told him what would bring him joy if there was life
after death. He wanted to play tennis. For his father, tennis reflected nirvana. Tennis was what he loved. For the group to encourage his father to move to another
place would be taking away this spirit's free will. It is not permissible to control a
being in that way, in or out of their body. The afterlife can take many forms, and
I see happiness as the ultimate freedom. When we pass from the physical structure, some spirits can become stuck in their earthly degenerative habits. Then they
need help moving on, but that was not the case here. Gene's father was clear. He
told his son his image of paradise is playing tennis. There was nothing to do but
accept that his father was happy and free.

When helping spirits, remember that by pretending to see them, the connection is made. Begin to imagine the deceased before you. By faking the scene, your
doubt will cease because you are playing, and there is no wrong way to do it. At
some point, something will happen that you didn't imagine, and later you may

find it to be true. A client asked that I see how her brother was doing because it was the tenth anniversary of his passing. Immediately I saw her brother on a bicycle but did not mention it because my client rode a Harley Davidson motorcycle. I was not going to tell her that her brother was on the other side with a meager bicycle. I heard "bike" in my thoughts three times, so I finally shared my vision carefully, saying bike, not bicycle. She smiled and said, "My brother was always on a bike. Not one like mine, he rode a bicycle."

There's about a three-month resting period that most spirits require. That prepares them for what awaits on higher planes. During these months they rest, free from the struggles of the world. Looking at a spirit soon after their death is permissible, but do not attempt to move them to the light right away, in fact, they will not let you.

A friend wanted me to look in on his deceased mother, but she had passed just a few weeks prior. I told him it was too soon, but because he was a dear friend and I wanted to ease his grief, I looked in on her with the help of my spiritual group. We saw her busily packing boxes, and she would not look at or acknowledge any of us. We did not attempt to alter her actions and left her packing. Three months later, we looked in again. This time the moving van was filled, and she was sitting in the passenger seat. The van drove away as she waved to us. I'd say she was heading to greener pastures—in the light.

Lessons Learned

Is it our destiny to repeat the same mistakes as our parents? NO! We are here to rise above the discontent in our lives and change the outcome for ourselves and those in our genetic line. Life is about healing, and it can go beyond our family, reaching every person we have encountered: clients, coworkers, and friends. We are all connected in a beautiful web of light, and as we progress through difficult situations, we attain insights and compassion that overflows out to others.

The connection to all life was highlighted in the hundredth monkey theory that was developed by observing primates on the island of Koshima. One monkey began to wash his sweet potato before eating it. Soon the others in the troop followed. This practice spread throughout the island and then to monkeys on other islands miles away, even though the original potato washing-monkeys were not on the other islands. Wikipedia says, "The hundredth monkey effect is a purported phenomenon in which a new behavior or idea is said to spread rapidly by unexplained means from one group to all related groups, once a critical number of members of one group exhibit the new behavior and acknowledge the new idea."

As the monkeys shared their discovery with other monkeys they never met, some people believe that it is easier for all humankind to advance as each individual advances. That is why extending kindness and compassion to all beings in the face of adversity becomes so important.

Even though we may be aware of our parents' flaws and try not to copy them, much to our dismay, we may find we have followed the model they set forth.

Here are the similarities I have seen between my parents and me:

Tony and Lorraine married one year after Tony came home from World War II.
They dated for three months and then married.
Their first child was born nine months after they wed.

Frank and I married one year after Frank returned from the war in Vietnam.
We dated for three months and then married.
Our first child was born nine months after we wed.

I so wanted to be different from my parents, yet I unconsciously followed in their footsteps. To see if I could release these genetic programs, I entered a deep relaxation through hypnosis. In this state, the mind sees images, which mimic the mind's language. Remember, the mind changes words into images; therefore, in hypnosis, stories will be created with pictures.

Follow the *Self-Hypnosis Guidelines* in The Courses of Action, Chapter 7. When you arrive at the library, instead of looking for books that give knowledge, look for books that hold unwanted, inherited behaviors. Some books may be tucked back on the shelf, hidden high, or sticking out from other books. Bring down the books, individually or in a stack, to a chair by a blazing fireplace. Scan each book and notice that the stories may be shown in pictures rather than words. Tear out all the pages to release the old programs and put them into a basket by your feet. Take time to feel any sensations or emotions that may arise. You will have the strength to rip the cover as well. After you demolish the books and the tendencies they hold, take the basket over to the fireplace. The flames will change from red and yellow to violet, which represents pure love. Clearing your unwanted qualities with love neutralizes your programming, so those qualities don't return.

Eliminating Unwanted Family Traits

1. List the unwanted characteristics you possess.

2. Compare this list to similar traits of your parents.

3. Decide which ones you want to keep and which ones no longer serve you.

4. Follow the *Self-Hypnosis Guidelines* in The Courses of Action, Chapter 7.

5. Once you step into the library, look for titles representing the genetic traits you would like to clear.

6. Remove each book and place them by a chair near the fireplace.

7. Open each book, see the images, feel the emotions, and then tear out the pages and throw them into a basket by your feet.

8. Rip the cover as well.

9. When you have destroyed all the books, carry the basket over to the fireplace.

10. The flames in the fire are violet to represent pure love.

11. As you put the pages into the fire, affirm your ability to release unwanted patterns of behavior from your family.

12. Move to the room filled with light across the hall.

13. Recall the good virtues you wish to keep and analyze each one, noticing how they may be similar to those of your parents.

14. See how these virtues are flavored with your individualized style.

15. Take a moment to claim yourself as an authentic, unique individual.

16. Be aware that owning your true self will not diminish your association with your parents but will build upon it.

17. Stay in this room until you feel good about who you are.

18. Revisit this room when you need to remind yourself of your virtues.

19. Confidently walk out of the room, down the hall, and into the elevator, and up to level A.

20. Step out of the elevator and slowly walk up seven stairs. As you ascend each stair, you will feel lighter and happier.

21. Know when you reach the top, you will feel better than you have felt in days, weeks, and even years.

Once you have cleared your hereditary patterns, you may need to revisit the previous steps 12 to 20 to remind yourself how you're different from your parents and can shine as an individual.

I knew my marriage had run its course, but I avoided the signs and refused to move forward. I did not want to repeat my mother's pattern of divorce. And yet I did! I stayed in an unhealthy marriage for twenty-three years. I discovered later that neither extending our time together nor ending the marriage would break the mold.

My marriage to Frank ended a few years after I met my father. Meeting my father removed the blinders I had worn for years. Knowing my father loved me gave me the strength I needed to view my situation with new eyes. Frank was my support when I stood on the steps and faced the unknown man. For that, he will always have a place in my heart, but after that time had passed, I needed to face the truth and move on. Some marriages last because the couples have found ways to grow together, but that was not our path. Our relationship had run its course, and it was time to end our unbalanced entanglement. We had been estranged long enough, making separation no surprise, yet it was still unexpected for Frank. When a relationship is crumbling, someone must be the one to crawl out from under the rubble and state the truth. On one fall afternoon, I spoke that truth.

Once I pointed out the obvious, Frank agreed we needed to divorce. Our next step was to share our decision with our children, ages eighteen, sixteen, and eight. Bringing them together that afternoon was effortless. Carmin, who suspected this move, was attending the University of Colorado in Boulder, and immediately jumped in her car and drove home. The other two children were in grammar and high school. They arrived home at about the same time as Carmin. We all sat in the family room as Frank and I looked at each other with tears in our eyes. I began, "Your dad and I have decided to divorce. We are still a family. It will just look different from now on." Carmin was the first to stand and hug her dad, "I'm sorry, Dad, I love you." Blake hugged me and cried, "I never wanted to see this happen, but I understand." Crystal held onto her dad and sobbed. We were honest with our emotions, knowing our family unit would never be the same again. The five of us determined how to divide the objects in our home, still making us feel like a harmonious family entity, even though the logistics were going to be different. We dealt with it well for the first month. Then, things went awry.

Frank quickly took up with another woman; and with her new ears to hear his complaints, it did not take long for him to reassess our situation. The divorce went smoothly; but in less than a year, Frank took me to court to reduce his share of child support, which was already a meager amount, not forty percent of his salary, like my father's had been.

Frank's request infuriated me. I felt emotionally and financially hit, adding to my burdens. Talking to him calmly, while pointing out what might be controlling his actions, did not have the result I desired. In my counseling practice, I would hear men share their concerns about how their former wives were not using their support checks for the children but rather for themselves. I approached Frank to see if this was an idea he held as well. Indeed, he too felt the same. I explained how the money he gave me and the finances I produced were all put into the same pot and used for all the incurred expenses. He seemed to hear what I was saying at the time but continued his court proceedings.

I allowed his fractured view of how I spent my income to agitate me. Analyzing my predicament became a constant chatter in my head that I found impossible to silence. Thoughts came to me unbidden; they confronted me as I tried to sleep, becoming my unwelcome companions, and I was cast into despair. I had physically removed the person from my life who stressed and enraged me, yet I was still aggravated by his actions and let him hold my attention. How stupid I had become, allowing him to continue to color my days and nights in despair; until one day, I had an epiphany.

Mental clarity and brilliant ideas happen not when we force them to appear, but when we let go and allow them to surface. My daily meditative practice built my intuitive awareness so that I could recognize divine advice. This guidance often floated to the surface of my thoughts when I least expected it. To become the one you truly are, an empowered being of light and truth, you must still your thoughts and actions on a regular basis, in order to hear this spiritual guidance.

My release from financial stress occurred on a warm summer day as I walked along the curved concrete path, bordered with flowers, up to the front door of my home. My realization hit me like a bolt of lightning. "My financial supply does not come from Frank." Affirming the source of my finances was brilliant and was full of light. Not only money but everything I receive comes from a higher source, one that I manifest through my thoughts and actions. Once I released the financial connection to Frank and plugged into the source of the Universe, my stress and anger subsided. I was surprised at how quickly it happened and how different I felt. When I changed my attitude, by relinquishing what Frank should be doing and turning the problem over to the oneness of the Universe, our unhealthy dependency was released. With my anger gone, I was not only liberated, but so was the one I held in contempt—Frank.

We do not travel through life alone. We stay connected to others through our thoughts, even when we are apart. Have you ever called someone, and they said, "I was just thinking about you," or you step into a place and felt a stranger's gaze? This unseen connection affects intimate relationships as well as relationships with friends and family. Therefore, when we change how we feel about others, their outlook may shift as well. It did not matter if Frank was conscious of the shift. I know my epiphany freed him along with me.

No one can make us angry. We allow others' acts to upset us or let them pass without confrontation. It can be like a fleeting moment or a constant reminder. We choose how long our discomfort stays.

Everything that happens to us comes from our preconceived thoughts, actions, judgments, visions, and beliefs. Blaming others for how they mistreat us drains our energy. Our negative reactions to a situation keep feeding those emotions. We can justify our feelings and hold onto them or allow the scenario to subside by being neutral to their words and actions. With mental clarity, confrontations can quickly dissolve into peace.

The clarity I received was not from some faraway place, handed to me by a wise guide or divine being. It was me! I figured out my anger was filling my days with dark thoughts, and I chose to release my frustration. Whether audibly, visually, or through body sensations, the messages we receive come from the divine essence of who we are. The guides, angels, and deities we call upon for help are merely an extension of ourselves. We are that which we seek. We are one with all that is. Embodying this concept will empower and free you from life's struggles, but you must feel it. It is not a mental concept, it resides within your heart, and then it becomes your truth.

We can choose to blame ourselves for something we deemed wrong or take a different approach to our confrontational memories. We do not need to hold negative patterns throughout our lives. When we carry bitterness, anger, and blame toward ourselves and others, we end up depressed, sad, and often physically and mentally ill. We have a choice. By reframing these scenarios into healthy experiences, we can rest in a loving place for ourselves and all involved. Use the process *Rewrite Your Story*, in The Courses of Action, Chapter 9, to reframe hurtful relationships.

Do Emotions Play a Part in Disease?

Mom kept her grief locked away as she had with the papers she kept locked in her safety deposit box and it festered in her mind. She never processed her lifetime struggles, and in time it infringed on her skewed memory. My father's deteriorating lungs could have been the sadness he never cleared, and eventually, his body gave out. The emotional component tied to lung cancer is grief or not having things your way. Indeed, this was true for my father. Yes, one can locate a physical reason for the body breaking down, but the emotional part needs also to be acknowledged.

Working in the healing arts, I have seen change occur when the patient addresses the physical body along with the mental, emotional, and spiritual bodies, thus covering issues in all areas. Reiki is one of the few healing modalities I know that will touch all the fore-mentioned bodies. Do not ignore your etheric bodies, for struggles affect us on many levels. All our thoughts, emotions, and judgments can trigger disease or injury. When your physical body is crying out for attention, listen. Your body is asking you to slow down. Take heed, and honor what you are feeling.

You cannot run from your own emotions. They inhabit your physical body and will cause physical distress if not addressed. Karol Truman, therapist and author of *Feelings Buried Alive Never Die*, has studied extensively how emotions affect the body. Her book lists physical ailments, along with the emotions often connected to those abnormalities. Look and see if her references to physical aliments apply to emotions you carry now or in the past. You may be surprised that Truman's findings mirror your story. Blocking or stuffing away the emotional pain will not change the discomfort; it only delays it.

Information found in Truman's book can help you heal. Don't become frustrated and angry with your discomfort. Harboring anger towards anyone or anything is never beneficial. Neither is pointing to your body and saying this is not fair or saying I will fight this disease. These thoughts only bring in more discontent. When illness or pain takes control, you have the opportunity to look deeper and reveal what needs to be addressed. Then make the adjustments required. Changing your thoughts, along with allopathic medicine, can be a great combination to bring permanent healing. When your illness mirrors your parents, it might be beneficial to take another approach.

Clearing Dis-ease from the DNA

When a parent develops a physical aliment and leaves the earth, their descendant may acquire the same affliction soon after or years later. Doctors will chalk it up to heredity, but there could be another reason other than the DNA repeating itself in an offspring.

It is not a conscious decision because no one wants to be ill, but when a person subconsciously manifests a disease similar to their loved one's, they feel their loved one is somehow still close. The desire to keep one who has departed close is so intense that the body decides to bring the loved one back by allowing their parent's illness to manifest in their own body. It is necessary to release the deceased fully into the light and visualize their pain and suffering dissolved. Then the dis-ease afflicting the one here on earth can also be healed.

Releasing an Unhealthy Hold to a Deceased Parent

1. Still your body and mind and be in a quiet place.

2. Remove all distractions: phones, family members, animals, and agendas.

3. Pay attention to the rhythm of your breath. Each time your chest rises, focus on being lighter.

4. Imagine your energy body of light—the aura, and see its color as in Chapter 3, *Connect to Your Divine Essence*. Allow that shade to wash over you and then into the room. You have now stepped into your divinity.

5. Relax in this still feeling for a while.

6. Invite the one who has passed to be present in your divine light.

7. In the high vibration of this light, ask for the divine medical team to assist your loved one and remove their pain and dis-ease.

8. Make up a scenario of the medical team's intervention, or one might

appear in your mind's eye; either is valid.

9. See the medical procedure complete, then direct the medical team to release the dis-ease from your body as well.

10. Lie down, feel, see, and accept the transformation that is occurring in your body.

11. Once you feel a difference, release the medical team, along with your loved one into the light.

12. Affirm, there is no need to hold onto your loved one through pain and illness. You are free, as are they.

13. Connect with your loved one in a new way. See an image of your heart's love blending with theirs, void of any dis-ease.

14. Depending on your belief system, the length you have held onto the affliction, or other reasons, you may find it helpful to repeat this action.

15. Notice how the process is different each time.

Clearing Sadness from Your Heart

When you're deeply sad, the heart physically records this emotion in the body. It could manifest as pain in the chest, shortness of breath, inability to stay focused, or mental anguish. If not addressed over the years, denying this emotion can create serious illness. Rather than focusing on the emotional cause of the pain, we will address the physical heart so that you can release the sadness.

In this exercise, it is important to focus on the heart's valves and the pericardium that incases the heart. During echocardiograms, I watched the screen to see how my valves functioned. Each time my heart beat, the valves looked like two arms raising, as if cheering. One technician felt the valves were reflecting two hands clapping. Either way, both observations give form to our loving hearts as our cheerleaders, giving a positive effect. We often look for love outside ourselves, but love first begins within us, and when we can see that fact in action, the world around us responds in a similar fashion.

Locate echocardiogram videos on the web and see what images come to mind for you. Hold that focus and see if you can experience the love that resides in your heart.

1. Silence your mind by stilling your body, closing your eyes, and sitting comfortably with your back straight.

2. Allow divine light to enter your head and fill your heart and body.

3. As your energy field receives this calming radiance, notice how your thoughts begin to diminish.

4. Wait to feel a shift in your body. It does not need to be a significant change, just a slight alteration.

5. Watch the movement of your lungs. Notice how they rise, fill with oxygen, and expand to the sides.

6. Bring white light into your lungs.

7. Move that color into the pericardium sack that encases your heart.

8. Notice how the light feels different in your heart rather than in your lungs.

9. Keep your attention on your heart and imagine the pericardium enveloping not only your physical heart but your emotional heart as well.

10. Bring your attention to the center of your heart and recall the video showing your heart's valves moving with the motion of clapping hands, cheering arms, or the picture you envisioned.

11. Imagine an audience applauding just for you.

12. Do not give way to the scenario that elicits pain in your heart.

13. Keep thinking about the sensation of loving hands around your heart.

14. If your mind wanders, bring it back to this image.

15. Release your pain into these hands. Feel and see sadness dissolve.

16. Watch for nuances as your heart releases its pain.

17. Allow radiant love to emanate from your core. Sense the joy it brings.

18. When your heart feels softer, take a moment and recall the words or actions that made you sad. Has anything changed, subsided, or diminished?

19. End your session by taking a deep breath and slowly open your eyes.

Returning to Source

Guided meditations and directions to clear old issues work best when you stand in your power, with a clear intention, knowing you can accomplish whatever you set forth to do. You will gain that power by affirming the divine presence held within you. When I was eight years old, I found the path to Source, but it took forty years to completely understand what had occurred that day.

Finding a place to be in nature is difficult when living in a city. The lawns in my neighborhood were off-limits to little tykes. These small properties, a mere twenty-five feet wide, were protected by the lords of these estates, older men who took pride in their emerald isles. The evenings found them hand watering their precious land, guarding against the dogs that intrude or child marauders who, in their excitement, would venture off the sidewalk onto the forbidden territory. Yet, during summer vacation, there was no one watching the small grassy area at the school entrance. I would cross the street to lie in the long, soft, green grass on those hot summer days. It was there that I felt the embrace of nature.

I recall lying on the grass, nuzzling my nose into the fragrant chlorophyll. I was content to be alone, happy in my private world, knowing nothing was required of me. There I stayed, tracking the clouds rolling by. One day, something happened that has stayed with me for decades. As I lay in the grass, I began to feel my body moving behind me even though I was still. I was rolling backward in somersaults, and it felt delightful. Later in my life, while studying metaphysics, I discovered what might have occurred that day. A metaphysician from Australia, whose name I do not recall, suggested that in order to return to Source, you must move back, out of your body.

Religious dogmas instruct that to connect to the divine, one must move above one's body, but I found moving backward could produce the same results. If we are made in the image of the divine, then our original connection to Source lies back in time, which can feel like a backward sensation. Buddhists believe the divine exists everywhere and in all things, so there would be no reason to imagine going anywhere, for we are always in the soup of the divine. But to appease our doubting minds, follow these directives and see what happens for you.

1. Set an intention to connect to the first time you took a body, eons ago.

2. Follow the *Basic Steps for Meditation* at the beginning of Part II.

3. In a relaxed state, allow your body to fill with the color of your divine light. Feel the sensation.

4. Call to your soul, spirit, or divine essence. Ask permission to return to Source, not one designated by religious figures unless that is your path.

5. Feel your light, soul, or spirit moving out of the back of your body as it journeys through space and time to your destination. Recalling the nebulae from outer space may help.

6. Stay in the backward movement and notice what transpires. You may see images or beings as you transition.

7. Allow the experience to unfold in its own time.

8. Return to it any time you wish because now the path is open.

Remember everything you seek is within your grasp, in fact, you already possess it. Now is the time to:

o   Claim your divinity
o   Stand in your light
o   Know your truth
o   Manifest your desires

Afterword

I carried pain from being left behind by my father, but I realized that abandonment served me on my spiritual path. By feeling there was no one to support and love me, I had to find another source for love. We cannot exist without love. It is as vital as air. When we don't feel the love from our family, friends, or partners, we must fill the void with our heart's love.

We practiced Christianity in my home, so I listened to the preacher at church and believed what he said to be true. I also took credence in what my elders told me, but I had a revelation at nineteen. It did not come from an angel whispering in my ear. It came from my teenage ego that wanted all life to be fair. I wondered how a person who lived a life of crime, murder, and injustice to others could affirm at the end of their life that they believed in Jesus and therefore be saved? I felt this was unfair! There must be remorse and the desire to make amends for one's unjust acts. I looked at the basic premise of religion and decided I could no longer abide by some of those principles. That insight led me to decide, for a short time, that God did not exist.

I was maturing in the 1960s, where protesting in the streets was common, young men were dying in Vietnam, and racial discrimination was rampant. It had to resolve.

As years passed, I explored various religions and found they are not so different. They all carry a common thread—love one another. But I did not feel comfortable giving my power to an organization, deity, or something outside myself. I found my power by acknowledging:

I am that which I seek
Spirit is in all things
People
Animals
Earth/Sky
and Me
Therefore God is me

I wanted to feel this connection, not merely perceive it in my mind, and access the sensation. That is how I began my journey and walked the path of light for decades. Through my experiences, I guide seekers to do the same. I trust my journey will help you find your way, claim your greatness, and share your findings to help others. Then we may grow together.

Acknowledgements

A book is not merely the ideas of a writer. Countless people add their wisdom and insights to make a publication hold the reader's interest, and for my books, enlighten them.

For hours spent toiling over my story, I send my praise to Nan, whose quest for knowledge has always put her at the head of the class. She stepped into her calling to be a teacher who guided children in how to master the English language and express themselves through writing. She took me under her wing by showing me an approach that held my readers' attention, yet she never drowned out my voice.

RobAnn kindly pointed out my infractions and directed me towards showing my family in a colorful new light. The hours we spent toiling over my text were filled with guidance, wisdom, and laughter. I will always be indebted to her. Sandra was my knight in shining armor. She fine-tuned the grammar I missed and added her metaphysical insights. Our time together warmed my heart while making my book better with each word we changed. And there were many! Thomas graciously took the time and used his linguistic gift to tweak my words to say precisely what I meant. Even though I resisted some of his counsel, he often turned out to be correct. Sigrid helped with the flow of the book by suggesting I redesign some of the chapters. Using her ideas superbly clarified the narrative. Finally, Beth made this book all come together. I thank her for her expertise in laying out my words and polishing up my photos so that my story would come alive. As they say, "It takes a village."

My father's sisters, Mary and Rose, were so eager to fill me in on the years I missed. My dear cousin Pam had tales that unfolded into an album of delightful characters. Her recollections enriched my writing and brought my relatives to life. Their stories then became my memory.

My days are filled with clients, everyday duties, writing blogs, and caring for my home and gardens. Once all those things were complete, came the sweetness of the day—writing about my family. Those hours became my candy. The sure thrill of writing was one aspect, but I equally enjoyed the time I spent researching about the family I never knew in my youth.

My life is magic. I am truly blessed.

Inspirational Materials

BOOKS

Empowerment Series:

Finding Your Inner Gift—Begin your journey of self-discovery and find the intuition, healing, and insights that you possess. Based on the healing style of Reiki, the information contained goes far beyond hands-on-healing.

Inner Gifts Uncovered—A complete manual for Reiki practitioners, teachers, and seekers of truth. Included are exercises to balance and understand all types of relationships. Learn processes that will allow you to send healing across the miles, into the past, and into the future.

Claiming Your Inner Gifts—Empower your life by following the guidance of a Reiki master's discoveries gained from decades of research to obtain advanced spiritual growth.

For Children:

The House Who Found Its Home—There once was a house that was not happy where it lived. Its place was too tight, too bright, and too noisy! So this whimsical character takes off to find a new place to live.

AUDIO

Meditation Made Easy—Meditation is simple with proper guidance. Follow along to relieve stress, pain, and emotional discomfort. Reiki hands-on healing positions are part of this recording.

Cosmic Connections—Be guided by meditations for personal empowerment, chakra clearing, gentle Kundalini activations, and self-love.

Meditation MP3 https://lightinternal.com/product-category/meditations

PRODUCTS

INSPIRATIONAL BLOG

How to scan the QR codes

1. Open the camera app on a smartphone
2. Point the phone at the QR code to scan it
3. Tap the pop-up banner to access information

About the Author

Marnie is devoted to assisting others in understanding how to see their talents and rise above life's challenges. She holds a sacred space for her students, clients, and readers, where they can easily access dimensions for higher learning and growth. For over three decades, Marnie has devoted her time to developing a unique way of transforming people's lives through intuitive sessions, energy clearing, mentoring, meditations, and books.

Marnie draws upon her extensive knowledge in the field of holistic health, and refined innate healing abilities. In her practice her clients are guided to understand and balance their emotional, mental, physical, and spiritual presence. She continues to explore new avenues of enlightenment to keep her energy clear while sharing her discoveries with others. Her other joys in life are gardening, dancing, and strolling through Colorado's breath-taking nature and making magic happen.

Marnie lives near Denver, Colorado. Her wisdom can be found at www.lightinternal.com.

WEBSITE

Made in the USA
Columbia, SC
01 November 2021